Embedded Web Control Panels on the Raspberry Pi

MSTMicro Publishing

MSTMicro Publishing
http://www.mstmicro.com

10 9 8 7 6 5 4 3 2 1 0

For Library of Congress Control Number go to www.mstmicro.com

ISBN 978-0-9970222-7-8 (paperback)

ISBN 978-0-9970222-8-5 (ebook)

~

First Edition
March 2022

Embedded Web Control Panels on the Raspberry Pi

A Design Reference

George L Babec

CONTENTS

1

INTRODUCTION

Programing and controlling an embedded computer like the Raspberry Pi can actually be really fun and rewarding. This book will help to open the door to some fabulous methods and sometimes unknown abilities of the user interface to control the physical hardware. You will learn things like how to play a wav file by pressing a button on a web page, turn on and off General Purpose Input Output (GPIO) pins for external control using relays and transistors to control lights, LEDs and other devices, or read and monitor the CPU temperature over time without refreshing the page. This book will walk you through the "Common Gateway Interface" (CGI) and how to create a static web control panel with dynamic elements that will update without performing a visible page refresh. CGI data input, output, and environment variables will be explained and demonstrated with real-life code examples. These secrets and much more will be presented within these pages.

So what is an embedded computer or an embedded application?

Embedded applications, commonly called firmware, are basically software that runs on an embedded target. An embedded target is a physical computing platform controlled by either a microcontroller, microprocessor, System on a Chip (SoC), or a Field Programmable Gate Array (FPGA) that is used to accomplish one or more specific tasks. For instance, an automobile computer that is responsible for controlling the engine, lighting, gauges, windshield wipers, and other functions is a great example of an embedded computer. Embedded computing systems have to have some center of control, normally in the form of a microcontroller with all the necessary peripherals internal to the Integrated Circuit (IC). Most, but not all, embedded systems will have limited user access once placed into operation.

Some embedded platforms will provide a remote interface where the user must access the device remotely by some means other than direct physical connection, i.e. keyboard, mouse, and monitor. One example of this is a home wireless router. One must configure the router by means of a web page where the user can access and control all the built-in features of the device. The web page is a visual interface that can act on user input resulting in an embedded action within the computing device, thus where the term "Embedded Web Page" originates.

This book covers basic and advanced methods of creating embedded web pages with real-life example code. The end product will be a virtual control panel with dynamic operations that will update on the page without reloading the page, simulating a real-life physical control panel. A Raspberry Pi will serve as the embedded target; however, the same concepts used here can be applied to any Linux® system running the Apache HTTP Server or potentially any plaform running a Web Server that supports CGI with only a few setup and path changes. This is also true of VxWorks systems when the web server is configured to use CGI, for individuals developing on an RTOS system.

Some of the techniques and methods used within this book are rather advanced and can be difficult for a beginner to fully understand; however, anyone can follow the tutorial-like examples and see the results. To fully understand the advanced concepts the reader will require at least some basic knowledge of the following:

- Linux Terminal Commands
- HTML
- Java Script
- 'C' Programming
- CGI (Common Gateway Interface)
- Raspberry Pi

The information within attempts to provide specific examples and precise explanations with only the elements required to understand the concepts or methods being presented. There are individual examples along the way that will be built upon and/or combined to reach the end goal. Since the final code is created over multiple chapters and built on over time, it is recommended that the steps in each chapter be followed in order or the resulting code may be missing pieces required for proper operation. Some of the examples will serve as great utilities when trying to debug a web application and can be used for any embedded web project. There are multiple approaches to accomplishing the end goal of creating virtual embedded web control panels. This book does not try to present all possible techniques but rather uses specific tried and tested real-world examples. This book serves as both a design reference and a tutorial for creating a Raspberry Pi-based web control panel.

The concepts explained in this book are not exclusive to the Raspberry Pi and can be applied to many embedded or PC-based computing systems. Virtually any platform that has a standard web server that supports CGI can be used to create Virtual Control Panels. The Raspberry Pi provides an inexpensive learning platform that is affordable for most budgets, thus it is the focus of most of the examples used here.

2

Preparing the Raspberry Pi

This chapter consists of two parts. Part one covers the process of setting up a new Raspberry Pi. Part two covers the installation of the supporting applications required to operate web control panels. If you already have an updated and working Raspberry Pi computer attached to a local network that can access the Internet then you can skip ahead to Part two. If your Operating System (OS) has not been updated in over a year it is suggested that you update your OS to the latest version. Optionally a new SD card can be used to set up a fresh install while saving the existing SD card if desired.

Steps covered in this chapter:

Part One, OS Setup -

- Download the Operating System Image
- Write the Operating System to the SD Flash Memory Card
- Configure the Raspberry Pi
- Network Configuration

Part Two, Web Server Setup -

- Set Up the Apache HTTP Server
- Enable CGI
- Setup and Verify Perl
- Setup and Verify CGI Operation

Part One

Raspbian/Raspberry Pi Operating System Installation

This section is provided for convenience only and is not part of the general subject matter of the book. Experienced users with a current OS installed can jump ahead to part two.

Required items for this section:

- Raspberry Pi computer
- Micro SD card reader/writer on a PC

- Micro SD card of at least 8GB in size; 32GB or more recommended
- Raspberry Pi USB power supply
- Keyboard, Mouse, and HDMI compatible Monitor or TV

Raspbian/Raspberry Pi Operating System

There are many operating systems available for the Raspberry Pi and quite a few of them will support the methods used in this book; however, some of the commands and paths used to set up and operate web control panels may differ. All of the examples in this book are based upon using the standard Raspbian or Raspberry Pi Operating System. If the decision is made to use a different Linux distribution, it will need to support Perl, CGI, and the Apache HTTP Server.

Operating System Install

The official Raspberry Pi OS can be downloaded at the following address:

https://www.raspberrypi.com/software/

Either use the Raspberry Pi Imager and follow the steps on the raspberrypi.org website from the link above or download the OS image and use the following steps to install the OS manually.

Manually Writing the SD Card Image

A program called BalenaEtcher can be used to write the Raspberry Pi OS image Zip file to an SD flash memory card. A SD card reader/writer will be required for this operation. Etcher is available for Windows, Mac, and Linux systems. Alternately, a program called "Win32 Disk Imager" can be used on Windows systems; however, a 64-Bit Zip utility like 7-Zip will be required to extract and uncompress the image file for before use. The example here will make use of BalenaEtcher to write the image file to a micro SD flash. In this case the image zip file can be used in the original compressed .zip format.

Step 1: Download and install BalenaEtcher from: https://www.balena.io/etcher/
Step 2: Open BalenaEtcher if it does not start automatically and click on the "Flash from file" button. Go to the location where the Raspberry Pi OS image zip file was previously saved. Click on the zip file and then the "Open" button.
Step 3: Insert the micro SD flash card into the SD reader/writer.
Step 4: If Etcher does not automatically select the SD drive with the SD card inserted then click on the "Select target" button and select the SD drive. Be sure to select the correct drive so no important information is erased on other storage media.
Step 5: When ready, click on the "Flash!" button to write the image file to the SD card.
Step 6: Be sure the Raspberry Pi is not powered and plug in the SD Flash Card, Keyboard, Mouse, and Monitor or TV.
Step 7: Power the Raspberry Pi with a USB power cord. Be sure the USB power supply can handle the current draw for the particular Raspberry Pi being used. If the power supply is not sufficient and limits the current needed then the Raspberry Pi can fail or periodically reboot without warning.

Note: *The first-time boot of a Raspberry Pi can take quite a bit of time to initialize so be patient. The setup process will require an Internet connection.*

Step 8: When the Raspberry Pi boots to the desktop, answer the questions when prompted.

If the Raspberry Pi Desktop does not fit the screen correctly or the desired screen size is not correct, it can be adjusted by running the application **raspi-config** at a Terminal Prompt. See the section "Accessing the Terminal Window" in this chapter if you are not sure how to access the Terminal Prompt. At the prompt type: **sudo raspi-config** When the configuration window opens, select -> **Advanced Options**-> **Resolution** and select the desired screen resolution for your TV or Monitor. For some TVs the overscan option may also need to be set if there are black bars around the edges of the screen. When complete, press the right arrow button on the keyboard selecting <Finish> then press Enter.

Step 9: If available, the Wi-Fi interface should have been set up during Step 8. If there is an issue connecting to the local network or the Internet, type **sudo raspi-config** at a Terminal Prompt to open the Raspberry Pi configuration menu. Once open, select Network Options and configure your network SSID and passphrase. For reference, network settings are normally saved to either of the following configuration files:

/etc/dhcpcd.conf or **/etc/wpa_supplicant/wpa_supplicant.conf**. Alternatively the **ifconfig** command may be used to view and configure various network settings including static IP addresses.

Step 10: Verify network access by typing the following command at a Terminal Prompt:

ping mstmicro.com

Example output:

pi@raspberrypi:/etc/network/interfaces.d $ ping mstmicro.com

PING mstmicro.com (65.60.38.10) 56(84) bytes of data.

64 bytes from chi102.greengeeks.net (65.60.38.10): icmp_seq=1 ttl=48 time=71.1 ms

64 bytes from chi102.greengeeks.net (65.60.38.10): icmp_seq=2 ttl=48 time=72.6 ms

64 bytes from chi102.greengeeks.net (65.60.38.10): icmp_seq=3 ttl=48 time=69.4 ms

64 bytes from chi102.greengeeks.net (65.60.38.10): icmp_seq=4 ttl=48 time=69.5 ms

Press <CTRL> C to stop the ping command.

If the ping command returns "host unreachable" then the network settings are not valid and need to be set properly before internet access is possible.

> **Note:** *To use the examples in this book the Raspberry Pi must be set up on your local network and have access to the internet.*

> **Note:** *When desiring to run an application with superuser privileges, the command sudo (superuser do) should precede the actual command. Without the sudo entry some commands will fail stating, "Permission Denied."*

Part Two

Accessing the Terminal Window

Before moving forward it is important to understand how to access the Terminal Prompt. Many of the examples and commands that are used in this book require the use of the system Terminal Window. To open a Terminal Window, click on the black screen icon on the top taskbar or hover over each icon until the help text showing "Terminal" pops up; then click the icon or simply press and hold CTRL+ALT+t on the keyboard for the

Terminal shortcut. To test once the Terminal Window opens, click inside the window with the mouse then type pwd at the prompt and press <ENTER>. The response should be your current directory:

pi@raspberrypi:~ $ pwd

/home/pi

Web Server Configuration

Prior to installing additional applications or servers on the Raspberry Pi, it's a good idea to update the available packages by typing the following command at the Terminal Prompt:

sudo apt-get update

First check to see if apache2 is installed by typing the following at the Terminal Prompt:

apache2 -v

If installed you should receive a response that displays the server version and the date of build:

Server version: Apache/2.4.38 (Raspbian)

Server built: 2019-10-15T19:53:42

Your response may look different depending on the OS installed and date of installation. If not installed or the command is not recognized then install the Apache HTTP Server by typing the following at a Terminal Prompt:

sudo apt-get install apache2

Enable CGI by typing:

sudo a2enmod cgi

The system may use cgid for the command automatically for systems with multi-threaded processors.

Restart the apache2 web server to make use of the CGI settings change by typing the following command:

sudo systemctl restart apache2

Test the newly installed web server by opening a web browser on the Raspberry Pi Desktop and typing the following address in the address bar: **localhost**

If the installation was successful then you should be looking at the default web page installed with Apache that displays helpful information and directory paths to Apache configuration files. An IP address of the Raspberry Pi is required to open a web page remotely from another computer. To obtain the IP address type one of the following at a Terminal Prompt:

hostname -I

ifconfig

When using ifconfig, look at the inet address for either eth0 (hardwired ethernet connection) or wlan0 (wireless connection). The inet address should look something like: 192.168.0.110 as an example. The actual address will be different but should have the same format of four numbers separated by periods.

Open a web browser on another computer on your local network and type the IP address in the address bar. Example: http://192.168.0.110 replacing the IP address with the one returned from the commands above. The resulting web page should look the same as the one returned on the Raspberry Pi after typing localhost in the address bar.

Setup and Verify Perl

Most Linux distributions will include Perl by default, making it a convenient and portable CGI solution. More about CGI and how it works later. Perl is only one solution as PHP, Python, or other scripting languages can also be used to accomplish the gateway between the web server and the embedded target. In the case of embedded web control panels there is normally only one line of code required to execute programs on the embedded target so it's not necessary to learn a new scripting language beyond the executable shell command regardless of the scripting language used.

Open a Terminal on the Raspberry Pi Desktop and type the following command at the prompt to test if Perl is already installed:

perl -v

If Perl is installed there should be a message including the perl version, otherwise the command will not be recognized. If Perl is not installed then type the following at the Terminal Prompt to start the installation: **sudo apt-get install perl**

Note: At the time of this writing, the following directory paths are used by default on the Raspberry Pi; if a path changes in the future or the Apache configuration file sets a new location then the path used in the examples will need to be changed respectfully.

CGI-BIN directory: **/usr/lib/cgi-bin**

Web HTML directory: **/var/www/html**

Perl directory: **/usr/bin/perl**

Apache2 Error Logs: **/var/log/apache2**

Apache2 Config Files: **/etc/apache2**

Verify CGI Operation

Now the CGI interface will be tested for proper operation using a simple script. Change directories to /usr/lib/cgi-bin by typing the following command at the Terminal Prompt:

cd /usr/lib/cgi-bin

Open the nano editor to quickly create a simple CGI file at a Terminal Prompt:

sudo nano test.cgi

Enter the following lines of code:

```
#!/usr/bin/perl
```

```
print "Content-type: text/html\n\n";
print "~~~~ CGI TEST OUTPUT ~~~~\n\n";
```

Press CTRL + O then ENTER to save edits.
Press CTRL + X to exit the nano editor.

You can type **cat test.cgi** to list the contents of the edited file.

Type **ls -als** to list the directory contents with permissions at the Terminal Prompt.

> **Note:** *Be sure to create and edit the test script on the Raspberry Pi. Files created on a Windows system will not have the standard unix style line endings, thus causing the script headers to fail. Linux expects a Line Feed (LF) character code "\n", or ASCII code 10, at the end of each line whereas Windows uses CRLF code "\r\n", or ASCII code 13 and then ASCII code 10. See the next chapter for information about converting line endings from Windows to Linux styles.*

Test the perl program locally by typing the following at the Terminal Prompt:

perl test.cgi

The output should look like the following:

Content-type: text/html

~~~~ CGI TEST OUTPUT ~~~~

Now make the CGI script executable and readable by typing the following at the Terminal Prompt:

sudo chmod +x+r test.cgi

Verify the program is executable using the following syntax:

./test.cgi

Don't forget to put the period before the "/" above. The output should look the same as before only now the CGI program is executable.

To test CGI operation, open a web browser on another computer and, using the IP address of the Raspberry Pi, as found in a previous step using hostname -I, type the following into the address bar: **http://192.168.0.110/cgi-bin/test.cgi** Don't forget to replace the IP address with the one for your device. The web page output should be displayed as follows in the web browser:

~~~~ CGI TEST OUTPUT ~~~~

Notice that the header line "Content-type: text/html" is not displayed as it basically provides the web server with information about the page content.

Now the CGI interface is tested and should be working properly. If the CGI script fails to run, refer to the Apache2 error log for possible details that can help debug the CGI interface by typing the following at the Terminal Prompt: **sudo cat /var/log/apache2/error.log**

For reference, the following are some helpful Terminal Commands relative to this chapter:

raspi-config	Set Raspberry Pi configuration options.
ifconfig	List or make modifications to network settings.
hostname -I	Display host IP addresses.
ls -als	List directory contents with formatting.
clear	Clears the Terminal Window.
exit	Exits and closes the Terminal Window.
ping	Try to verify an Internet Address is accessible.
pstree	Show all running processes.
a2enmod	Enable an Apache2 module.
a2dismod	Disable an Apache2 module.
a2ensite	Enable an Apache2 site / virtual host.
a2dissite	Disable an Apache2 site / virtual host.
a2enconf	Enable an Apache2 configuration.
a2disconf	Disable an Apache2 configuration.
systemctl restart apache2	Restart the Apache Web Server.
sudo pcmanfm	Run file manager as root.
service apache2 status	Get the state of the Apache Server.
service apache2 restart	Restart the Apache HTTP Server.

3

CGI Shell

CGI stands for Common Gateway Interface. It provides a method for a web server to access the low-level system on which it operates. A developer can use CGI to execute script files through a client browser and then view the results on a web page. The script files can be written in various languages like Bash shell, Perl, Python, PHP, Java, and others. Several examples of CGI scripting will be presented here. Each script will demonstrate the use of a shell command to run an executable program.

Some of the approaches used here are for reference only and will not be used in control panel examples; however, they are provided for those who may want to take an alternate approach to accessing the system shell and to demonstrate commonality between the various CGI technologies.

The primary purpose of CGI when creating virtual control panels is to execute commands or perform operations on the underlying computing system, like turning port pins on and off on the Raspberry Pi and then updating page elements dynamically based on the results without reloading the control panel. This gives it a more realistic feeling for the user. Understanding CGI concepts and knowing how to access things like POST data sent from a form on a web page is an important aspect of system control through a web interface.

This chapter demonstrates the basics of CGI operation and program execution through a web browser by means of executable scripts. Later chapters will dive down into the finite details of the CGI interface to examine GET and POST data, Environment Variables, and program INPUT/OUTPUT when executed via a web browser.

It is recommended that the Raspberry Pi be operated behind a firewall to prevent undesired access while developing and testing the script files. A local network router will normally serve the purpose of a firewall when connected to the internet via a modem. In some cases the modem will have an integrated router that acts as a firewall. When testing is complete, it may be desirable to remove the script files from the cgi-bin directory or change the permissions so they are no longer executable. One should always consider security risks when exposing a script to the outside world and consider adding username and password protection to script execution.

> **Note:** *All of the example text and graphics used in this book may be downloaded from the following URL:* ***https://www.mstmicro.com/projects/webpanels.tgz*** *If used, this file will need to be extracted into the /home/pi directory. The example instructions in each chapter will still need to be followed for correct operation of the code examples.*

Code Sandbox

In the previous chapter the simple test code was edited directly in the **/usr/lib/cgi-bin** directory and required superuser access using the sudo command. This makes editing a little more difficult as desktop editors cannot save to protected directories unless they were started with superuser access. It will be much easier to create code listings by using a local user project directory that does not require superuser access. The user sandbox should be in the user's home directory. This is user "pi" by default on the Raspberry Pi. If using a different user name then simply replace the "pi" directory in the path with the user account name being used.

In a Terminal Window, change the directory into the "pi" user folder: **cd /home/pi**

At the Terminal Prompt, or using the File Manager; create a sub-directory named "webproj": **mkdir webproj**

Change the path to the new directory: **cd webproj**

This directory is where all future code examples will be created. The finished examples will then be moved after completion to either the CGI or WWW directories as needed.

> **Note:** The Terminal command **pwd** can be used to determine the current Terminal path. For example, type pwd at the Terminal Prompt:
>
> pi@raspberrypi:~ $ **pwd**
> **/home/pi/webproj**
> pi@raspberrypi:~ $

Now create a new directory under the webproj directory named "chapter3":

mkdir chapter3

CD into the new directly: **cd chapter3**

The current path should now be: /home/pi/webproj/chapter3

Bash Script

The first script presented in this chapter will be a Bash Script designed to be executed through CGI. This example will run a simple shell command to retrieve a directory listing of the root directory and then display the results on a web page. One main difference between writing a Bash script to run at the command prompt versus through CGI is that the standard output device will be redirected to the web page rather than the normal console output. In this manner a standard HTML web page will be created in the script with the directory listing inserted within the body of the text.

Create a text file in the directory /home/pi/webproj/chapter3 with the filename bash1.sh. The file can be created by using a favorite text editor on the desktop or by typing the following two commands at a Terminal Prompt:

```
cd /home/pi/webproj/chapter3
nano bash1.sh
```

Enter the text from Program Listing 3.1 below. When finished, save the file by pressing CTRL+O then ENTER on the keyboard then CTRL+X to exit the nano editor. Make the shell program executable and readable by typing at the Terminal Prompt: **chmod +x+r bash1.sh**

To test the CGI script it needs to be copied to the path: /usr/lib/cgi-bin by typing the following at the Terminal Prompt: **sudo cp bash1.sh /usr/lib/cgi-bin/bash1.sh**

Open a web browser on the Raspberry Pi Desktop and type the path to the CGI script into the URL box: **localhost/cgi-bin/bash1.sh**

The script can also be viewed on a remote computer by opening a web browser and typing the Raspberry Pi IP address followed by the path to the CGI script as in the following example (remember to replace the IP address with the address of your Raspberry Pi):

192.168.0.3/cgi-bin/bash1.sh or basically **(IP Address)/cgi-bin/bash1.sh**

```
Directory Listing of root:

total 88
drwxr-xr-x  21 root root  4096 Feb 13  2020 .
drwxr-xr-x  21 root root  4096 Feb 13  2020 ..
drwxr-xr-x   2 root root  4096 Mar  4 09:53 bin
drwxr-xr-x   4 root root  4096 Dec 31  1969 boot
drwxr-xr-x  18 root root  3920 Mar  4 10:02 dev
drwxr-xr-x 123 root root 12288 Mar  4 10:05 etc
drwxr-xr-x   3 root root  4096 Feb 13  2020 home
drwxr-xr-x  17 root root  4096 Mar  4 09:50 lib
drwx------   2 root root 16384 Feb 13  2020 lost+found
drwxr-xr-x   3 root root  4096 May 28  2020 media
drwxr-xr-x   2 root root  4096 Feb 13  2020 mnt
drwxr-xr-x   6 root root  4096 Feb 13  2020 opt
dr-xr-xr-x 227 root root     0 Dec 31  1969 proc
drwx------   5 root root  4096 Feb 16  2020 root
drwxr-xr-x  29 root root   840 Mar  4 10:05 run
drwxr-xr-x   2 root root  4096 Mar  4 09:55 sbin
drwxr-xr-x   2 root root  4096 Feb 13  2020 srv
dr-xr-xr-x  12 root root     0 Dec 31  1969 sys
drwxrwxrwt   2 root root  4096 Mar  4 10:06 tmp
drwxr-xr-x  11 root root  4096 Feb 13  2020 usr
drwxr-xr-x  12 root root  4096 Mar  4 10:05 var
```

Figure 3.1 Web page output of the bash1.sh CGI script.

Program Listing 3.1: bash1.sh

```bash
#!/bin/bash

# This is a comment, start with a normal web page output.
echo "Content-type: text/html"
echo  #This blank echo line must be present for the HTML header to function correctly.
echo "<!DOCTYPE HTML PUBLIC \"-//W3C//DTD HTML 4.0 Transitional//EN\">"
echo "<html>"
echo "<head>"
echo "<title>Bash Shell CGI Script Example</title>"
echo "</head>"
echo "<body text='#191966' bgcolor='#FFFFFF' link='#F9DF77' vlink='#F9DF77' alink='#FFFF00' nosave>"
echo "<br/><br/><h3>"
echo "<font face='FreeMono, Lucida Console, Consolas'>"

# Change directory to root
cd /

# Command to list the contents of the current directory (root)
# and save the output in a buffer variable named (files).
files=$(ls -1al)

# Modify the files variable to replace all occurrences of a carriage return
# with a <br> so that new lines will show up in the web browser. Otherwise
# all of the directory contents will show up on one line.
files="${files//$'\n'/<br/>}"

# Modify the files variable to replace all occurrences of a space with a web
# non breaking space ( ) so that extra spaces will not be ignored on the web page.
files="${files//$' '/ }"

# Print a title over the directory listing.
echo "<font style='color:#660033'>Directory Listing of root:</font><br><br>"

# Send the directory listing buffer to the web page.
printf "$files"

# Finish the rest of the web page html information.
echo "</font></h3>"
echo "<br/>"
echo "</body></html>"
```

Avoiding Common Mistakes

There are several common errors that can easily cause a script to fail. When developing CGI code, it's important to know how to identify these errors and how to correct them. Four of the most common reasons for script failures are:

- Improper Case (URLs and File Names)
- Line Endings
- File Permissions
- Malformed Page Header

Improper Case

Unix and Linux have case-sensitive file systems. For example, two scripts with basically the same name can be created in the same directory as long as their case is different. Prog1.py and porg1.py can exist in the same directory as two distinct files and must be accessed by using the same case. In this example, the only difference is the "p" versus "P" as the first letter of the script name. The same is true of directory names. The following two URLs demonstrate the correct and incorrect case when executing a shell script through the Raspberry Pi web browser:

localhost/cgi-bin/bash1.sh   Correct!

localhost/CGI-BIN/bash1.sh   Incorrect!

If the latter was entered then the web browser would display a message on the page similar to the following:

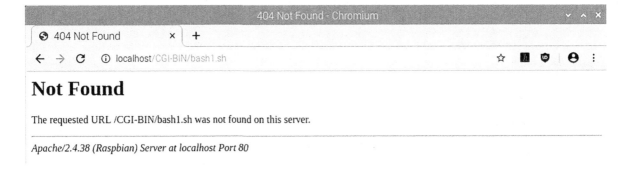

The URL case should be verified when encountering this type of error. Similarly, when accessing an application through a CGI script shell command, the path and program name are case sensitive. When an internal script failure occurs, the cause may not be easily determined. In some cases the only indication of a failure may be due to strange script behaviour or incorrect web page results. If the cause of a failure is not obvious then it's always best to refer to the Apache2 error logs normally found at the following location:

/var/log/apache2/(error logs)

Line Endings

For a script file to operate correctly on Linux the file must not contain MS DOS line endings or the script header will fail, causing the web page to report an error. If the script fails and the /var/log/apache2/error.log shows the following issue: **End of script output before headers: bash1.sh** or if trying to run the script from the Terminal Prompt: **sudo ./bash1.sh** returns a message like: **bash: ./bash1.sh: /bin/bash^M: bad interpreter: No such file or directory**, then most likely the text was originally edited on a windows system and then copied to the Raspberry Pi. The resulting web page may look similar to the following:

Linux systems use the Line Feed (LF) character code '\n', or ASCII code 10, at the end of each line whereas Windows systems use Carriage Return Line Feed (CRLF) character codes "\r\n", or ASCII code 13 and 10.

There are several methods available to fix this issue by changing the line endings back to unix style. Two automatic options are presented here:

Option1: Use the following Terminal commands:

```
sudo sed -e "s/\r//g" bash1.sh > bash1
sudo cp bash1 bash1.sh
sudo rm bash1
```

The sed command with the above options will create a new temporary file with the extra '\r' characters removed. The commands following then overwrite the original file with the new temporary one and then the temporary file is deleted.

Option2: Use the following Perl command at the Terminal Prompt:

```
perl -pi -e 's/\r\n/\n/' bash1.sh
```

This perl command will replace all instances of "\r\n" with '\n', thus removing all of the carriage returns from the text. Invalid line endings are very common when using a Raspberry Pi Remote Desktop, where the files are edited in Windows and then copied into an editor on the Raspberry Pi Desktop, or simply transferring files from a flash thumb drive that were edited on a Windows system. It's best to create and edit the example files on the Raspberry Pi to avoid invalid line endings.

File Permissions

CGI scripts are placed into the cgi-bin directory to make them available for execution by the web server; however, for the server to run the script it must have executable permissions, otherwise the following internal server error (500) may occur:

Since there are multiple issues that can cause error 500 it is necessary to consult the Apache error log /var/log/apache2/error.log to determine the cause. In this instance the log records "Permission denied" because the script is not executable or is not readable:

[Sun Aug 11 19:59:51.578150 2019] [cgid:error] [pid 2152] (13)Permission denied: AH01241: exec of '/usr/lib/cgi-bin/bash1.sh' failed

Before a script can be executed by the web server it must be made executable and readable by using the chmod +x+r command: **sudo chmod +x+r bash1.sh**

Malformed Page Header

All CGI scripts and applications must return a valid content-type header ending with two new line ('\n') characters or the server will incur a malformed page header error, normally indicated by an Internal Server Error 500 being displayed on the web page. As mentioned previously, there are many issues that can cause an error 500 so the Apache error log will need to be examined. In the case of the malformed header the following log entry exists:

[Sun Aug 11 20:26:43.219986 2019] [cgid:error] [pid 533] [client ::1:47888] malformed header from script 'bash1.sh': Bad header: <!DOCTYPE HTML PUBLIC "-//W3C/

This error was created by commenting out the second line of the Bash1.sh script:

#echo #This blank echo line must be present for the HTML header to function correctly.

The extra echo with no command creates a second line ending that is required by the HTML header. Since that line was commented out, the server encountered an internal error. A correct HTML header looks like the following:

Content-type: text/html\n\n

PHP Script

Although PHP seems to be losing popularity to Python, it's still widely used across the internet. PHP is an acronym for *Hypertext Preprocessor* and is a very powerful server-side scripting language. PHP files can contain text, HTML, CSS, JavaScript and PHP code. Because of the popularity of PHP it runs on various platforms like Windows, Mac OS X, Linx, Unix, Raspberry Pi, and others. The embedded control panel examples will not make use of PHP; however, due to the similarities to Perl, PHP could easily be substituted as the GCI language of choice. Many Linux distributions do not include PHP by default. The current release of the Raspberry Pi distribution does not include PHP.

To test if PHP is installed, open a Terminal Window and type the following at the command prompt: **php -v**

If the command does not return the PHP version string then the application is not installed.

To install php type the following at the prompt:

sudo apt-get install php libapache2-mod-php -y

To test PHP change directories to: **cd /home/pi/webproj/chapter3**
At the Terminal Prompt type: **nano phptst.php**
Enter the following line into the editor: **<?php echo "\n\nHello PHP!\n\n"; ?>**

Press CTRL + O then ENTER to save the file then CTRL + X to exit the program. Run the PHP script by typing:

php phptst.php

The following text should be displayed:

Hello PHP!

Now a PHP CGI script may be created and tested through a web browser. As in the previous Bash Shell example, the following PHP script will create a directory listing of the root filesystem and will add another element, a list of disk usage on the Raspberry Pi. In a Terminal Window, change to the **cd /home/pi/webproj/ selection3** directory. Using either a favorite desktop editor or nano, create a file with the name php1.php:

nano php1.php

Enter the script from Program Listing 3.2 below and then type CTRL + O then ENTER to save then CTRL + X to exit nano. At the Terminal Prompt, type in the command to make the script executable and readable:

chmod +x+r php1.php

Copy the PHP CGI script to: /usr/lib/cgi-bin by typing the following at the Terminal Prompt:

sudo cp php1.php /usr/lib/cgi-bin/php1.php

Open a web browser on the Raspberry Pi Desktop and type the path to the CGI script into the URL box:

localhost/cgi-bin/php1.php

The script can also be viewed on a remote computer by opening a web browser and typing the Raspberry Pi IP address followed by the path to the CGI script:

(IP Address)/cgi-bin/php1.php

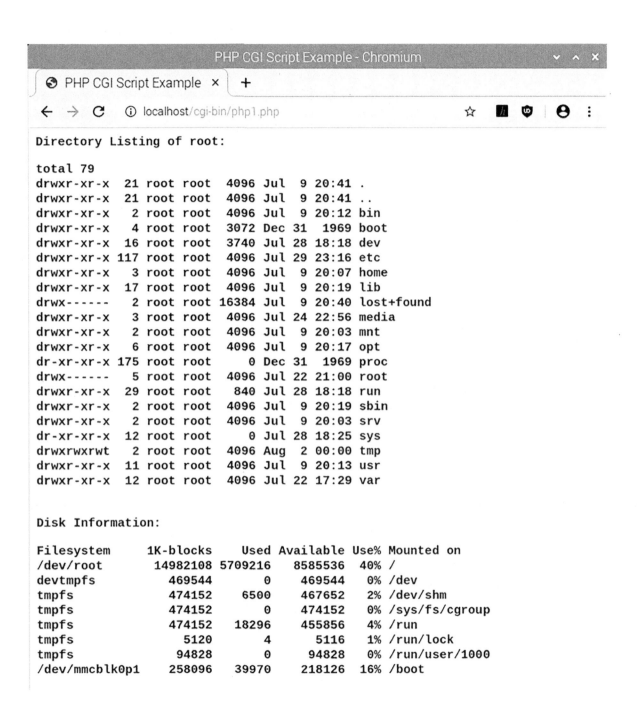

Figure 3.2 Web page output of php1.php CGI script.

Program Listing 3.2: php1.php

```php
<?php

// This line is a comment
echo "<title>PHP CGI Script Example</title>";
echo "<body text='#191966' bgcolor='#FFFFFF' nosave>";
echo "<h3>";
echo "<pre><font style='color:#660033'>Directory Listing of root:";
echo "</font><br></pre>";

// Change the working directory to root.
chdir('/');

// Get the directory listing of root.
$output = shell_exec('ls -1al');

// Use pre tag to keep proper spacing and formatting
// of the directory listing.
echo "<pre>";

// Output the directory listing to the web page.
echo $output;


// Get the amount of disk space available
$output = shell_exec('df');

echo "<br/><pre><font style='color:#660033'>Disk Information:";
echo "</font><br></pre>";

// Send the disk usage information to the web page.
echo $output;

echo "</pre></h3>";
?>
```

Python Script

Python is a popular programming language that can be used to create server-side web applications but can also be used to write desktop applications. Python can be run on most platforms including Mac, Windows, Linux, Raspberry Pi, and others. It has an English-like syntax that requires fewer lines of code compared to some interpreted languages. Unlike writing a program in 'C', Python uses line endings to complete a command where most others require a semicolon or parenthesis. Indentation and whitespace are used to define the scope of loops, functions, and classes rather than using curly brackets. Python will not be used when creating the web control panel examples; however, it is included here because it is a powerful programming language that could easily be substituted in place of Perl, and like Perl it is normally included with most popular Linux distributions. At the time of this writing, Python is included with the Raspberry Pi OS distribution. Several chapters will provide Python examples for both shell access and hardware I/O control. To verify that the latest version is installed, type the following at the Terminal Prompt:

python3 -c "print(__import__('sys').version)"

The output should look something like the following:

3.7.3 (default, Apr 3 2019, 05:39:12)
[GCC 8.2.0]

If the command is not found then Python needs to be installed:

sudo apt-get install python3-picamera

Test Python3 by opening a Python shell and following the commands listed below. At the Terminal type the following:

sudo python3

Python 3.7.3 (default, Apr 3 2019, 05:39:12)
[GCC 8.2.0] on linux
Type "help", "copyright", "credits" or "license" for more information.
>>>

Next type:

>>> print("Hello!!!")
Hello!!!
>>>

Use exit() or CTRL+Z to exit the Python shell.

>>> exit()

Time for a little twist! The following Python script will perform two shell access commands that will read the system date and time and then run the **cal** command to read the current month's calendar. The interesting part will be that the resulting web page will dynamically display the information by continually cycling through the base RED, GREEN, and BLUE color codes for all text within a <DIV> tag. Several new elements will be added to this script; first, a table is used to center the textual output with a surrounding border then, secondly, a JavaScript function is used to cycle through the color codes based on a callback timer. Make sure the calander package is installed by typeing the following at the Terminal Prompt: **sudo apt-get install ncal**

In a Terminal Window change to the **cd /home/pi/webproj/chapter3** directory. Using either a favorite desktop editor or nano, create a file with the name python1.py: **nano python1.py**

Enter the script from Program Listing 3.3 below and then type CTRL + O then ENTER to save then CTRL + X to exit nano. At the Terminal Prompt, type in the command to make the script executable:

chmod +x+r python1.py

Copy the Python script to: /usr/lib/cgi-bin by typing the following at the Terminal Prompt:

sudo cp python1.py /usr/lib/cgi-bin/python1.py

Open a web browser on the Raspberry Pi Desktop and type the path to the CGI script into the URL box:

localhost/cgi-bin/python1.py

The script can also be viewed on a remote computer by opening a web browser and typing the Raspberry Pi IP address followed by the path to the CGI script:

(IP Address)/cgi-bin/python1.py

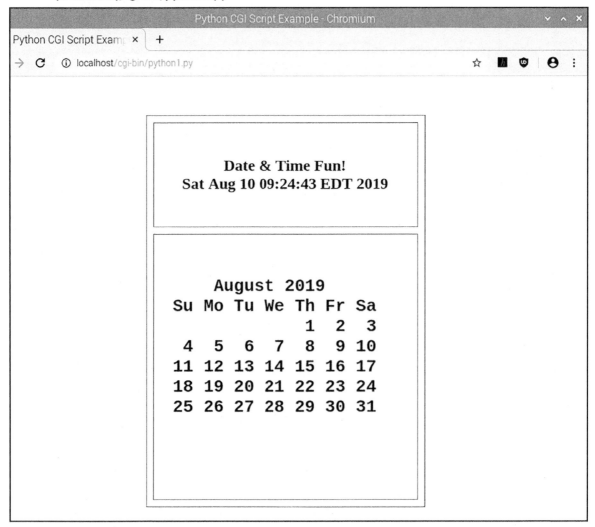

Figure 3.3 Web page output of python1.py CGI script.

Program Listing 3.3: python1.py

```python
#!/usr/bin/python3
import os

#This line is a comment.
print("Content-type:text/html\r\n\r\n")
print()
print("<!DOCTYPE html>")
print("<html>")
print("<head>")
print("<title>Python CGI Script Example</title>")
print("<meta charset=\"utf-8\"/>")

#JavaScript code
print("<script>")
print("var r = 30;")
print("var g = 30;")
print("var b = 30;")
print("var state = 1;")
print("setTimeout(colorChange, 1000);")
print("// JavaScript comment visible when viewing page source.")
print("// Timer callback function.")
print("function colorChange()")
print("{")
print("var caltxt = document.getElementById(\"funtxt\");")
print("switch(state)")
print("{")
print("  case 1: r+=10;")
print("       if(r > 0xF0) state = 2;")
print("  break;")
print("  case 2: r-=10;")
print("       if(r <= 30) state = 3;")
print("  break;")
print("  case 3: g+=10;")
print("       if(g > 0xF0) state = 4;")
print("  break;")
print("  case 4: g-=10;")
print("       if(g <= 30) state = 5;")
```

```
print("    break;")
print("    case 5: b+=10;")
print("        if(b > 0xF0) state = 6;")
print("    break;")
print("    case 6: b-=10;")
print("        if(b <= 30) state = 1;")
print("    break;")
print("}")
print("val = (r << 16) + (g << 8) + (b);")
print("caltxt.style.color = ")
print("\"#\" + (\"000000\" + val.toString(16)).substr(-6).toUpperCase();")
print("setTimeout(colorChange, 100);")
print("}")
print("</script>")


print("</head>")


#Start of the HTML body
print("<body text='#000000' bgcolor='#FFFFFF' nosave>")
print("<DIV name='funtxt' id='funtxt' style='color:BLACK;position: relative;")
print("top:50px;'>")
print("<table width='200' border='1' cellspacing='10' cellpadding='30'")
print(" align='center'><tbody>")


#Shell command, read the date and time
Cmd = os.popen('date').read()


print("<tr><td align='center'>")
print("<h2>Date & Time Fun!<br/>")
#Print the date and time in the body of the page.
print(Cmd)
print("</h2>")
print("</td></tr>")
print("<tr><td>")


print("<h1><p><pre>")


#Shell command to get the current month's calendar.
Cmd = os.popen('cal').read()
#Remove special characters from the calendar display.
Cmd = Cmd.replace("\x5f\x08", "")
```

```
#Print the calendar result.
print(Cmd)

print("</pre></p><h1>")
print("</td></tr>")
print("</tbody></table>")
print("</DIV>")
print("</body>")
print("</html>")
```

Script Details

The script in Program Listing 3.3 has a dynamic element that uses techniques that are well suited for updating static virtual web control panels. Notice the opening and closing <DIV> tag that surrounds the textual information. The <DIV> tag has an ID and a NAME attribute defined as **"funtxt"** that is used to identify the <DIV> page element. The JavaScript code gets a reference to the page element by its ID that is saved in the variable caltxt using the following command: **var caltxt = document.getElementById(\"funtxt\");**

Once the reference to the element is obtained, the contents within the <DIV> tag can be dynamically modified. In this case the color style of all text contained within the surrounding <DIV> tag is updated each time the JavaScript callback function is called by a timer. The JavaScript portion of the Python script is listed below with additional formatting and functional comments to provide additional clarity:

```
var r = 30;
var g = 30;
var b = 30;
var state = 1;
// Create a timer that calls the function "colorChange" 1000 milliseconds (one
second)
// after the web page loads.
setTimeout(colorChange, 1000);

// Timer callback function.
function colorChange()
{
        // Get a reference to the <DIV> element based on its ID attribute.
var caltxt = document.getElementById("funtxt");

// State machine that cycles through the RGB color values.
switch(state)
{
  case 1: r+=10;
      if(r > 0xF0) state = 2;
```

```
  break;
  case 2: r-=10;
      if(r <= 30) state = 3;
  break;
  case 3: g+=10;
      if(g > 0xF0) state = 4;
  break;
  case 4: g-=10;
      if(g <= 30) state = 5;
  break;
  case 5: b+=10;
      if(b > 0xF0) state = 6;
  break;
  case 6: b-=10;
      if(b <= 30) state = 1;
  Break;
}
// Combine the current RGB color values into one HEX value.
val = (r << 16) + (g << 8) + (b);

// Convert the HEX number into text and set the color style for all text in the
<DIV> tag.
caltxt.style.color = "#" + ("000000" + val.toString(16)).substr(-6).
toUpperCase();

// Set the next timer interval to 100 milliseconds for the next color change
update.
setTimeout(colorChange, 100);
}
```

Perl Script

Perl is a very well-defined and seasoned general-purpose programming language. It is available for most operating systems and comes by default with most Linux distributions. Perl can be used to create both Desktop and Server-Side Applications and has supporting debuggers to help detect and fix code issues. Perl is very powerful and can do almost anything, from opening ethernet sockets for streaming communications to sending automatic emails. Many libraries and modules are available to expand the language beyond its base functionality.

Perl can accomplish complex operations with a small amount of code. The resulting file sizes are small, making it ideal for embedded development with targets that have limited disk space. The Raspberry Pi Raspbian distribution includes Perl by default and is the scripting language of choice for the development of embedded web control panels. Only the shell interface will be used for most examples except for a few CGI debugging tools that will be created along the way. It would be easy to substitute another scripting language if so desired as long as the replacement language has shell access similar to the examples presented in this chapter.

The following Perl shell example will function in the same manner as the web control panels by executing a simple program written in 'C'. The static virtual web control panels use Perl scripts as a form of "back end" communications that are transparent to the user, hidden from view. The 'C' code created in this chapter will be expanded on over time and will become part of a framework that works together with the CGI script to form an interactive HTML control panel.

Program Listing 3.4 is a program written in 'C' that must be compiled into an executable program. The program file may be created using a favorite text editor or using nano as demonstrated here. First change into the chapter 3 folder previously created by typing at the Terminal Prompt: **cd /home/pi/webproj/chapter3**

Create the program file with the following operations:

1. Type the terminal command: **nano cgimain.c**
2. Enter the text from Program Listing 3.4. Be sure to enter the text exactly as listed or compiler errors could occur that will need to be corrected.
3. Type CTRL + O then ENTER to save then CTRL + X to exit nano.
4. Compile the program by typing: **gcc cgimain.c -o cgimain**
5. Make sure the program is executable and readable: **chmod +x+r cgimain**
6. Test the application by typing: **./cgimain**
7. Create a folder to place web applications that will be executed by the script. In this case a "webapp" folder will be created in the /var/www directory:

    sudo mkdir /var/www/webapp
8. Copy the **"cgimain"** program to the new webapp folder:

    sudo cp cgimain /var/www/webapp/cgimain

Program Listing 3.4: cgimain.c

```c
/*****************************************************************************
* File: cgimain.c
* Purpose: Program to control various Raspberry Pi operations from the web.
*
*****************************************************************************/
#include <stdio.h>

/*****************************************************************************
* Function: main()
* Receives: int argc - Number of command line arguments.
*           char *argv[] - Command line argument strings.
* Returns 0 = OK or ERROR CODE
*****************************************************************************/
int main(int argc, char *argv[])
{
```

```
    int retval = 0;

    printf("%s%c%c","Content-Type:text/html;charset=iso-8859-1",10,10);

    /* Start of web page. */
    printf("<!DOCTYPE html>\n");
    printf("<html>\n<head>\n\n<title>CGI Interface</title>\n\n</head>\n\n");
    printf("<body bgcolor=\"#669999\" text=\"#FFFFFF\">\n\n");

    /* HTML Web Output. */
    printf("<br/><br/><center>\n");
    printf("<h1>Hello CGI Application!</h1>\n");
    printf("<h3>This is the initial CGI application framework.</h3>\n\n");
    printf("</center><br/><br/>\n");
    printf("</body></html>\n");

    return retval;
}
```

The next step is to create a Perl script that will be used to launch the "cgimain" application for the web panel framework. Use a text editor or follow the commands to create the Perl script:

1. Change directories: **cd /home/pi/webproj/chapter3**

2. Create the Perl script by typing: **nano webpanel.cgi**

3. Enter the text for program listing 3.5 below.

4. Type CTRL + O then ENTER to save then CTRL + X to exit nano.

5. Make the script executable: **chmod +x+r webpanel.cgi**

6. Copy the script to the cgi-bin directory:

    sudo cp webpanel.cgi /usr/lib/cgi-bin/webpanel.cgi

7. Open a web browser on the Raspberry Pi Desktop and type the path to the CGI script into the URL box: **localhost/cgi-bin/webpanel.cgi**

The script can also be viewed on a remote computer by opening a web browser and typing the Raspberry Pi IP address followed by the path to the CGI script:

(IP Address)/cgi-bin/webpanel.cgi

Program Listing 3.5 : webpanel.cgi

```
#!/usr/bin/perl -w

my $retval = system("/var/www/webapp/cgimain");
if($retval != 0)
{
```

```
    print "Content-Type: text/html\n\n";
    print "<!DOCTYPE html>\n<html>\n<head>\n";
    print "<title>ERROR PAGE</title></head>\n";
    print "<body>\n";
    print "<h1>Error! \'cgimain\' failed.\n";
    print "<br />See Apache error log.</h1>\n";
    print "</body>\n</html>\n";
}
```

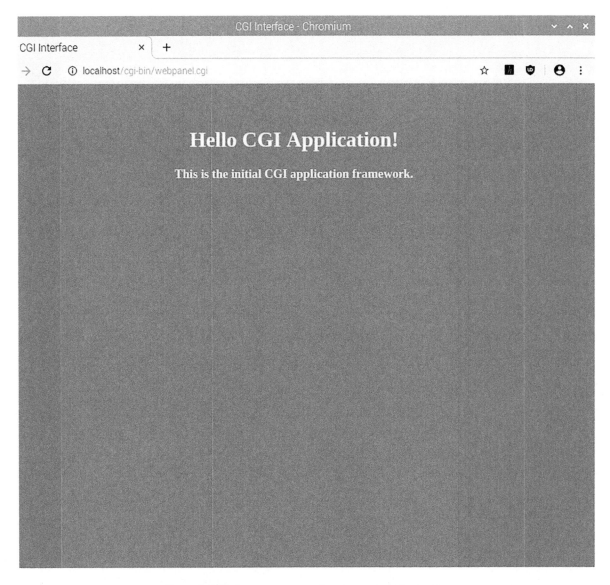

Figure 3.4 Web page output of webpanel.cgi Perl script.

Script Details

The "cgimain" program was executed by using the Perl system() function. The system() command basically creates a fork process that waits for the program to either succeed or fail and will return a value. The normal operation for a program is to return a zero on success or a non-zero error code on failure. In the case of this script, a non-zero value will cause a minimal web page to be output from Perl that alerts the developer that an error has occurred. When this script is used with the full web control panel framework, the output will be hidden from the user when in release mode. In developer mode the hidden script output will be displayed and alert the developer that an error has occurred.

The framework program and script files will be explained in more detail in the next chapter as the interface is examined and expanded upon.

Java Notes

Notice that Java is not mentioned as being a scripting language. All of the scripting languages demonstrated above are interpreted at the time of execution. An interpreter reads each line of script and creates actions based on the content; whereas Java has to be compiled into byte-codes first, before being executed. A Java Virtual Machine (JVM) is then required to execute the precompiled byte codes, which are loaded and executed at run-time. Java can achieve faster operations when executing because it has already been compiled into instructions that run efficiently by the JVM.

Java is a powerful high-level Object-Oriented programming language that is not dissimilar to 'C++' and 'C#'. Java can be run on any platform that has a JVM installed and can be used to create Desktop Applications, Java Servlets, and Java Applets. Java Desktop applications are like programs that run on the system. Java Servlets are server-side applications that are launched by a web server in a similar fashion to CGI scripts. Java Applets are actual Java programs that run within the web browser, not to be confused with JavaScript, which is not related to Java or Java development. JavaScript can be used by Java when serving up web pages, but JavaScript is not part of the Java programming language.

4

CGI Environment Variables

Web Control Panels rely heavily on the CGI interface for system control and monitoring. When a web browser makes a request for a CGI script, the web server creates a special environment in order to execute a new process on the target device. The environment uses two standard mechanisms to interface with the new process:

- Environment Variables
- Application Input/Output

This chapter covers environment variables and how they interact with the web control panel application. Web server environment variables are not the same as system environment variables as the CGI interface provides a custom environment specific to the CGI process. Some system environment variables are passed on to the CGI interface, but most are not. The Apache HTTP Server configuration file can be modified to add additional system environment variables as well as custom user environment variables to the CGI interface that is accessible by CGI applications.

During the execution of a CGI script, the web server provides a wealth of information through Environment Variables that are readable by the script or underlying application. They hold information about the Web Client, Web Server, CGI script, and CGI request information. Some Environment Variables are required to obtain user input from the Web Client and others are informational, not necessarily required by all applications. Environment Variables can be helpful when debugging web applications, thus several examples will be covered in this chapter. The examples presented here can be used as debugging tools when developing any CGI application. Later chapters will demonstrate how to make use of these tools within a web control panel framework that makes hidden CGI calls that are transparent to the user.

Reading Environment Variables

There are two methods for accessing CGI Environment Variables. They can be read directly by name or by reading a full list of [name:value] pairs. It's helpful to be able to read and display a full list of supported environment variables on a web page because some web servers will provide more environment variables than others; however, there is a base subset that almost all web servers will provide. Displaying environment variables on a web page should only be used as a tool that is implemented when developing web applications. It would be risky to allow external users access to internal server information in such a manner. Testing and development should be accomplished behind a secure firewall for local network access only. Optionally the environment variables could be read and saved into a text file for reference. Web security is not as much of an issue when using a Raspberry Pi on a local home network provided it's not placed into a router's DMZ and router port forwarding is disabled.

Read by Name

The first script example will demonstrate how to read some of the most important environment variables by name. Create a script file by following these steps:

1. To get started, a new folder must be created within the webproj directory for this chapter. At a Terminal Prompt, change into the project directory:

   cd /home/pi/webproj

2. Create a new directory where the chapter 4 code will be stored:

   mkdir chapter4

3. Change into the chapter4 directory: **cd chapter4**

4. Using either a favorite desktop editor or nano, create a file with the name cgidbg1.cgi:

   nano cgidbg1.cgi

5. Enter the script from Program Listing 4.1 below and then type CTRL + O then ENTER to save then CTRL + X to exit nano.

6. At the Terminal Prompt, type in the command to make the script executable and readable:

   chmod +x+r cgidbg1.cgi

7. Copy the Perl script to: /usr/lib/cgi-bin by typing the following at the Terminal Prompt:

   sudo cp cgidbg1.cgi /usr/lib/cgi-bin/cgidbg1.cgi

8. Open a web browser on the Raspberry Pi Desktop and type the path to the CGI script into the URL box:

   localhost/cgi-bin/cgidbg1.cgi

9. The script can also be viewed on a remote computer by opening a web browser and typing the Raspberry Pi IP address followed by the path to the CGI script:

   (IP Address)/cgi-bin/cgidbg1.cgi

Program Listing 4.1: cgidbg1.cgi

```perl
#!/usr/bin/perl -wT


# Add important runtime and compile-time script checks.
use strict;
# A script failure requires a look at the Apache error log.



print "Content-type: text/html\n\n";
print "<!DOCTYPE html>\n";
print "<html>\n<head>\n";
print "<title>CGI Environment Variables</title>\n</head>\n\n";
```

```perl
print "<body bgcolor='#235d80' text='#cadaea'>\n\n";
print "<center><i><strong><u>\n";
print "<font color='#cadaea' size='7'>CGI Environment Variables</font>\n";
print "</u></strong></i></center>\n\n";

my $TimeStr = ServerTime();
my $DateStr = ServerDate();
print "<br/><center><i><strong><font color='#cadaea' size='5'>";
print "Server Time: $DateStr $TimeStr</font></strong></i></center>\n\n";
ListEnvByName();

print "</body>\n</html>";


sub ServerTime
{
     my $Servertime;
     my @timeValue = localtime(time);
     (my $sec, my $min, my $hour) = @timeValue;
     $Servertime = sprintf "%d:%02s:%02s %s", ($hour > 12) ? ($hour - 12) :
          ($hour), $min, $sec, ($hour > 12) ? "PM" : "AM";
     return $Servertime;
}

sub ServerDate
{
     my $ServerDate;
     my @months = qw(Jan Feb Mar Apr May Jun Jul Aug Sep Oct Nov Dec);
     my @timeValue = localtime(time);
     (my $sec, my $min, my $hour, my $DAY, my $MONTH, my $YEAR) = @timeValue;
     $ServerDate = sprintf "%s-%s-%d", $months[$MONTH], $DAY, ($YEAR + 1900);
     return $ServerDate;
}


sub ListEnvByName
{
    print "<br/><br/>\n";
    print "<table style='width:800px;' ALIGN='center' border='1' ";
    print "cellspacing='1' cellpadding='10' bgcolor='#555555'\n";
    print "bordercolor='354f6a'>\n";
```

```perl
print "<tr><td ALIGN='center' COLSPAN='2' bgcolor='#354f6a'>\n";
print "<font color='#cadaea' size='4'>\n";
print "Table of Available Enviroment Variables</font>\n";
print "</td></tr>\n\n";

printf"<tr bgcolor='#114170'><td>HTTP_USER_AGENT:</td>";
printf"<td>  %s<br></td></tr>\n",
    $ENV{HTTP_USER_AGENT} ? $ENV{HTTP_USER_AGENT} : " ";
printf"<tr bgcolor='#15487a'><td>HTTP_REFERER:</td>";
printf"<td> %s<br></td></tr>\n",
    $ENV{HTTP_REFERER} ? $ENV{HTTP_REFERER} : " ";
printf"<tr bgcolor='#114170'><td>CONTENT_TYPE:";
printf"</td><td> %s<br></td></tr>\n",
    $ENV{CONTENT_TYPE} ? $ENV{CONTENT_TYPE} : " ";
printf"<tr bgcolor='#15487a'><td>CONTENT_LENGTH:";
printf"</td><td>  %s<br></td></tr>\n",
    $ENV{CONTENT_LENGTH} ? $ENV{CONTENT_LENGTH} : " ";
printf"<tr bgcolor='#114170'><td>SERVER_SOFTWARE:";
printf"</td><td>  %s<br></td></tr>\n",
    $ENV{SERVER_SOFTWARE} ? $ENV{SERVER_SOFTWARE} : " ";
printf"<tr bgcolor='#15487a'><td>SERVER_ADDR:";
printf"</td><td>  %s<br></td></tr>\n",
    $ENV{SERVER_ADDR} ? $ENV{SERVER_ADDR} : " ";
printf"<tr bgcolor='#114170'><td>SERVER_PORT:";
printf"</td><td>  %s<br></td></tr>\n",
    $ENV{SERVER_PORT} ? $ENV{SERVER_PORT} : " ";
printf"<tr bgcolor='#15487a'><td>REMOTE_ADDR:";
printf"</td><td>  %s<br></td></tr>\n",
    $ENV{REMOTE_ADDR} ? $ENV{REMOTE_ADDR} : " ";
printf"<tr bgcolor='#114170'><td>DOCUMENT_ROOT:";
printf"</td><td>  %s<br></td></tr>\n",
    $ENV{DOCUMENT_ROOT} ? $ENV{DOCUMENT_ROOT} : " ";
printf"<tr bgcolor='#15487a'><td>SCRIPT_FILENAME:";
printf"</td><td>  %s<br></td></tr>\n",
    $ENV{SCRIPT_FILENAME} ? $ENV{SCRIPT_FILENAME} : " ";
printf"<tr bgcolor='#114170'><td>GATEWAY_INTERFACE:";
printf"</td><td>  %s<br></td></tr>\n",
    $ENV{GATEWAY_INTERFACE} ? $ENV{GATEWAY_INTERFACE} : " ";
printf"<tr bgcolor='#15487a'><td>REQUEST_METHOD:";
printf"</td><td>  %s<br></td></tr>\n",
    $ENV{REQUEST_METHOD} ? $ENV{REQUEST_METHOD} : " ";
```

```perl
    printf"<tr bgcolor='#114170'><td>REQUEST_URI:";
    printf"</td><td>  %s<br></td></tr>\n",
       $ENV{REQUEST_URI} ? $ENV{REQUEST_URI} : " ";
    printf"<tr bgcolor='#15487a'><td>SCRIPT_NAME:";
    printf"</td><td>  %s<br></td></tr>\n",
       $ENV{SCRIPT_NAME} ? $ENV{SCRIPT_NAME} : " ";
    printf"<tr bgcolor='#114170'><td>QUERY_STRING:";
    printf"</td><td>  %s<br></td></tr>\n",
       $ENV{QUERY_STRING} ? $ENV{QUERY_STRING} : " ";

    print"</table>\n";
}
```

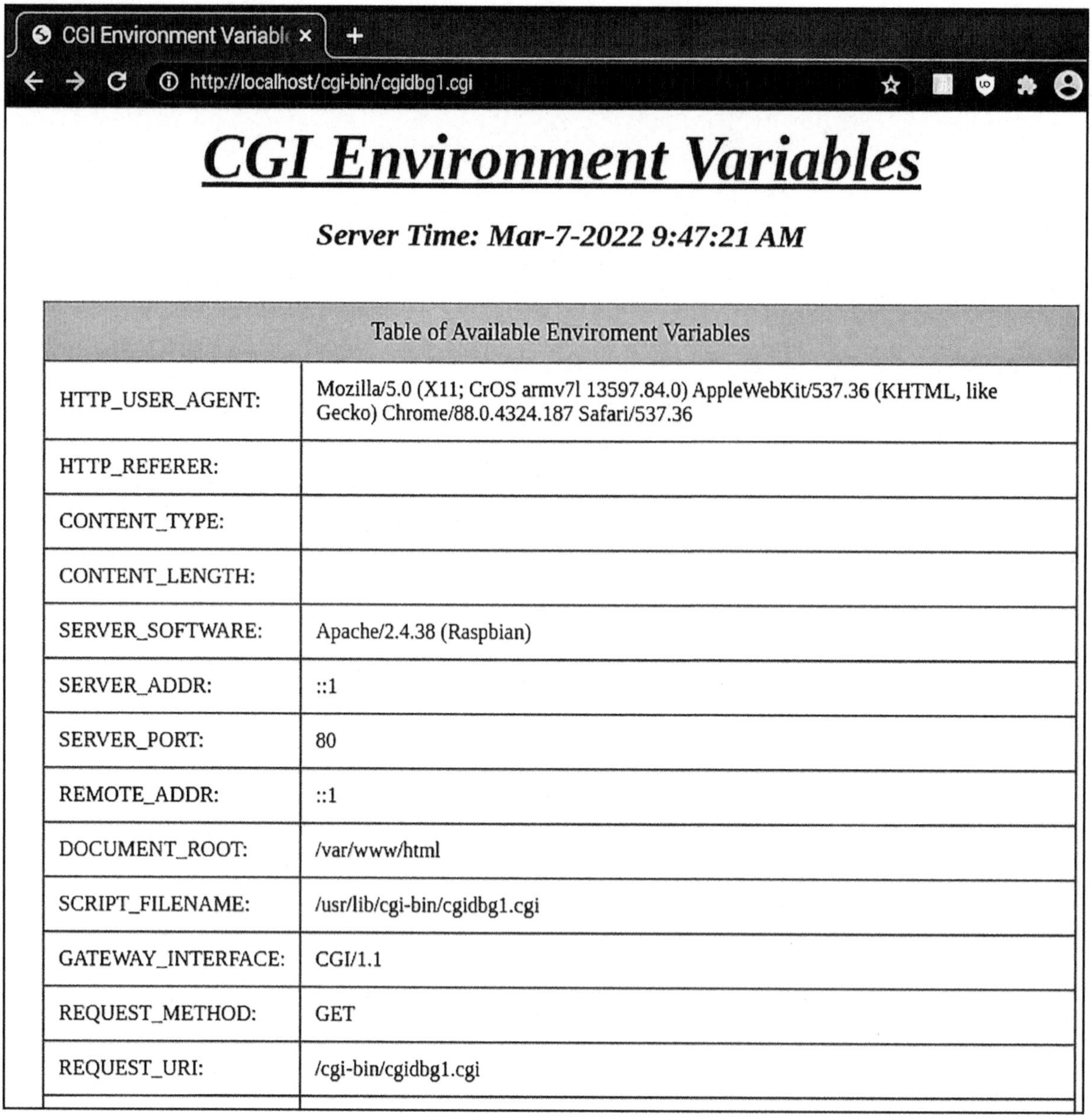

Table of Available Enviroment Variables	
HTTP_USER_AGENT:	Mozilla/5.0 (X11; CrOS armv7l 13597.84.0) AppleWebKit/537.36 (KHTML, like Gecko) Chrome/88.0.4324.187 Safari/537.36
HTTP_REFERER:	
CONTENT_TYPE:	
CONTENT_LENGTH:	
SERVER_SOFTWARE:	Apache/2.4.38 (Raspbian)
SERVER_ADDR:	::1
SERVER_PORT:	80
REMOTE_ADDR:	::1
DOCUMENT_ROOT:	/var/www/html
SCRIPT_FILENAME:	/usr/lib/cgi-bin/cgidbg1.cgi
GATEWAY_INTERFACE:	CGI/1.1
REQUEST_METHOD:	GET
REQUEST_URI:	/cgi-bin/cgidbg1.cgi

Figure 4.1 Web page output of cgidbg1.cgi Perl script.

Remember to check the Apache error log in the event of an error. It's a good practice to check the error logs after creating and running a script just to make sure an error has not occurred even though the web page is displayed properly. **/var/log/apache2/(error logs)**

It's also a good practice to find the developer menu in the browser client and select the "View Source" option. This will provide a display of the final HTML output sent to the browser. The HTML language is very forgiving and tends to work with subtle errors in coding so viewing the source may uncover small typos that need to be fixed in the source code.

Script Output

Figure 4.1 shows the output of cgidbg1.cgi. Notice that several of the environment variables do not have any content. This is because the script can be called by different methods that will vary the content of the environment variables. For instance, try changing the URL in the browser address box to add query parameters as follows:

(IP Address)/cgi-bin/cgidbg1.cgi?Device=Raspberry%20Pi

The "%20" is a URL-encoded space character. After accessing the page with the URL text above, there should now be content in the previously empty environment variable named QUERY_STRING and the contents of REQUEST_URI should have changed also. Please note that printing the contents of the QUERY_STRING in a script can be very dangerous if on a public network as an individual could type command line information that could cause damage to the underlying system when the print method is called. Use the QUERY_STRING environment variable with caution and always verify the input to make sure it's as expected.

If the same URL listed above is opened in a browser on a mobile device connected to the local network, then the content of some of the environment variables will be different. Pay special attention to the HTTP_USER_AGENT environment variable; its content can be used to identify mobile devices, allowing the page displayed to differ depending on device type.

Table 4.1 below provides a definition of the environment variables used in the cgidbg1.cgi script.

Table 4.1 Partial list of environment variable descriptions.

Environment Variable	Description
HTTP_USER_AGENT	The request browser information.
HTTP_REFERER	The document that submitted form data, if any.
CONTENT_TYPE	POST or PUT request MIME type.
CONTENT_LENGTH	The byte length of the data for POST or PUT requests.
SERVER_SOFTWARE	Name and version of the web server software.
SERVER_ADDR	The server IP address for this instance. A server may have more than one IP address across multiple physical networks.
SERVER_PORT	The server port number of the request. Port 80 by default.
REMOTE_ADDR	IP address of the client making the request.
DOCUMENT_ROOT	The path to the www root folder containing web page files.
SCRIPT_FILENAME	The path to the script file being executed on the server.
GATEWAY_INTERFACE	The CGI specification version.
REQUEST_METHOD	The method used by the request: GET or POST.
REQUEST_URI	The full URL of the request.
SCRIPT_NAME	Relative path of the script being executed.
QUERY_STRING	Any string that follows the ? in a request URL.

Read All Environment Variables

The next script example will read all available environment variables and display them on a web page. The number of available variables will vary depending on platform and web server. Except for the QUERY_STRING, only the variables with content will be in the list so the list will vary depending on the request type. Generally, POST requests will have more variables than GET requests due to the additional fields required to read web page form data. Create a debug script file with the following steps:

1. Change into the chapter4 directory: **cd /home/pi/webproj/chapter4**

2. Using either a favorite desktop editor or nano, create a file with the name cgidbg2.cgi:

   nano cgidbg2.cgi

3. Enter the script from Program Listing 4.2 below and then type CTRL + O then ENTER to save then CTRL + X to exit nano.

4. At the Terminal Prompt, type in the command to make the script executable and readable:

   chmod +x+r cgidbg2.cgi

5. Copy the Perl script to: /usr/lib/cgi-bin by typing the following at the Terminal Prompt:

   sudo cp cgidbg2.cgi /usr/lib/cgi-bin/cgidbg2.cgi

6. Open a web browser on the Raspberry Pi Desktop and type the path to the CGI script into the URL box:

   localhost/cgi-bin/cgidbg2.cgi

7. The script can also be viewed on a remote computer by opening a web browser and typing the Raspberry Pi IP address followed by the path to the CGI script:

   (IP Address)/cgi-bin/cgidbg2.cgi

Program Listing 4.2: cgidbg2.cgi

```perl
#!/usr/bin/perl -wT


# Add important runtime and compile-time script checks.
use strict;
# A script failure requires a look at the Apache error log.

print "Content-type: text/html\n\n";
print "<!DOCTYPE html>\n";
print "<html>\n<head>\n";
print "<title>CGI Environment Variables</title>\n</head>\n\n";
print "<body bgcolor='#235d80' text='#cadaea'>\n\n";
print "<center><i><strong><u>\n";
print "<font color='#cadaea' size='7'>CGI Environment Variables</font>\n";
print "</u></strong></i></center>\n\n";


my $TimeStr = ServerTime();
my $DateStr = ServerDate();
```

```perl
print "<br/><center><i><strong><font color='#cadaea' size='5'>";
print "Server Time: $DateStr $TimeStr</font></strong></i></center>\n\n";
DispEnvironmentVariables();

print "</body></html>";

sub ServerTime
{
    my $Servertime;
    my @timeValue = localtime(time);
    (my $sec, my $min, my $hour) = @timeValue;
    $Servertime = sprintf "%d:%02s:%02s %s", ($hour > 12) ? ($hour - 12) :
        ($hour), $min, $sec, ($hour > 12) ? "PM" : "AM";
    return $Servertime;
}


sub ServerDate
{
    my $ServerDate;
    my @months = qw(Jan Feb Mar Apr May Jun Jul Aug Sep Oct Nov Dec);
    my @timeValue = localtime(time);
    (my $sec, my $min, my $hour, my $DAY, my $MONTH, my $YEAR) = @timeValue;
    $ServerDate = sprintf "%s-%s-%d", $months[$MONTH], $DAY, ($YEAR + 1900);
    return $ServerDate;
}


sub DispEnvironmentVariables
{
    my $lineToggle = 0;
    print "<br/><br/>\n";
    print "<table style='width:800px;' ALIGN='center' border='1' ";
    print "cellspacing='1' cellpadding='10' bgcolor='#555555' ";
    print "bordercolor='354f6a'>\n";
    print "<tr><td ALIGN='center' COLSPAN='2' bgcolor='#354f6a'>\n";
    print "<font color='#cadaea' size='4'> ";
    print "Table of Available Environment Variables</font>\n";
    print "</td></tr>\n\n";

    #Print each environment variable key-Value pair.
    foreach my $env_vars (sort keys(%ENV))
    {
```

```perl
    print "<!-- Table Row -->\n";

    # Alternate the background color for each table row
    # to help the content stand out.
    if($lineToggle == 0) { print "<tr bgcolor='#114170'>\n"; }
    else { print "<tr bgcolor='#15487a'>\n"; }

    # Key name text
    print "<td><font color='#cadaea' size='3'>$env_vars</font></td>\n";

    # Value text
    print "<td><font color='#cadaea' size='3'>";
     print "$ENV{$env_vars}</font></td>\n";
    print "</tr>\n\n";

    # Alternate the lineToggle variable between 0 and 1
    # using exclusive or operator.
    $lineToggle ^= 1;
  }
  print"\n</table>\n";
}
```

CGI Environment Variables

Server Time: Sep-7-2019 11:51:23 PM

Table of Available Enviroment Variables	
CONTEXT_DOCUMENT_ROOT	/usr/lib/cgi-bin/
CONTEXT_PREFIX	/cgi-bin/
DOCUMENT_ROOT	/var/www/html
GATEWAY_INTERFACE	CGI/1.1
HTTP_ACCEPT	text/html,application/xhtml+xml,application/xml;q=0.9,image/webp, exchange;v=b3
HTTP_ACCEPT_ENCODING	gzip, deflate
HTTP_ACCEPT_LANGUAGE	en-US,en;q=0.9
HTTP_CACHE_CONTROL	max-age=0
HTTP_CONNECTION	keep-alive
HTTP_HOST	192.168.40.113
HTTP_UPGRADE_INSECURE_REQUESTS	1
HTTP_USER_AGENT	Mozilla/5.0 (X11; Linux armv7l) AppleWebKit/537.36 (KHTML, like Gecko) Raspbian Chromium/74.0.3729.157 Chrome/74.0.3729.157 Safari/537.36
PATH	/usr/local/sbin:/usr/local/bin:/usr/sbin:/usr/bin:/sbin:/bin
QUERY_STRING	
REMOTE_ADDR	192.168.40.113
REMOTE_PORT	60792
REQUEST_METHOD	GET
REQUEST_SCHEME	http
REQUEST_URI	/cgi-bin/cgidbg2.cgi
SCRIPT_FILENAME	/usr/lib/cgi-bin/cgidbg2.cgi
SCRIPT_NAME	/cgi-bin/cgidbg2.cgi

Figure 4.2 Web page output of cgidbg2.cgi Perl script.

Adding Environment Variables

Additional environment variables may be added to the list of available CGI server parameters. The Apache HTTP Server supports both custom environment variables and passing additional system environment variables to the CGI interface using the following two commands:

SetEnv [Variable Name] ["Variable Value String"]

PassEnv [System Environment Variable Name]

Only system-level environment variables that are loaded at boot time when the web service is started may be passed to the CGI interface. User environment variables that are created when a user logs in are not available to the web server. For instance, the UID variable is not accessible because it is created when the user logs into the system. Custom environment variables can be created by editing the Apache configuration file. Follow the next steps to create a new custom environment variable that will be available to CGI applications:

1. At a Terminal Prompt, change into the Apache sites-available directory:

   cd /etc/apache2/sites-available

2. Make a backup copy of the 000-default.conf configuration file:

   sudo cp 000-default.conf 000-default.conf.bak

3. Edit the file 000-default.conf using nano at the user prompt:

   sudo nano 000-default.conf

4. Press the down arrow in the nano editor until the following line is found:

   <VirtualHost *:80>

5. Listing 4.3 shows an example of how to enter a user environment variable between the opening and closing <VirtualHost> xml tags. Enter the following line somewhere between the two tags as in the example listing:

   SetEnv HTTP_USER_ENV1 "Custom user env string"

   The contents of the text between the <VirtualHost> xml tags may differ slightly from the example Listing 4.3.

6. When finished editing, type CTRL + O then ENTER to save then CTRL + X to exit nano.

7. For the changes to take effect, the Apache HTTP Server must be restarted. Type the following at the Terminal Prompt: **sudo service apache2 restart**

8. If the web server fails to start then run the following command to view the issue:

   service apache2 status

9. If unable to correct any issue, the backup copy of the config file may be restored.

10. Once the web server has restarted the CGI debug script may be run to view the results. Open a web browser and type in the Raspberry Pi IP address followed by the path to the CGI script: **(IP Address)/ cgi-bin/cgidbg2.cgi** or open a web browser on the Raspberry Pi Desktop and type the path to the CGI script into the URL box: **localhost/cgi-bin/cgidbg2.cgi**

11. The new user environment variable should show up in the table on the debug web page.

Listing 4.3

```
<VirtualHost *:80>
        # The ServerName directive sets the request scheme, hostname and port t$
        # the server uses to identify itself. This is used when creating
        # redirection URLs. In the context of virtual hosts, the ServerName
        # specifies what hostname must appear in the request's Host: header to
        # match this virtual host. For the default virtual host (this file) this
        # value is not decisive as it is used as a last resort host regardless.
        # However, you must set it for any further virtual host explicitly.
        #ServerName www.example.com

        ServerAdmin webmaster@localhost
        DocumentRoot /var/www/html
        SetEnv HTTP_USER_ENV1 "Custom user env string"

        # Available loglevels: trace8, ..., trace1, debug, info, notice, warn,
        # error, crit, alert, emerg.
        # It is also possible to configure the loglevel for particular
        # modules, e.g.
        #LogLevel info ssl:warn

        ErrorLog ${APACHE_LOG_DIR}/error.log
        CustomLog ${APACHE_LOG_DIR}/access.log combined

        # For most configuration files from conf-available/, which are
        # enabled or disabled at a global level, it is possible to
        # include a line for only one particular virtual host. For example the
        # following line enables the CGI configuration for this host only
        # after it has been globally disabled with "a2disconf".
        #Include conf-available/serve-cgi-bin.conf
</VirtualHost>
```

5

CGI ENVIRONMENT VARIABLES IN 'C'

CGI Environment variables are available to 'C' programs when executed through a web server. This is true if called directly or by means of a server-side script. In this chapter, web page output will be created to mimic the two Perl examples from the preceding chapter by means of a web control panel application project. This project will serve as the default structure that will be built upon over the remaining chapters for all web control panel operations.

Project Overview

The initial project 'C' source code will provide a debug interface to display CGI Environment variables by accessing them both by Name and by iterating through the full list of available variables. This will be accomplished by two function calls that will depend on the Perl command line that executes the cgimain application. The application web page output will depend on the Perl script command line options.

The web control panel application project consists of a total of seven files. Below is a list of the file names and a brief description:

1. **cgimain.c** - The application main() function and entry point into the web panel control code.

2. **cgimain.h** - The header file for the cgimain application code to contain function prototypes and definitions.

3. **cgitools.c** - This file will contain all of the application interface functions used to process CGI GET and POST data as well as environment variable parsing.

4. **cgitools.h** - The header file for cgitools.c to contain function prototypes, definitions, and structures.

5. **cgidebug.c** - This file is used to hold CGI interface debugging functions that include reading CGI environment variables.

6. **cgidebug.h** - Header file for cgidebug.c to contain function prototypes and definitions.

7. **webpanel.cgi** - This file is the Perl script that is called from the web server to execute the cgimain web control panel application.

8. **makefile** - Project makefile is used to build and install the web control panel application on the Raspberry Pi.

First Steps

Before creating the web control panel application structure, the chapter5 directory needs to be created and initial project files copied into the new directory and then modified.

Follow these steps to get started:

1. From a Raspberry Pi Terminal Prompt, change into the project directory:

   cd /home/pi/webproj

2. Create the chapter5 directory: **mkdir chapter5**

3. Copy the file cgimain.c from the chapter3 directory to the chapter5 directory:

   cp ./chapter3/cgimain.c ./chapter5/cgimain.c

4. Copy the file webpanel.cgi from the chapter3 directory to the chapter5 directory:

   cp ./chapter3/webpanel.cgi ./chapter5/webpanel.cgi

5. Change into the chapter5 directory:

   cd chapter5

Next, the individual project files will be created or edited in the chapter 5 project directory. Alternatively, *all of the example text and graphics used in this book may be downloaded from the following URL:*

   https://www.mstmicro.com/projects/webpanels.tgz

Program Listing 5.1, cgimain.c, contains the main( ) application entry point and two additional functions used to process debug and POST data input. Notice the main( ) function has three input variables, int argc, char *argv[], and char *env[]. The first two are the standard command line arguments list, but the third variable is a pointer to a list of environment variables. Not all systems support the third input variable, thus it will not be used in the control panel application but is included for reference. The environment variable list will be accessed by the use of an external global variable that will be used by the cgidebug.c source code.

The main( ) function checks to make sure the application is called by the Perl script by checking for the "CGI" text input string and, if valid, continues to check for a debug or POST data request. POST data requests result in the calling of the PostDataOperations( ) function and will be covered in the next chapter. Debug requests will result in a call of the DebugOperations( ) function that will provide web page output similar to the environment variable display demonstrated in the previous chapter. This serves to provide a web control panel debug interface and to demonstrate using CGI environment variables in 'C'.

Follow these steps to edit the main program file cgimain.c

1. From a command prompt change into the chapter5 project directory:

   cd /home/pi/webproj/chapter5

2. Using nano or a favorite text editor, open cgimain.c:

   nano cgimain.c

3. Edit cgimain.c to match Program Listing 5.1 below.

4. When finished editing, press CTRL + O then ENTER to save then CTRL + X to exit nano.

Program Listing 5.1: cgimain.c

```c
/*****************************************************************************
* File: cgimain.c
* Purpose: Program to control various Raspberry Pi operations from the web.
*
*****************************************************************************/
#include <stdio.h>
#include <string.h>
#include <stdlib.h>

#include "cgimain.h"
#include "cgitools.h"
#include "cgidebug.h"



/*****************************************************************************
* Function: main()
* Receives: int argc - Number of command line arguments.
*           char *argv[] - Command line argument strings.
*           char *env[]  - Optionally add for systems that support
*                   environment variables passed to the main function.
*
* Returns 0 = OK or ERROR CODE
*****************************************************************************/
int main(int argc, char *argv[], char *env[])
{
    int retval = 0;

    /* Start of web page. */
    printf("%s%c%c","Content-Type:text/html;charset=iso-8859-1",10,10);
    printf("<!DOCTYPE html>\n");

    /* Verify the application is called by the CGI script. If the argument
     * text "CGI" is not found then don't run anything. */
    if(argc > 1 && strncmp(argv[1], "CGI", 3) == 0)
    {
        /* If debug operations specified. */
        if(argc >= 3 && strncmp(argv[2], "DEBUG", 5) == 0)
        {
            retval = DebugOperations(argc, argv, env);
```

```
        }

        /* Act on control panel POST data, if any. */
        else
        {
            retval = PostDataOperations(argc, argv, env);
        }

    }
    else
    {
        printf("<html>\n<head>\n<title>Execution Error</title>\n\n</head>\n\n");
        printf("<body bgcolor=\"#669999\" text=\"#FFFFFF\">\n\n");
        printf("<br/><br/><center>\n<h1>Application Error!</h1>\n</center>\n");
        printf("<br/><br/>\n</body></html>\n");
        retval = 0;
    }
    return retval;
}


/******************************************************************************
* Function: PostDataOperations()
* Purpose: Act on POST data form information to perform various control
*          panel operations.
*
* Receives: int argc - Number of script command line arguments.
*           char *argv[] - Command line argument strings.
*           char *env[]  - Environment variables passed to the main function,
*                          only on supported operating systems.
*
* Returns 0 on success
******************************************************************************/
int PostDataOperations(int argc, char *argv[], char *env[])
{
    int retval = 0;

    /* To be continued in the next chapter. */

    printf("<html>\n<head>\n\n<title>CGI Response</title>\n\n</head>\n\n");
    printf("<body bgcolor=\"#669999\" text=\"#FFFFFF\">\n\n");
```

```c
    printf("<br/><br/><center>\n");
    printf("<h1>(Control panel form input processing.)\n");
    printf("<br/>To be continued...</h1>\n");
    printf("</center><br/><br/>\n");
    printf("</body></html>\n");

    return retval;
}



/*****************************************************************************
* Function: DebugOperations()
* Purpose: Call various debug functions relative to the script command line
*          options.
*
* Receives: int argc - Number of script command line arguments.
*           char *argv[] - Command line argument strings.
*           char *env[]  - Environment variables passed to the main function,
*                          only on supported operating systems.
*
* Returns 0 on success
*****************************************************************************/
int DebugOperations(int argc, char *argv[], char *env[])
{
    int retval = 0;

    /* Request ENV variables by name. */
    if(argc >= 4 && strncmp(argv[3], "ENV_NAME", 8) == 0)
    {
        retval = CGIDebugByName(argc, argv);
    }

    /* If environment variable debug information requested.
     * Request variables by name. */
    else if(argc >= 4 && strncmp(argv[3], "ENV_ALL", 7) == 0)
    {
        retval = CGIDebugAll(argc, argv);
    }

    return retval;
}
```

Program Listing 5.2, cgimain.h, is the header file for cgimain.c and contains all of the function prototypes and definitions related to the cgimain.c source code.

Follow these steps to create the header file cgimain.h:

1. From a command prompt, change into the chapter5 project directory:

    cd /home/pi/webproj/chapter5

2. Using nano or a favorite text editor, create the file cgimain.h:

    nano cgimain.h

3. Add the source code from Program Listing 5.2 into the editor.

4. When finished editing, press CTRL + O then ENTER to save then CTRL + X to exit nano.

Program Listing 5.2: cgimain.h

```
/****************************************************************************
* File: cgimain.h
* Purpose: Header file for the cgimain CGI application.
*
****************************************************************************/



/* Function prototypes. */
int DebugOperations(int argc, char *argv[], char *env[]);
int PostDataOperations(int argc, char *argv[], char *env[]);
```

Program Listing 5.3, cgitools.c, contains the CGI interface support code that will handle contributory functionality like Key/Value pair parsing, extraction of POST form data, reading server time and date, and other operations. This file will develop over the next few chapters to add increased support. Follow these steps to create cgitools.c:

1. From a command prompt change into the Chapter 5 project directory:

    cd /home/pi/webproj/chapter5

2. Using nano or a favorite text editor, create the file cgitools.c:

    nano cgitools.c

3. Add the source code from Program Listing 5.3 into the nano editor.

4. When finished editing, press CTRL + O then ENTER to save then CTRL + X to exit nano.

Program Listing 5.3: cgitools.c

```
/****************************************************************************
* File: cgitools.c
* Purpose: CGI supporting functions.
*
****************************************************************************/
```

```c
#include <stdio.h>
#include <string.h>
#include <unistd.h>
#include <time.h>
#include "cgitools.h"


/****************************************************************************
* File: serverTime()
* Purpose: Get current time then format and send to web page.
*
* Returns: void
****************************************************************************/
void serverTime(void)
{
    time_t timeval;
    struct tm *timeinfo;
    char buf[100];


    if(time(&timeval) != ERROR)
    {
        timeinfo = localtime(&timeval);
        strftime(buf,100,"%h-%-d-%Y %I:%M:%S %p",timeinfo);

        printf("<br/><center><i><strong><font color='#cadaea' size='5'>");
        printf("Server Time: %s</font></strong></i></center>\n\n", buf);


    }


}




/****************************************************************************
* Function: GetNameValuePairs()
* Purpose: Get the string pointers of a name-value pair based on delimiter.
* Inserts null in place of the delimiter.
*
* Receives: char *Name - name-value pair string on input, Name string on output.
*           char *Value - null on input, value string on output.
*           char *delimiters - Delimiter character string.
```

```
*
* Returns: 0 on success else ERROR.
*****************************************************************************/
int GetNameValuePairs(char **Name, char **Value, char *delimiters)
{
    int retval = 0, position = 0;

    /* Get string position of first occurrence of any delimiter characters. */
    position = strcspn(*Name, delimiters);

    /* If delimiter found. */
    if (position > 0)
    {
        /* Make sure the string had a delimiter. */
        if (Name[0][position] == delimiters[0])
        {
            if (strlen(&Name[0][position + 1]) > 0)
            {
                /* Get the value string address. */
                *Value = &Name[0][position + 1];
            } else Value = NULL;
        } else Value = NULL;

        /* Insert an end of line in the Name field. */
        Name[0][position] = '\0';
    }
    else if(strlen(&Name[0][0]) == 0)
    {
        retval = ERROR;
    }

    return retval;
}
```

Program Listing 5.4, cgitools.h, is the header file for cgitools.c and contains all of the function prototypes and definitions related to the cgitools.c source code. Additional type definitions and linked list structures will be added here in later chapters to handle POST data processing.

Follow these steps to create cgitools.c:

1. From a command prompt change into the chapter5 project directory:

    cd /home/pi/webproj/chapter5

2. Using nano or a favorite text editor, create the file cgitools.h:

        nano cgitools.h

3.   Add the source code from Program Listing 5.4 into the nano editor.

4.   When finished editing, press CTRL + O then ENTER to save then CTRL + X to exit nano.

Program Listing 5.4: cgitools.h

```
/****************************************************************************
* File: cgitools.h
* Purpose: Header file for the cgitools functionality.
*
****************************************************************************/


#define ERROR -1


/* Function prototypes. */
void serverTime(void);
int GetNameValuePairs(char **Name, char **Value, char *delimiters);
```

Program Listing 5.5, cgidebug.c, contains CGI interface debugging code that includes the reading and displaying of CGI environment variables. Additional functionality will be added to this file in the next chapter to display POST data submitted by web page forms.

Follow these steps to create cgidebug.c:

1.   From a command prompt change into the chapter5 project directory:

        cd /home/pi/webproj/chapter5

2.   Using nano or a favorite text editor, create the file cgidebug.c:

        nano cgidebug.c

3.   Add the source code from Program Listing 5.5 into the nano editor.

4.   When finished editing, press CTRL + O then ENTER to save then CTRL + X to exit nano.

Program Listing 5.5: cgidebug.c

```
/****************************************************************************
* File: cgidebug.c
* Purpose: CGI debug functions.
*
****************************************************************************/
#include <stdio.h>
#include <string.h>
#include <stdlib.h>
```

```c
#include "cgimain.h"
#include "cgitools.h"
#include "cgidebug.h"


/*****************************************************************************
* Function: CGIDebugByName()
* Purpose: Read a set of CGI environment variables by name and generate web
* page output.
*
* Returns 0 on success
*****************************************************************************/
int CGIDebugByName(int argc, char *argv[])
{
    int toggle = 0, retval = 0;
    char color[10];

    printf("<html>\n<head>\n\n");
    printf("<title>CGI Environment Variables</title>\n</head>\n\n");
    printf("<body bgcolor='#235d80' text='#cadaea'>\n\n");
    printf("<center><i><strong><u>\n");
    printf("<font color='#cadaea' size='7'>CGI Environment Variables</font>\n");
    printf("</u></strong></i></center>\n\n");


    serverTime();


    printf("<br/><br/>\n");
    printf("<table style='width:800px;' ALIGN='center' border='1' ");
    printf("cellspacing='1' cellpadding='10' bgcolor='#555555' ");
    printf("bordercolor='354f6a'>\n");
    printf("<tr><td ALIGN='center' COLSPAN='2' bgcolor='#354f6a'>\n");
    printf("<font color='#cadaea' size='4'>Command Line Arguments</font>\n");
    printf("</td></tr>\n\n");

    /* Display application command line arguments. */
    for(int i=0; i < argc; i++)
    {
        if(toggle^=1) strcpy(color, "114170");
        else strcpy(color, "15487a");
        printf("<tr bgcolor='#%s'>", color)    ;
        printf("<td align='center'>%d</td><td>%s<br></td></tr>\n", i, argv[i]);
```

```c
}
printf("</table>\n");

/* Display environment variables by name. */
printf("<br/><br/>\n");
printf("<table style='width:800px;' ALIGN='center' border='1' ");
printf("cellspacing='1' cellpadding='10' bgcolor='#555555' ");
printf("bordercolor='354f6a'>\n");
printf("<tr><td ALIGN='center' COLSPAN='2' bgcolor='#354f6a'>\n");
printf("<font color='#cadaea' size='4'>");
printf("Table of Available Environment Variables</font>\n");
printf("</td></tr>\n\n");


printf("<tr bgcolor='#114170'><td>HTTP_USER_AGENT:</td><td>%s<br></td></tr>",
          getenv("HTTP_USER_AGENT") ? getenv("HTTP_USER_AGENT") : " ");
printf("<tr bgcolor='#15487a'><td>HTTP_REFERER:</td><td>%s<br></td></tr>\n",
          getenv("HTTP_REFERER") ? getenv("HTTP_REFERER") : " ");
printf("<tr bgcolor='#114170'><td>CONTENT_TYPE:</td><td>%s<br></td></tr>\n",
          getenv("CONTENT_TYPE") ? getenv("CONTENT_TYPE") : " ");
printf("<tr bgcolor='#15487a'><td>CONTENT_LENGTH:</td><td> %s<br></td></tr>",
    getenv("CONTENT_LENGTH") ? getenv("CONTENT_LENGTH") : " ");
printf("<tr bgcolor='#114170'><td>SERVER_SOFTWARE:");
printf("</td><td> %s<br></td></tr>",
    getenv("SERVER_SOFTWARE") ? getenv("SERVER_SOFTWARE") : " ");
printf("<tr bgcolor='#15487a'><td>SERVER_ADDR:</td><td>%s<br></td></tr>\n",
    getenv("SERVER_ADDR") ? getenv("SERVER_ADDR") : " ");
printf("<tr bgcolor='#114170'><td>SERVER_PORT:</td><td>%s<br></td></tr>\n",
    getenv("SERVER_PORT") ? getenv("SERVER_PORT") : " ");
printf("<tr bgcolor='#15487a'><td>REMOTE_ADDR:</td><td>%s<br></td></tr>\n",
    getenv("REMOTE_ADDR") ? getenv("REMOTE_ADDR") : " ");
printf("<tr bgcolor='#114170'><td>DOCUMENT_ROOT:</td><td>%s<br></td></tr>\n",
    getenv("DOCUMENT_ROOT") ? getenv("DOCUMENT_ROOT") : " ");
printf("<tr bgcolor='#15487a'><td>SCRIPT_FILENAME:</td><td>%s<br></td></tr>",
    getenv("SCRIPT_FILENAME") ? getenv("SCRIPT_FILENAME") : " ");
printf("<tr bgcolor='#114170'><td>GATEWAY_INTERFACE:");
printf("</td><td>%s<br></td></tr>\n",
    getenv("GATEWAY_INTERFACE") ? getenv("GATEWAY_INTERFACE") : " ");
printf("<tr bgcolor='#15487a'><td>REQUEST_METHOD:");
printf("</td><td>%s<br></td></tr>\n",
    getenv("REQUEST_METHOD") ? getenv("REQUEST_METHOD") : " ");
printf("<tr bgcolor='#114170'><td>REQUEST_URI:</td><td>%s<br></td></tr>\n",
```

```c
        getenv("REQUEST_URI") ? getenv("REQUEST_URI") : " ");
    printf("<tr bgcolor='#15487a'><td>SCRIPT_NAME:</td><td>%s<br></td></tr>\n",
        getenv("SCRIPT_NAME") ? getenv("SCRIPT_NAME") : " ");
    printf("<tr bgcolor='#114170'><td>QUERY_STRING:</td><td>%s<br></td></tr>\n",
        getenv("QUERY_STRING") ? getenv("QUERY_STRING") : " ");
    printf("</table>\n<br/>\n");


    /* Display form data. */
    CGIPostDataDisplay();


    printf("</body></html>\n");


    return retval;
}




/*****************************************************************************
* Function: CGIDebugAll()
* Purpose: Read all available environment variables and generate web
* page output.
*
* Returns 0 on success
*****************************************************************************/
int CGIDebugAll(int argc, char **argv)
{
    extern char **environ;
    char *env = *environ;
    char *name, *value;
    char maxenv[1024];
    int toggle = 0, retval = 0;
    char color[10];

    printf("<html>\n<head>\n\n");
    printf("<title>CGI Environment Variables</title>\n</head>\n\n");
    printf("<body bgcolor='#235d80' text='#cadaea'>\n\n");
    printf("<center><i><strong><u>\n");
    printf("<font color='#cadaea' size='7'>CGI Environment Variables</font>\n");
    printf("</u></strong></i></center>\n\n");

    serverTime();
```

```c
printf("<br/><br/>\n");
printf("<table style='width:800px;' ALIGN='center' border='1' ");
printf("cellspacing='1' cellpadding='10' bgcolor='#555555' ");
printf("bordercolor='354f6a'>\n");
printf("<tr><td ALIGN='center' COLSPAN='2' bgcolor='#354f6a'>\n");
printf("<font color='#cadaea' size='4'>Command Line Arguments</font>\n");
printf("</td></tr>\n\n");

/* Display application command line arguments. */
for(int i=0; i < argc; i++)
{
    if(toggle^=1) strcpy(color, "114170");
    else strcpy(color, "15487a");
    printf("<tr bgcolor='#%s'>", color)      ;
    printf("<td align='center'>%d</td><td>%s<br></td></tr>\n", i, argv[i]);
}
printf("</table>\n");

/* Table to display all environment variables. */
printf("<br/><br/>\n");
printf("<table style='width:800px;' ALIGN='center' border='1' ");
printf("cellspacing='1' cellpadding='10' bgcolor='#555555'");
printf("bordercolor='354f6a'>\n");
printf("<tr><td ALIGN='center' COLSPAN='2' bgcolor='#354f6a'>\n");
printf("<font color='#cadaea' size='4'>");
printf("Table of Available Environment Variables</font>\n");
printf("</td></tr>\n\n");

toggle = 0;

/* Loop through all environment variables and output to web page. */
for(int cnt=1; (env != NULL); cnt++)
{
    strncpy(maxenv, env, sizeof(maxenv));
    name = maxenv;

    if(GetNameValuePairs(&name, &value, "=") != ERROR)
    {
        if(toggle^=1) strcpy(color, "114170");
        else strcpy(color, "15487a");
        printf("<tr bgcolor='#%s'><td>%s</td><td>%s<br></td></tr>\n",
```

```
                color, name, value);
        }

        env = *(environ+cnt);
    }

    printf("</table>\n<br/>\n");

    /* Display form data. */
    CGIPostDataDisplay();

    printf("</body></html>\n");

    return retval;
}



/******************************************************************************
* Function: CGIPostDataDisplay()
* Purpose: To get the POST data content length and read in all form data to
* be displayed on the web page.
*
* Returns 0 on success
******************************************************************************/
int CGIPostDataDisplay(void)
{
        int retval = 0;

        /* To be continued in the next chapter. */

        return retval;
}
```

Program Listing 5.6, cgidebug.h, is the header file for cgidebug.c and contains all of the function prototypes and definitions related to the cgidebug.c source code.

Follow these steps to create cgidebug.h:

1. From a command prompt change into the chapter5 project directory:

    cd /home/pi/webproj/chapter5

2. Using nano or a favorite text editor, create the file cgidebug.h:

    nano cgidebug.h

3.   Add the source code from Program Listing 5.6 into the nano editor.

4.   When finished editing, press CTRL + O then ENTER to save then CTRL + X to exit nano.

Program Listing 5.6: cgidebug.h

```
/*****************************************************************************
* File: cgidebug.h
* Purpose: Header file for the CGI debug functions.
*
*****************************************************************************/



/* CGI Debug function prototypes. */
int CGIDebugByName(int argc, char **argv);
int CGIDebugAll(int argc, char **argv);
int CGIPostDataDisplay(void);
```

Program Listing 5.7, webpanel.cgi, is a Perl script that will be called from the web server to execute the cgimain web control panel application. Currently there are three different system calls to run the cgimain application within this file. Two of the system calls are commented out with the preceding "#" comment character. This file will be modified later in this chapter to exercise the different command line arguments in these system calls to cause different web page output from the cgimain application. The behavior of the cgimain application changes based on the Perl command line options used in the system calls.

To create the Perl script, follow these steps:

1.   From a command prompt change into the chapter5 project directory:

     cd /home/pi/webproj/chapter5

2.   Using nano or a favorite text editor, create the file webpanel.cgi:

     nano webpanel.cgi

3.   Add the source code from Program Listing 5.7 into the nano editor.

4.   When finished editing, press CTRL + O then ENTER to save then CTRL + X to exit nano.

Program Listing 5.7: webpanel.cgi

```
#!/usr/bin/perl -w

#my $retval = system("/var/www/webapp/cgimain", "CGI", "DEBUG", "ENV_NAME");
#my $retval = system("/var/www/webapp/cgimain", "CGI", "DEBUG", "ENV_ALL");
my $retval = system("/var/www/webapp/cgimain", "CGI");
if($retval != 0)
{
     print "Content-Type: text/html\n\n";
```

```
print "<!DOCTYPE html>\n<html>\n<head>\n";
print "<title>ERROR PAGE</title></head>\n";
print "<body>\n";
print "<h1>Error! \'cgimain\' failed.\n";
print "<br />See Apache error log...</h1>\n";
print "</body>\n</html>\n";


}
```

Building the Project

A project makefile is used to compile and install the cgimain application. The makefile makes the process much easier as it will perform multiple steps with a single command line entry. The install command will make the required changes to the output file attributes to make them executable and copy the application and script files to the perper directories for web access.

Note: The multiple spaces before makefile commands have to be set as tabs and not spaces. The tab separator is required for the makefile parser. If the makefile commands fail be sure to verify the multiple spaces before each command are actually a single tab character without spaces.

Take the following steps to create and use the makefile to compile and install the web control panel application:

1. From a command prompt change into the chapter5 project directory:

   cd /home/pi/webproj/chapter5

2. Using nano or a favorite text editor, create the makefile:

   nano makefile

3. Add the makefile contents from Listing 5.8 below into the nano editor.

4. When finished editing, press CTRL + O then ENTER to save then CTRL + X to exit nano.

5. There are three operations that can be performed by the makefile:

   a. **make cgimain** - build the project.

   b. **sudo make install** - change file attributes and copy the output files.

   c. **make clean** - remove all output files to be able to perform a fresh build.

6. While at a Terminal Prompt in the chapter5 project directory, type the following to compile all of the project files previously entered: **make cgimain**

7. If everything worked correctly the output should look similar to the following:

   pi@raspberrypi:~/webproj/chapter5 $ make cgimain

   gcc -c cgimain.c

   gcc -c cgitools.c

   gcc -c cgidebug.c

gcc -lm -o cgimain cgimain.o cgitools.o cgidebug.o

pi@raspberrypi:~/webproj/chapter5 $

8. If there were any typos or invalid code entered for any of the steps in this chapter then those errors will be listed in the terminal from the build output. The compiler issues will have associated file name and line numbers listed so the mistakes in the files can be corrected. Be sure the proper line endings were used. Any compiler errors will have to be fixed before the cgimain application will be created.

9. Once the build output is successful, run the make install command:

sudo make install

10. Open a web browser on the Raspberry Pi Desktop and type the path to the CGI script into the URL box: **localhost/cgi-bin/webpanel.cgi** The script can also be viewed on a remote computer by opening a web browser and typing the Raspberry Pi IP address followed by the path to the CGI script:

(IP Address)/cgi-bin/webpanel.cgi

Based on the current system call command line options, the web page will display the text "To be continued..."

11. Next modify the Perl script to run the system call with the "ENV_NAME" option.

12. From a command prompt, change into the chapter5 project directory:

cd /home/pi/webproj/chapter5

13. Using nano or a favorite text editor, edit the Perl script:

nano webpanel.cgi

14. Comment out the current system command by placing a '#' character before the line:

 # my $retval = system("/var/www/webapp/cgimain", "CGI");

15. Now uncomment the line that contains the text "ENV_NAME" and save the changes:

my $retval = system("/var/www/webapp/cgimain", "CGI", "DEBUG", "ENV_NAME");

16. Install the new script file changes by typing the following command:

sudo make install

17. Refresh the previous web page and view the new results. There should now be a web page listing similar to the environment variable output of the previous chapter. This web page also provides a table showing the Perl script command line options used when calling the cgimain application.

18. Repeat steps 12 to 17 again except comment out the current system call and uncomment the line with the "ENV_ALL" text. After running the make install command, refresh the web page again to see a list of all environment variables displayed using 'C' code. See Figure 5.1 below for final web page output.

Note: *If the script fails to execute, be sure to examine the Apache error log to diagnose the issue.*

Listing 5.8: makefile

```
# type 'make cgimain' to build the project.
cgimain: cgimain.o cgitools.o cgidebug.o
    gcc -lm -o cgimain cgimain.o cgitools.o cgidebug.o
```

```
cgimain.o: cgimain.c
    gcc -c cgimain.c

cgitools.o: cgitools.c
    gcc -c cgitools.c

cgidebug.o: cgidebug.c
    gcc -c cgidebug.c

# type 'sudo make install' to copy files and change their attributes.
install:
    if test -d /var/www/webapp; then echo -n;  else mkdir /var/www/webapp/; fi
    cp cgimain /var/www/webapp
    cp webpanel.cgi /usr/lib/cgi-bin
    chmod 755 /var/www/webapp/cgimain
    chmod 755 /usr/lib/cgi-bin/webpanel.cgi

# type 'make clean 'to remove objects for a fresh build.
clean:
    rm cgitools.o cgimain.o cgidebug.o cgimain
```

CGI Environment Variables

Server Time: Jan-28-2022 10:43:19 AM

Command Line Arguments	
0	/var/www/webapp/cgimain
1	CGI
2	DEBUG
3	ENV_ALL

Table of Available Environment Variables	
HTTP_HOST	192.168.40.113
HTTP_USER_AGENT	Mozilla/5.0 (Windows NT 10.0; Win64; x64; rv:96.0) Gecko/20100101 Firefox/96.0
HTTP_ACCEPT	text/html,application/xhtml+xml,application/xml;q=0.9,image/avif,image/webp,*/*;q=0.8
HTTP_ACCEPT_LANGUAGE	en-US,en;q=0.5
HTTP_ACCEPT_ENCODING	gzip, deflate
HTTP_CONNECTION	keep-alive
HTTP_UPGRADE_INSECURE_REQUESTS	1
HTTP_CACHE_CONTROL	max-age=0
PATH	/usr/local/sbin:/usr/local/bin:/usr/sbin:/usr/bin:/sbin:/bin
SERVER_SIGNATURE	*Apache/2.4.38 (Raspbian) Server at 192.168.40.113 Port 80*
SERVER_SOFTWARE	Apache/2.4.38 (Raspbian)

Figure 5.1 Web page output of Perl system command:

system("/var/www/webapp/cgimain", "CGI", "DEBUG", "ENV_ALL"); .

6

CGI INPUT/OUTPUT

When a CGI application is executed, the web server creates a special environment that provides a custom set of file descriptors for STDIN, STDOUT, and STDERR. This is accomplished through the use of pipes. The result is the redirection of all program output to the web server to be displayed on a web page. The pipe acts as a FIFO (First In First Out) buffer that will store the program output until execution is complete; then that output is sent over the network to the client browser as web page content. Similarly, all input from the client browser will appear on the application STDIN. This normally encompases form submission data made by a POST request. A user enters form fields on a web page and clicks the submit button, which starts the process. A POST method request is sent to the web server, which results in a CGI call. POST data is then sent to the CGI program through the STDIN pipe. The application may then read and process the form data and create a resulting web page to send back to the client browser through STDOUT. STDERR output normally results in a "500 Internal Server Error" reply back to the web browser. Such errors will show up in the web server error logs.

In this chapter, the web control panel application will be modified to add support for CGI POST data handling that includes parsing form data that is URL encoded to escape special characters using a percent encoding with all spaces replaced by a "+" character. The POST data is formatted as key=value pairs with an "&" character separating each pair. Key=value pairs may be repeated within the input. In other words, a single key may be repeated multiple times with different values assigned to each instance.

Web page form data can be generated using multiple methods. The most common is to use a form that displays fields a user can interact with and then post to a web server using a submit button. Hidden form data with fixed information may also be added as in the following example of the form depicted in **Figure 6.1**:

```
<form method="post" action="/cgi-bin/webpanel.cgi">
  <br>Name:<input name="Name" type="text" value="Enter Name">
  <br>Date:<input name="Date" type="text" value="Enter Date">
  <input name="COMMAND" type="hidden" value="PlaySound">
  <input name="VAR1"        type="hidden" value="RaspberryPi.wav">
  <input name="fncybtn" type="submit" value="Click Me!">
</form>
```

Notice the two input tags of type="hidden" within the form html code. These two lines are transparent to the user and produce no visible output on the web page yet provide a powerful interface in which various commands can be used to control embedded actions within the Raspberry Pi. When this form is submitted, the following URL Encoded Post Data is sent to the CGI application and is available through STDIN:

Name=Enter+Name&Date=Enter+Date&COMMAND=PlaySound&VAR1=RaspberryPi. wav&fncybtn=Click+Me

Take note of the correlation between the post data output and the name and value attributes of the from fields. After parsing and converting the URL Encoded Post Data the following Key=Value pairs are found:

Key	Value
Name	Enter Name
Date	Enter Date
COMMAND	PlaySound
VAR1	RaspberryPi.wav
fncybtn	Click Me

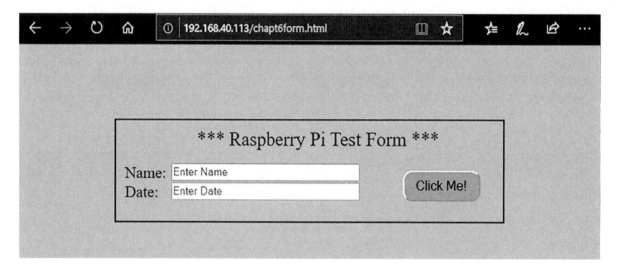

Figure 6.1 Web page form example.

Another method of creating post data is to build form data programmatically using JavaScript. Hidden form information can be manipulated in such a way that various commands can be invoked through an array of buttons where each button performs a different embedded action on the Raspberry Pi. A timer can also be created in a web page to perform background updates of dynamically changing information like the Raspberry Pi CPU temperature.

Subsequent chapters will provide methods of performing programmatic actions using embedded forms and background updates that are transparent to the user while maintaining a static web control panel with dynamically updated elements. A static control panel with dynamically updated elements is much preferred over a panel that has to be reloaded after each button press.

Adding Support for CGI POST Data

Several of the control panel project files will need to be updated to provide support for handling CGI post data. The first of two main feature enhancements is supporting code for reading and parsing CGI POST data into a special structure called a "linked list". Linked lists are common structures normally used to hold dynamic data in which the size and length of the fields are initially unknown. The POST data linked list is built dynamically as each Key-Value pair is parsed and URL decoded. Each linked list entry contains a single Key-Value pair. Each entry is linked to the next entry such that the software can easily iterate through the list to quickly pull out the desired Key so the Value can be accessed and used in the code. The second main feature enhancement is the addition of a CGI command operations function, which evaluates and acts on CGI commands to perform various tasks.

First Steps

Before updating the project source files, a new chapter6 project directory needs to be created and the web control panel files copied to the new directory.

Follow these steps to prepare the new directory:

1. From the Terminal Prompt change into the user project directory:

   cd /home/pi/webproj

2. Copy the contents of the chapter5 directory to the new chapter6 directory:

   cp -R chapter5 chapter6/

Web Audio Setup

The chapter 6 project includes a demonstration of how to play a wav file through a CGI command. For this to occur, the Raspberry Pi must be configured to allow the web user to access the audio services, otherwise the command will fail and the faulty results will be added to the Apache2 error log.

Follow these steps to update the Raspberry Pi to allow the web user, www-data, to access audio services:

1. From a Terminal Prompt, add the web user to the audio group:

   sudo usermod -a -G audio www-data

2. This next step is very important. For the new change to take effect the web server must be restarted: **sudo service apache2 restart**

3. The audio group addition can be verified by typing the following command at the Terminal Prompt: **getent group**

4. If the group modification was successful then something similar to the following should be found in the group listings showing www-data: **audio:x:29:pi,www-data**

5. Next, at the terminal, change into the html directory: **cd /var/www/html/**

6. Get the wav file from the MST server by typing the following case-sensitive command:

   sudo wget https://www.mstmicro.com/projects/RaspberryPi.wav

7. At the Terminal Prompt, type **ls -als** to view the contents of the directory and verify the RaspberryPi. wav file is present.

8. The wav file can be played from the prompt by typing: **aplay RaspberryPi.wav** If not using HDMI for sound then be sure to have a set of speakers plugged into the Raspberry Pi so the sound can

be heard. If no sound is heard then try rebooting the Raspberry Pi. If no sound persists check the Raspberry Pi settings to make sure your audio is set to the correct output device (HDMI or Speakers) by typing **sudo alsamixer** at the Terminal Promopt. To verify the output for the web user www-data, type the following:

sudo runuser -u www-data alsamixer

Make sure your output device is selected and the volume is at the desired level. Since the www-data user is not a real user it may not be possible to change the sound settings. Most likely the default HDMI sound output will be selected so there will only be sound if a compatible HDMI monitor with sound option or a TV is used.

Program Listing 6.1, chapt6form.html, contains the full html listing of the form depicted in Figure 6.1. The code has two options for submitting the form. The normal submit button entry is commented out:

<!-- <input id="fncybtn" name="fncybtn" type="submit" value="Click Me!"> -->

The active form submit option uses script to submit the form programmatically, similar to the method that will be used in subsequent chapters:

<input id="fncybtn" name="fncybtn" type="button" value="Click Me!"
  onclick="document.getElementById('exform').submit();">

Submitting a form programmatically can be a powerful mechanism when creating actions from web page elements that can be embedded with virtually any CGI command desired. In most cases the form element can be accessed by the use of the "id" or "name" field by use of the getElementById() function. This function will be used heavily in the static web control panel examples.

 There are two Cascading Style Sheets (CSS) entries used in this code. The CSS classes are used to provide formatting options to web page elements. Styles can be used inline within an HTML tag or by linking styles either by class or by element id in the head section of the html document. A separate CSS style sheet file may also be used. Notice the commands in the html code in Program Listing 6.1 specifying how each of the two CSS styles are applied after the line:

<style type="text/css">

Follow these steps to create the chapt6form.html file:

1.   From a Terminal Prompt, change into the chapter6 project directory created earlier in this chapter:
     cd /home/pi/webproj/chapter6
2.   Using nano or a favorite text editor, create the html file:
     nano chapt6form.html
3.   Enter the code from Program Listing 6.1 below.
4.   When complete, press CTRL + O then ENTER to save then CTRL + X to exit nano.

Program Listing 6.1: chapt6form.html

```
<!DOCTYPE html>
<html>
<head>
<title>Raspberry Pi X - Form Example</title>
```

```
<style type="text/css">

    /* Alignment styles for inputs by class. */
    .inclass {
        position:absolute;
        left:60px;
    }

    /* Fancy button styles by ID/Name. */
    #fncybtn {
        position:absolute;
        top:59px;
        left:359px;
        height:37px;
        width:100px;
        background-color:#2D82C7;
        border-radius:12px;font-size:16px;
    }

</style>
</head>

<body bgcolor="#559BC7" text="#0E1923">
<center>
<!-- Set up DIV tag with inline styles to create a form container. -->
<div id="FormDisp" name="FormDisp" style="position:relative;top:80px;width:500px;
     height:120px;border-style:solid;border:2px solid black;font-size:20px">

    <div style="position:relative;left:12px;text-align:left;">

        <form id="exform" name="exform" target="_blank" method="post"
            action="/cgi-bin/webpanel.cgi?Device=RaspberryPi">

            <div style="position:relative;top:8px;color:#050952;
            text-align:center;font-size:24px">
                *** Raspberry Pi Test Form ***
            </div>

            <br>Name:<input class="inclass" name="Name" type="text"
                value="Enter Name" style="width:240px;">
```

```
             <br>Date:<input class="inclass" name="Date" type="text"
                 value="Enter Date" style="width:240px;">

             <input name="COMMAND" type="hidden" value="PlaySound">
             <input name="VAR1" type="hidden" value="RaspberryPi.wav">

             <input id="fncybtn" name="fncybtn" type="button" value="Click Me!"
                    onclick="document.getElementById('exform').submit();">

    <!-- Normal submit button example. -->
    <!-- <input id="fncybtn" name="fncybtn" type="submit" value="Click Me!">  -->
       </form>
     </div>
</div>
</center>
</body></html>
```

Program Listing 6.2, cgimain.c, is the next file that needs to be updated. Several interesting modifications have been made to this file starting with a global definition of the main structure that will hold the CGI POST data linked list, **CGIPostData CGIData**, and is defined near the top of the file. All of the data in the CGI linked list is parsed, allocated, and stored by calling the ReadCGIPostData( ) function within the main( ) function. Notice that the function DeleteLinkedList( ) is called at the end of main( ) before the program exists so that the allocated memory may be freed. The process of reading, storing, and then deleting CGI data will ensue each time the program is called.

The PostDataOperations( ) function has been modified to handle the first two CGI operations. The first is a command to play a wav file and the second a command to get drive space information. These two operations can be called simply by changing the web form to post the required command options.

One of the most substantial additions to cgimain.c is the new function GenericSystemCall( ), which can be used to execute a command on the Raspberry Pi from the web program. The resulting web page will display any program output. Later, this output will be hidden as CGI calls will be made to run in the background, transparent to the user from a static web control panel.

Follow these steps to update cgimain.c:

1.   From a Terminal Prompt, change into the chapter6 project directory:
     cd /home/pi/webproj/chapter6
2.   Using nano or a favorite text editor, edit the source file:
     nano cgimain.c
3.   Edit cgimain.c to match the code from Program Listing 6.2 below.
4.   When complete, press CTRL + O then ENTER to save then CTRL + X to exit nano.

Program Listing 6.2: cgimain.c

```c
/*****************************************************************************
* File: cgimain.c
* Purpose: Program to control various Raspberry Pi operations from the web.
*
*****************************************************************************/
#include <stdio.h>
#include <string.h>
#include <stdlib.h>

#include "cgimain.h"
#include "cgitools.h"
#include "cgidebug.h"


/* Global Post data linked list variable. */
CGIPostData CGIData;



/*****************************************************************************
* Function: main()
* Receives: int argc - Number of command line arguments.
*           char *argv[] - Command line argument strings.
*           char *env[]  - Optionally add for systems that support
*                          environment variables passed to the main function.
*
* Returns 0 = OK or ERROR CODE
*****************************************************************************/
int main(int argc, char *argv[], char *env[])
{
    int retval = 0;
    CGIPostData *CGIDataPtr = &CGIData;

    /* Preinitialize the linked list to prevent unallocation errors. */
    CGIData.ListHead = NULL;
    CGIData.Count = 0;

    /* Start of web page. */
    printf("%s%c%c","Content-Type:text/html;charset=iso-8859-1",10,10);
    printf("<!DOCTYPE html>\n");
```

```c
    /* Verify the application is called by the CGI script. If the argument
     * text "CGI" is not found then don't run anything. */
    if(argc > 1 && strncmp(argv[1], "CGI", 3) == 0)
    {
        /* Load CGI POST data, if any. */
        ReadCGIPostData(CGIDataPtr);

        /* If debug operations specified. */
        if(argc >= 3 && strncmp(argv[2], "DEBUG", 5) == 0)
        {
            retval = DebugOperations(argc, argv, env);
        }

        /* Act on control panel POST data, if any. */
        else
        {
            retval = PostDataOperations(argc, argv, env);
        }

    }
    else
    {
        printf("<html>\n<head>\n\n<title>Execution Error</title>\n\n</head>\n\n");
        printf("<body bgcolor=\"#669999\" text=\"#FFFFFF\">\n\n");
        printf("<br/><br/><center>\n<h1>Application Error!</h1>\n</center>\n");
        printf("<br/><br/>\n</body></html>\n");
        retval = 0;
    }

    /* Free CGI POST data allocated memory, if any. */
    DeleteLinkedList(CGIDataPtr);

    return retval;
}


/*****************************************************************************
* Function: PostDataOperations()
* Purpose: Act on POST data form information to perform various control
*          panel operations.
```

```
 *
 * Receives: int argc - Number of script command line arguments.
 *           char *argv[] - Command line argument strings.
 *           char *env[]  - Environment variables passed to the main function,
 *                          only on supported operating systems.
 *
 * Returns 0 on success
 **************************************************************************/
int PostDataOperations(int argc, char *argv[], char *env[])
{
    int retval = 0;
    char *COMMAND = NULL;
    char *VAR1 = NULL, *VAR2 = NULL, *VAR3 = NULL, *VAR4 = NULL, *VAR5 = NULL;
    char buf[512];

    printf("<html>\n<head><title>CGI COMMAND RESULTS</title>\n\n</head>\n\n");
    printf("<body bgcolor=\"#559BC7\" text=\"#0E1923\">\n\n");

    /* Get the POST command string. */
    COMMAND = GetKeyValue(&CGIData, "COMMAND", 0);

    /* Act on POST data submission. */
    if(strncmp(COMMAND, "PlaySound", 9) == 0)
    {
        /* POST Data command to play a wav file. */
        /* Get the sound file name from the web form data named 'VAR1'. */
        VAR1 = GetKeyValue(&CGIData, "VAR1", 0);

        /* Prepare to play wav file. The file must be in the html directory. */
        sprintf(buf, "aplay /var/www/html/%s", VAR1);

        /* Make a system call to play the wav file.           */
        /* Be sure the www-data user is in the audio group */
        /* and the Apache HTTP Server has been restarted.    */
        /* If command fails see the apache error log.        */
        GenericSystemCall(buf);

    }
    else if(strncmp(COMMAND, "DriveSpace", 10) == 0)
    {
        GenericSystemCall("df");
```

```c
    }


    /* Display CGI command information. */
    printf("\n<br><table border='1' cellspacing='2' cellpadding='15px'>\n");
    printf("\n<tr align='left'>\n<th>\n");
    serverTime();
    printf("\n<h3>CGI COMMAND REPLY:</h3><p>");
    printf("\n  COMMAND: %s<br>", COMMAND);
    printf("\n  VAR1: %s<br>", VAR1);
    printf("\n  VAR2: %s<br>", VAR2);
    printf("\n  VAR3: %s<br>", VAR3);
    printf("\n  VAR4: %s<br>", VAR4);
    printf("\n  VAR5: %s\n</p>", VAR5);
    printf("\n</th>\n</tr>");
    printf("\n</table><br><br>");
    printf("\n</body>\n</html>\n");


    return retval;
}



/*****************************************************************************
* Function: DebugOperations()
* Purpose: Call various debug functions relative to the script command line
*          options.
*
* Receives: int argc - Number of script command line arguments.
*           char *argv[] - Command line argument strings.
*           char *env[]  - Environment variables passed to the main function,
*                          only on supported operating systems.
*
* Returns 0 on success
*****************************************************************************/
int DebugOperations(int argc, char *argv[], char *env[])
{
    int retval = 0;

    /* Request ENV variables by name. */
    if(argc >= 4 && strncmp(argv[3], "ENV_NAME", 8) == 0)
    {
```

```c
        retval = CGIDebugByName(argc, argv);
    }

    /* If environment variable debug information requested.
     * Request variables by name. */
    else if(argc >= 4 && strncmp(argv[3], "ENV_ALL", 7) == 0)
    {
        retval = CGIDebugAll(argc, argv);
    }

    return retval;
}



/****************************************************************************
* Function: GenericSystemCall()
* Purpose: Executes and displays the results of a Raspberry Pi system call.
*
* Receives: char *sysComand - Command line for system call.
*
* Returns: 0 on success else ERROR.
****************************************************************************/
int GenericSystemCall(char *sysComand)
{
    FILE *fp;
    char buf[1024];
    int strpos;
    int retval = ERROR;

    /* Make a system call based on the sysCommand string. */
    fp = popen(sysComand, "r");

    /* Create a table to hold any command line output. */
    printf("<center>");
    printf("<table width='95%' border='1' cellspacing='2' cellpadding='1'>\n");
    printf("<tr bgcolor=\"#65ABD7\">\n\t<th>\n\t\t<h3>");
    printf("COMMAND OUTPUT - IF ANY</h3>\n\t</th>\n</tr>\n");
    printf("<tr align='left'>\n\t<th>\n");

    if(fp == NULL)
    {
```

```c
        printf("<br/><h1>ERROR: Could not execute command! bye...</h1>\n");
}
else
{
    retval = 0;

    printf("\n\t<div style='color:#00134F;font:14pt,courier, arial;'>\n");
    printf("\n\t<strong>\n");
    printf("\t<font face='FreeMono, Lucida Console, Consolas'>\n\t<p>");
    printf("\n\t ");

    /* Display command output on web page, if any. */
    while(fgets(buf, sizeof(buf), fp))
    {
        /* For each character in text string. */
        for(strpos = 0; strpos < strlen(buf); strpos++)
        {
            switch(buf[strpos])
            {
                case '\n': printf("\n<br>");
                break;

                case ' ': printf(" ");
                break;

                case '\t': printf("    ");
                break;

                default: putchar(buf[strpos]);
                break;
            }
        }
    }

    printf("\n\t</P>\n\t</font>");
    printf("\n\t</strong>\n\t</div>");
    /* Close the file pointer to the command. */
    pclose(fp);
}

/* Close the table. */
```

```
    printf("</th>\n\t</tr>\n");
    printf("\n</table></center>\n<br><hr>\n\n");
}
```

Program Listing 6.3, cgimain.h, needs to be updated to add the function prototype for the GenericSystemCall() function.

Follow these steps to update cgimain.h:

1. From a Terminal Prompt change into the chapter6 project directory:

    cd /home/pi/webproj/chapter6

2. Using nano or a favorite text editor, edit the source file:

    nano cgimain.h

3. Edit cgimain.h to match the code from Program Listing 6.3 below.

4. When complete, press CTRL + O then ENTER to save then CTRL + X to exit nano.

Program Listing 6.3: cgimain.h

```
/***************************************************************************
* File: cgimain.h
* Purpose: Header file for the cgimain CGI application.
*
***************************************************************************/


/* Function prototypes. */
int DebugOperations(int argc, char *argv[], char *env[]);
int PostDataOperations(int argc, char *argv[], char *env[]);
int GenericSystemCall(char *);
```

Program Listing 6.4, cgitools.c, has been heavily modified to add support for parsing, storing and deleting CGI POST data using a linked list structure and a new header file has been added to the top of the file. The following functions have been added to support linked list operations:

1. ReadCGIPostData() - Reads CGI key-value pairs from STDIN.
2. ExtractKeyValuePairs( ) - Extracts the key-value pairs into a linked list.
3. GetNextRecord( ) - Gets a key-value pair and stores it in a list record.
4. AddLinkedListRecord( ) - Adds a new linked list record to the list.
5. DeleteLinkedList( ) - Unallocates and destroys the linked list.
6. GetNumRecords( ) - Gets the number of key-value pairs in the list.
7. GetNextKeyValuePair( ) - Retrieves records stored in the list.
8. GetKeyValue( ) Gets the value of a specified key.
9. UnescapeURI( ) - Unescapes the URL encoded CGI data.

Follow these steps to make the code changes to cgitools.c:

1. From a Terminal Prompt, change into the chapter6 project directory:

    cd /home/pi/webproj/chapter6

2. Using nano or a favorite text editor, edit the source file:

    nano cgitools.c

3. Edit cgitools.c to match the code from Program Listing 6.4 below.

4. When complete, press CTRL + O then ENTER to save then CTRL + X to exit nano.

Program Listing 6.4: cgitools.c

```c
/*****************************************************************************
 * File: cgitools.c
 * Purpose: CGI supporting functions.
 *
 *****************************************************************************/
#include <stdio.h>
#include <string.h>
#include <unistd.h>
#include <time.h>
#include "cgitools.h"

#include <stdlib.h>


/*****************************************************************************
 * File: serverTime()
 * Purpose: Get current time then format and send to web page.
 *
 * Returns: void
 *****************************************************************************/
void serverTime(void)
{
   time_t timeval;
   struct tm *timeinfo;
   char buf[100];


   if(time(&timeval) != ERROR)
   {
      timeinfo = localtime(&timeval);
      strftime(buf,100,"%h-%-d-%Y %I:%M:%S %p",timeinfo);
```

```c
        printf("<br/><center><i><strong><font color='#cadaea' size='5'>");
        printf("Server Time: %s</font></strong></i></center>\n\n", buf);


    }
}



/****************************************************************************
* Function: GetNameValuePairs()
* Purpose: Get the string pointers of a name-value pair based on delimiter.
* Inserts null in place of the delimiter.
*
* Receives: char *Name - name-value pair string on input, Name string on output.
*        char *Value - null on input, value string on output.
*        char *delimiters - Delimiter character string.
*
* Returns: 0 on success else ERROR.
****************************************************************************/
int GetNameValuePairs(char **Name, char **Value, char *delimiters)
{
    int retval = 0, position = 0;

    /* Get string position of first occurrence of any delimiter characters. */
    position = strcspn(*Name, delimiters);

    /* If delimiter found. */
    if (position > 0)
    {
        /* Make sure the string had a delimiter. */
        if (Name[0][position] == delimiters[0])
        {
            if (strlen(&Name[0][position + 1]) > 0)
            {
                /* Get the value string address. */
                *Value = &Name[0][position + 1];
            } else Value = NULL;
        } else Value = NULL;

        /* Insert an end of line in the Name field. */
        Name[0][position] = '\0';
    }
```

```c
    else if(strlen(&Name[0][0]) == 0)
    {
       retval = ERROR;
    }


    return retval;
}



/*****************************************************************************
* File: ReadCGIPostData()
* Purpose: Read CGI post data from STDIN, if any, then extract the
* key-value pairs into a link list.
* Receives: CGIPostData *CGIPostList - Pointer to the POST data linked list.
*
* Returns: 0 if okay else ERROR if list not created.
*****************************************************************************/
int ReadCGIPostData(CGIPostData *CGIPostList)
{
    char *Env, *postDataStr;
    char *key, *value;
    int ContentLength = 0;
    int retval = ERROR;

    /* Read the CONTENT_LENGTH environment variable to get the
     * size of the post data string. */
    Env = getenv("CONTENT_LENGTH");

    /* Make sure there is POST data available. */
    if( (Env != NULL) && ((ContentLength = atoi(Env)) > 0) )
    {
        /* Allocate memory to hold the post data content. */
        postDataStr = (char *) malloc(ContentLength + 2);
        if(postDataStr != NULL)
        {
            /* Read POST data from STDIN. */
            ContentLength = read(0, postDataStr, ContentLength);
            /* Add null terminator to the end of the POST data string. */
            postDataStr[ContentLength] = '\0';

            /* Extract the POST data Key-Value pairs into the linked list. */
```

```
            if(ExtractKeyValuePairs(CGIPostList, postDataStr) != ERROR)
            {
                /* Save the original POST data string length. */
                CGIPostList->ContentLength = ContentLength;

                /* The post data was successfully read. */
                retval = 0;
            }

            /* Free up the original POST data memory. */
            free(postDataStr);
        }
    }
    return retval;
}



/****************************************************************************
* File: ExtractKeyValuePairs()
* Purpose: Read the CGI form data key-value pairs into a link list.
* Receives: CGIPostData *CGIPostList - Pointer to the POST data linked list.
*           char *PostDataStr - String pointer to the POST data.
*
* Returns: 0 if okay else ERROR if list not created.
****************************************************************************/
int ExtractKeyValuePairs(CGIPostData *CGIPostList, char *PostDataStr)
{
    int retval=0;
    key_value_pair *key_value_record;
    char delimiter[] = "&";
    char *tok = NULL;
    char *pstr = NULL;
    char *pData = PostDataStr;

    /* Initialize the head of the linked list. */
    CGIPostList->Count = 0;
    CGIPostList->ListHead = NULL;


    /* Break down the post data into its individual key/value pairs. */
    if((pstr = strtok_r(pData, delimiter, &tok)) != NULL)
```

```
   {
      /* Extract the key and value pair into a linked list element. */
      key_value_record = GetNextRecord(pstr);

      /* Create a linked list record and check for memory ERROR. */
      if((retval = AddLinkedListRecord(CGIPostList, key_value_record)) == ERROR)
      {
         DeleteLinkedList(CGIPostList);
         return ERROR;
      }

      /* Add the rest of the key/value pairs. */
      while((pstr = strtok_r(NULL, delimiter, &tok)) != NULL)
      {
         /* Extract the key and value pair into a linked list element. */
         key_value_record = GetNextRecord(pstr);

         /* Create a linked list record and check for memory ERROR. */
         if((retval = AddLinkedListRecord(CGIPostList, key_value_record))
             == ERROR)
         {
            DeleteLinkedList(CGIPostList);
            return ERROR;
         }
      }
   }
   return 0;
}



/****************************************************************************
* File: GetNextRecord()
* Purpose: Separate a key-value pair, unescape the data, and store in a record.
* Receives: char *key_val_str - Form data key-value string.
*
* Returns: key_value_pair structure or ERROR.
****************************************************************************/
key_value_pair *GetNextRecord(char *key_val_str)
{
   key_value_pair *key_value_record;
   char *key=NULL,*value=NULL, *temp=NULL;
```

```c
char delimiter[] = "=";
unsigned int loc=0;

/* Create memory to hold this key-value pair. */
key_value_record = (key_value_pair *) malloc(sizeof(key_value_pair));
if(key_value_record == NULL) return NULL;

/* Separate the CGI post data key-value pair. */
if( (GetNameValuePairs(&key_val_str, &temp, delimiter) == ERROR) ||
            (key_val_str == NULL) )
{
   free(key_value_record);
   return NULL;
}

/* Allocate memory for the KEY string. */
key = (char*) malloc(sizeof(char) * (strlen(key_val_str) + 1));

/* Copy the key name. */
strncpy(key, key_val_str, strlen(key_val_str) + 1);
UnescapeURI(key);

/* Save the key in the allocated record. */
key_value_record->key = key;

if(temp != NULL)
{
   /* Allocate memory for the Value string. */
   value = (char *) malloc(sizeof(char) * (strlen(temp) + 1));

   /* Copy the value string, */
   strncpy(value, temp, strlen(temp) + 1);
   value = UnescapeURI(value);

   /* Save the key value in the allocated record.*/
   key_value_record->value = value;
}
else
{
   key_value_record->value = NULL;
}
```

```c
   /* Return the address of our record. */
   return key_value_record;
}



/***************************************************************************
* Function: UnescapeURI()
* Purpose: Convert special '%' characters back to original and change the '+'
*          characters back to spaces.
*
* Returns: Pointer to updated string.
***************************************************************************/
char *UnescapeURI(char *URI)
{
   int rdloc = 0, wrloc = 0;
   char hexenc[3];
   unsigned long hexch;

   /* Unescape null terminated URI string. */
   while(URI[rdloc] != '\0')
   {
      switch (URI[rdloc])
      {
         /* Unescape hexadecimal codes. */
         case '%':
            hexenc[0]=URI[rdloc+1];
            hexenc[1]=URI[rdloc+2];
            hexenc[2]='\0';

            /* Get special character represented by
             * escaped hexadecimal code. */
            hexch = strtoul(hexenc, NULL, 16);
            URI[wrloc] = (char) hexch;
            rdloc += 2;
         break;

         /* Unescape spaces. */
         case '+':
            URI[wrloc]=' ';
         break;
```

```
          /* Nothing to escape. */
          default:
              URI[wrloc] = URI[rdloc];
          break;
      }
      rdloc++;
      wrloc++;
    }
    URI[wrloc]='\0';

    return URI;
}



/***************************************************************************
* Function: DeleteLinkedList( )
* Purpose: Free all memory used for the linked list.
*
* Receives: CGIPostData *List - Pointer to the list.
***************************************************************************/
void DeleteLinkedList(CGIPostData *List)
{
    list_record *thisrecord=NULL;
    list_record *nextrecord=NULL;

    if(List->Count == 0 || List->ListHead == NULL)
    {
        return;
    }

    /* Get first record. */
    thisrecord = List->ListHead;

    /* Free all records and associated memory. */
    while(thisrecord != NULL)
    {
        /* Get pointer to next record. */
        nextrecord = thisrecord->nextrecord;

        /* Free key and value pair memory. */
```

```c
        free(thisrecord->record->key);
        free(thisrecord->record->value);

        /* Free the record memory. */
        free(thisrecord->record);

        /* Free the list entry memory. */
        free(thisrecord);

        /* Next record to free. */
        thisrecord = nextrecord;
    }
}


/****************************************************************************
* Function: GetNumRecords( )
* Purpose: Get the total number of records in the list.
*
* Receives: CGIPostData *List - Pointer to the list.
*
* Returns: Record count.
****************************************************************************/
int GetNumRecords(CGIPostData *List)
{
    return List->Count;
}



/****************************************************************************
* Function: AddLinkedListRecord( )
* Purpose: Add a key-value pair to the linked list.
*
* Receives: CGIPostData *List - Pointer to the list.
*        key_value_pair *Record - Pointer of the element to add to the list.
*
* Returns: 0 if okay else ERROR if memory error.
****************************************************************************/
int AddLinkedListRecord(CGIPostData *List, key_value_pair *Record)
{
    list_record *NewRecord=NULL;
```

```c
list_record *LastRecord=NULL;

/* Get the first linked list element. */
LastRecord = List->ListHead;

NewRecord = (list_record *) malloc(sizeof(list_record));
if(NewRecord == NULL)
{
   /* Free memory for the key and value pair. */
   free(Record->key);
   free(Record->value);
   return -1;
}

/* If no records stored. */
if(LastRecord == NULL)
{
   NewRecord->nextrecord = NULL;
   NewRecord->record = Record;
   List->ListHead = NewRecord;
   List->Count++;
}

/* Add next record. */
else
{
   /* Find the end of the list. */
   while(LastRecord->nextrecord != NULL)
   {
       LastRecord = LastRecord->nextrecord;
   }

   /* Insert record at list end. */
   NewRecord->nextrecord = NULL;
   NewRecord->record = Record;
   LastRecord->nextrecord = NewRecord;
   List->Count++;
}
return 0;
}
```

```
/**************************************************************************
* Function: GetNextKeyValuePair( )
* Purpose:  Iterate through the post data linked list one record at a time.
*           Each function call will retrieve the next record in the list.
*
* Receives: CGIPostData *List - Pointer to the linked list on first call
*                   then NULL for all remaining calls until end of list reached.
*         char **key - A pointer to hold the address of the key string.
*         char **Value - A pointer to hold the address of the value string.
*
* Returns: 0 if record valid else -1 if end of list.
**************************************************************************/
int GetNextKeyValuePair(CGIPostData *List, char **key, char **value)
{
   static CGIPostData *LinkedList = NULL;
   static list_record *thisrecord = NULL;

   /* If first time, list is provided, start at the beginning of the list. */
   if (List != NULL)
   {
      LinkedList = List;
      thisrecord = List->ListHead;
   }

   /* Make sure the record is valid. */
   if(LinkedList == NULL || thisrecord == NULL)
      return ERROR;

   /* Return the key value pair for the current record. */
   *key = thisrecord->record->key;
   *value = thisrecord->record->value;

   /* Get the next record. */
   thisrecord = thisrecord->nextrecord;

   return 0;
}


/**************************************************************************
```

```
* Function: GetKeyValue( )
* Purpose:  Gets the value of the specified key.
*
* Receives: CGIPostData *List - Pointer to the list.
*         char *Name - The key name string.
*          int Instance - The zero based key instance number for when there
*                          is more than one key of the same name. 0 = 1st instance.
*
* Returns: Pointer to the value string else NULL if the instance does not exist.
*************************************************************************/
char *GetKeyValue(CGIPostData *List, char *Name, int Instance)
{
    char* ValueStr = NULL;
    list_record *thisrecord=NULL;
    int recordInstance = 0;

    /* exit the function if empty list or no nodes exist */
    if(List->ListHead == NULL) return NULL;

    thisrecord = List->ListHead;

    /* Find the record instance if it exists. */
    while(thisrecord != NULL)
    {
        /* Compare the current record key name string. */
        if(strcmp(thisrecord->record->key, Name) == 0)
        {
            if(recordInstance == Instance)
            {
                return thisrecord->record->value;
            }
            else recordInstance++;
        }
        /* Get next record. */
        thisrecord = thisrecord->nextrecord;
    }
    return NULL;
}
```

Program Listing 6.5, cgitools.h, has been modified to add the typedef definitions to support the CGI linked list structures as well as the addition of function prototypes for performing linked list operations.

Follow these steps to make the code changes to cgitools.h:

1. From a Terminal Prompt, change into the chapter6 project directory:

    cd /home/pi/webproj/chapter6

2. Using nano or a favorite text editor, edit the source file:

    nano cgitools.h

3. Edit cgitools.h to match the code from Program Listing 6.5 below.

4. When complete, press CTRL + O then ENTER to save then CTRL + X to exit nano.

Program Listing 6.5: cgitools.h

```
/*****************************************************************************
* File: cgitools.h
* Purpose: Header file for the cgitools functionality.
*
*****************************************************************************/

#define ERROR -1

/* Linked list record (node) structure. */
typedef struct key_value_pair_t
{
    char *key;
    char *value;
} key_value_pair;

/* Node entry structure. */
typedef struct list_record_t
{
    /* Single record pointer. */
    key_value_pair *record;
    /* Points to the next record in the linked list. */
    struct list_record_t *nextrecord;
} list_record;


/* Top of linked list structure declaration. */
typedef struct linked_list_t
{
    /* Pointer to the first linked list record. */
    list_record *ListHead;
    /* Number of records in list. */
    int Count;
    /* For storing the original POST data content length for reference. */
```

```
    int ContentLength;
} CGIPostData;

extern CGIPostData CGIData;

/* Function prototypes. */
void serverTime(void);
int GetNameValuePairs(char **Name, char **Value, char *delimiters);

/* Post data function prototypes. */
int ReadCGIPostData(CGIPostData *);
int ExtractKeyValuePairs(CGIPostData *, char *);
key_value_pair *GetNextRecord(char *);
char *UnescapeURI(char *);

/* Linked list function prototypes. */
void DeleteLinkedList(CGIPostData *);
int GetNumRecords(CGIPostData *);
int AddLinkedListRecord(CGIPostData *, key_value_pair *);
int GetNextKeyValuePair(CGIPostData *, char **, char **);
char *GetKeyValue(CGIPostData *, char *, int);
```

Program Listing 6.6, cgidebug.c, has been modified to add code to the function CGIPostDataDisplay( ) that is used to provide a list of CGI key-value pairs when debugging a web page posting form data. The header file cgidebug.h did not change.

Follow these steps to make the code changes to cgidebug.c:

1. From a Terminal Prompt, change into the chapter6 project directory:

    cd /home/pi/webproj/chapter6

2. Using nano or a favorite text editor, edit the source file:

    nano cgidebug.c

3. Edit cgidebug.c to match the code from Program Listing 6.6 below.

4. When complete, press CTRL + O then ENTER to save then CTRL + X to exit nano.

Program Listing 6.6: cgidebug.c

```
/******************************************************************************
 * File: cgidebug.c
 * Purpose: CGI debug functions.
 *
 ******************************************************************************/
#include <stdio.h>
#include <string.h>
#include <stdlib.h>
```

```c
#include "cgimain.h"
#include "cgitools.h"
#include "cgidebug.h"


/******************************************************************************
* Function: CGIDebugByName()
* Purpose: Read a set of CGI environment variables by name and generate web
* page output.
*
* Returns 0 on success
******************************************************************************/
int CGIDebugByName(int argc, char *argv[])
{
    int toggle = 0, retval = 0;
    char color[10];

    printf("<html>\n<head>\n\n");
    printf("<title>CGI Environment Variables</title>\n</head>\n\n");
    printf("<body bgcolor='#235d80' text='#cadaea'>\n\n");
    printf("<center><i><strong><u>\n");
    printf("<font color='#cadaea' size='7'>CGI Environment Variables</font>\n");
    printf("</u></strong></i></center>\n\n");

    serverTime();

    printf("<br/><br/>\n");
    printf("<table style='width:800px;' ALIGN='center' border='1' ");
    printf("cellspacing='1' cellpadding='10' bgcolor='#555555' ");
    printf("bordercolor='354f6a'>\n");
    printf("<tr><td ALIGN='center' COLSPAN='2' bgcolor='#354f6a'>\n");
    printf("<font color='#cadaea' size='4'>Command Line Arguments</font>\n");
    printf("</td></tr>\n\n");

    /* Display application command line arguments. */
    for(int i=0; i < argc; i++)
    {
        if(toggle^=1) strcpy(color, "114170");
        else strcpy(color, "15487a");
        printf("<tr bgcolor='#%s'>", color)   ;
        printf("<td align='center'>%d</td><td>%s<br></td></tr>\n", i, argv[i]);
    }
    printf("</table>\n");
```

```
/* Display environment variables by name. */
printf("<br/><br/>\n");
printf("<table style='width:800px;' ALIGN='center' border='1' ");
printf("cellspacing='1' cellpadding='10' bgcolor='#555555' ");
printf("bordercolor='354f6a'>\n");
printf("<tr><td ALIGN='center' COLSPAN='2' bgcolor='#354f6a'>\n");
printf("<font color='#cadaea' size='4'>");
printf("Table of Available Environment Variables</font>\n");
printf("</td></tr>\n\n");

printf("<tr bgcolor='#114170'><td>HTTP_USER_AGENT:</td><td>%s<br></td></tr>",
    getenv("HTTP_USER_AGENT") ? getenv("HTTP_USER_AGENT") : " ");
printf("<tr bgcolor='#15487a'><td>HTTP_REFERER:</td><td>%s<br></td></tr>\n",
    getenv("HTTP_REFERER") ? getenv("HTTP_REFERER") : " ");
printf("<tr bgcolor='#114170'><td>CONTENT_TYPE:</td><td>%s<br></td></tr>\n",
    getenv("CONTENT_TYPE") ? getenv("CONTENT_TYPE") : " ");
printf("<tr bgcolor='#15487a'><td>CONTENT_LENGTH:</td><td> %s<br></td></tr>",
    getenv("CONTENT_LENGTH") ? getenv("CONTENT_LENGTH") : " ");
printf("<tr bgcolor='#114170'><td>SERVER_SOFTWARE:");
printf("</td><td> %s<br></td></tr>",
    getenv("SERVER_SOFTWARE") ? getenv("SERVER_SOFTWARE") : " ");
printf("<tr bgcolor='#15487a'><td>SERVER_ADDR:</td><td>%s<br></td></tr>\n",
    getenv("SERVER_ADDR") ? getenv("SERVER_ADDR") : " ");
printf("<tr bgcolor='#114170'><td>SERVER_PORT:</td><td>%s<br></td></tr>\n",
    getenv("SERVER_PORT") ? getenv("SERVER_PORT") : " ");
printf("<tr bgcolor='#15487a'><td>REMOTE_ADDR:</td><td>%s<br></td></tr>\n",
    getenv("REMOTE_ADDR") ? getenv("REMOTE_ADDR") : " ");
printf("<tr bgcolor='#114170'><td>DOCUMENT_ROOT:</td><td>%s<br></td></tr>\n",
    getenv("DOCUMENT_ROOT") ? getenv("DOCUMENT_ROOT") : " ");
printf("<tr bgcolor='#15487a'><td>SCRIPT_FILENAME:</td><td>%s<br></td></tr>",
    getenv("SCRIPT_FILENAME") ? getenv("SCRIPT_FILENAME") : " ");
printf("<tr bgcolor='#114170'><td>GATEWAY_INTERFACE:");
printf("</td><td>%s<br></td></tr>\n",
    getenv("GATEWAY_INTERFACE") ? getenv("GATEWAY_INTERFACE") : " ");
printf("<tr bgcolor='#15487a'><td>REQUEST_METHOD:");
printf("</td><td>%s<br></td></tr>\n",
    getenv("REQUEST_METHOD") ? getenv("REQUEST_METHOD") : " ");
printf("<tr bgcolor='#114170'><td>REQUEST_URI:</td><td>%s<br></td></tr>\n",
    getenv("REQUEST_URI") ? getenv("REQUEST_URI") : " ");
printf("<tr bgcolor='#15487a'><td>SCRIPT_NAME:</td><td>%s<br></td></tr>\n",
    getenv("SCRIPT_NAME") ? getenv("SCRIPT_NAME") : " ");
printf("<tr bgcolor='#114170'><td>QUERY_STRING:</td><td>%s<br></td></tr>\n",
    getenv("QUERY_STRING") ? getenv("QUERY_STRING") : " ");
```

```c
    printf("</table>\n<br/>\n");

    /* Display form data. */
    CGIPostDataDisplay();

    printf("</body></html>\n");

    return retval;
}


/****************************************************************************
 * Function: CGIDebugAll()
 * Purpose: Read all available environment variables and generate web
 * page output.
 *
 * Returns 0 on success
 ****************************************************************************/
int CGIDebugAll(int argc, char **argv)
{
    extern char **environ;
    char *env = *environ;
    char *name, *value;
    char maxenv[1024];
    int toggle = 0, retval = 0;
    char color[10];

    printf("<html>\n<head>\n\n");
    printf("<title>CGI Environment Variables</title>\n</head>\n\n");
    printf("<body bgcolor='#235d80' text='#cadaea'>\n\n");
    printf("<center><i><strong><u>\n");
    printf("<font color='#cadaea' size='7'>CGI Environment Variables</font>\n");
    printf("</u></strong></i></center>\n\n");

    serverTime();

    printf("<br/><br/>\n");
    printf("<table style='width:800px;' ALIGN='center' border='1' ");
    printf("cellspacing='1' cellpadding='10' bgcolor='#555555' ");
    printf("bordercolor='354f6a'>\n");
    printf("<tr><td ALIGN='center' COLSPAN='2' bgcolor='#354f6a'>\n");
    printf("<font color='#cadaea' size='4'>Command Line Arguments</font>\n");
    printf("</td></tr>\n\n");
```

```c
/* Display application command line arguments. */
for(int i=0; i < argc; i++)
{
    if(toggle^=1) strcpy(color, "114170");
    else strcpy(color, "15487a");
    printf("<tr bgcolor='#%s'>", color) ;
    printf("<td align='center'>%d</td><td>%s<br></td></tr>\n", i, argv[i]);
}
printf("</table>\n");

/* Table to display all environment variables. */
printf("<br/><br/>\n");
printf("<table style='width:800px;' ALIGN='center' border='1' ");
printf("cellspacing='1' cellpadding='10' bgcolor='#555555'");
printf("bordercolor='354f6a'>\n");
printf("<tr><td ALIGN='center' COLSPAN='2' bgcolor='#354f6a'>\n");
printf("<font color='#cadaea' size='4'>");
printf("Table of Available Environment Variables</font>\n");
printf("</td></tr>\n\n");


toggle = 0;

/* Loop through all environment variables and output to web page. */
for(int cnt=1; (env != NULL); cnt++)
{
    strncpy(maxenv, env, sizeof(maxenv));
    name = maxenv;

    if(GetNameValuePairs(&name, &value, "=") != ERROR)
    {
        if(toggle^=1) strcpy(color, "114170");
        else strcpy(color, "15487a");
        printf("<tr bgcolor='#%s'><td>%s</td><td>%s<br></td></tr>\n",
          color, name, value);
    }

    env = *(environ+cnt);
}

printf("</table>\n<br/>\n");

/* Display form data. */
CGIPostDataDisplay();
```

```c
        printf("</body></html>\n");

        return retval;
}



/****************************************************************************
* Function: CGIPostDataDisplay()
* Purpose: To get the POST data content length and read in all form data to
* be displayed on the web page.
*
* Returns 0 on success else ERROR.
****************************************************************************/
int CGIPostDataDisplay(void)
{
        CGIPostData *CGIDataPtr = &CGIData;
        char *key, *value;
        char color[10];
        int retval = ERROR;
        int toggle = 0;

        /* Table to display POST Data. */
        printf("<br/><br/>\n");
        printf("<table style='width:800px;' ALIGN='center' border='1' ");
        printf("cellspacing='1' cellpadding='10' bgcolor='#555555' ");
        printf("bordercolor='354f6a'>\n");
        printf("<tr><td ALIGN='center' COLSPAN='2' bgcolor='#354f6a'>\n");
        printf("<font color='#cadaea' size='4'>");
        printf("Table of POST Data Key-Value Pairs</font>\n");
        printf("</td></tr>\n\n");


        toggle = 0;

        /* Get and display each post data key-value pairs. */
        if(GetNextKeyValuePair(CGIDataPtr, &key, &value) != ERROR)
        {
                if(toggle^=1) strcpy(color, "114170");
                else strcpy(color, "15487a");

                printf("<tr bgcolor='#%s'><td>%s</td><td>%s<br></td></tr>\n",
                        color, key, value);

                while (GetNextKeyValuePair(NULL, &key, &value) != ERROR)
                {
```

```
            if(toggle^=1) strcpy(color, "114170");
            else strcpy(color, "15487a");

            printf("<tr bgcolor='#%s'><td>%s</td><td>%s<br></td></tr>\n",
                color, key, value);
        }
        printf("</table>\n<br/>\n");
        retval = 0;
    }
    return retval;
}
```

Program Listing 6.7, webpanel.cgi, did not change, but there are three options available when executing the Perl script. Only one of the three options can be used at a time and the other two commented out, as was the case in the previous chapter. For the first test of the new code make sure that webpanel.cgi looks like Program Listing 6.7 below by following these steps:

1. From a Terminal Prompt, change into the chapter6 project directory:

   cd /home/pi/webproj/chapter6

2. Using nano or a favorite text editor, edit the source file:

   nano webpanel.cgi

3. Edit webpanel.cgi to match the code from Program Listing 6.7 below by making sure the proper lines are commented out.

4. When complete, press CTRL + O then ENTER to save then CTRL + X to exit nano.

Program Listing 6.7: webpanel.cgi

```perl
#!/usr/bin/perl -w

#my $retval = system("/var/www/webapp/cgimain", "CGI", "DEBUG", "ENV_NAME");
my $retval = system("/var/www/webapp/cgimain", "CGI", "DEBUG", "ENV_ALL");
#my $retval = system("/var/www/webapp/cgimain", "CGI");
if($retval != 0)
{
    print "Content-Type: text/html\n\n";
    print "<!DOCTYPE html>\n<html>\n<head>\n";
    print "<title>ERROR PAGE</title></head>\n";
    print "<body>\n";
    print "<h1>Error! \'cgimain\' failed.\n";
    print "<br />See Apache error log...</h1>\n";
    print "</body>\n</html>\n";
}
```

Program Listing 6.8, makefile, has been modified to add one line to the install script to copy the chapt6form. html file to the html directory:

1. From a Terminal Prompt, change into the chapter6 project directory:

    cd /home/pi/webproj/chapter6

2. Using nano or a favorite text editor, edit the makefile to match Program Listing 6.8 below:

    nano makefile

3. When complete, press CTRL + O then ENTER to save then CTRL + X to exit nano.

Program Listing 6.8: makefile

```
# type 'make cgimain' to build the project.
cgimain: cgimain.o cgitools.o cgidebug.o
        gcc -lm -o cgimain cgimain.o cgitools.o cgidebug.o

cgimain.o: cgimain.c
        gcc -c cgimain.c

cgitools.o: cgitools.c
        gcc -c cgitools.c

cgidebug.o: cgidebug.c
        gcc -c cgidebug.c

# type 'sudo make install' to copy files and change their attributes.
install:
        if test -d /var/www/webapp; then echo -n;  else mkdir /var/www/webapp/; fi
        cp cgimain /var/www/webapp
        cp webpanel.cgi /usr/lib/cgi-bin
        cp chapt6form.html /var/www/html
        chmod 755 /var/www/webapp/cgimain
        chmod 755 /usr/lib/cgi-bin/webpanel.cgi

# type 'make clean 'to remove objects for a fresh build.
clean:
        rm cgitools.o cgimain.o cgidebug.o cgimain
```

Building the Project

Now that all of the source code files have been updated, it's time to build and install the project. Follow the next steps to make and install the updated application:

1. From a Terminal Prompt, change into the chapter6 project directory:

    cd /home/pi/webproj/chapter6

2. Next, start with a fresh build by typing the following at the prompt: **make clean**

3. Build the project by typing: **make cgimain**

4. If there are any compiler errors, the erroring files will need to be fixed.

5. Once the project has built successfully, install the project updates into the proper directories by typing: **sudo make install**

6. To execute the new project, open a web browser on the Raspberry Pi Desktop and type the path to the chapt6form.html file in the URL box:

   localhost/chapt6form.html

7. The script can also be viewed on a remote computer by opening a web browser and typing in the Raspberry Pi IP address followed by the path to the form:

   (IP Address)/chapt6form.html

8. The debug output should look similar to the output of the previous chapter except for the addition of the POST data key-value pair table at the bottom as seen in Figure 6.2 below. Feel free to edit the text boxes in the form and view the changes in the POST data table.

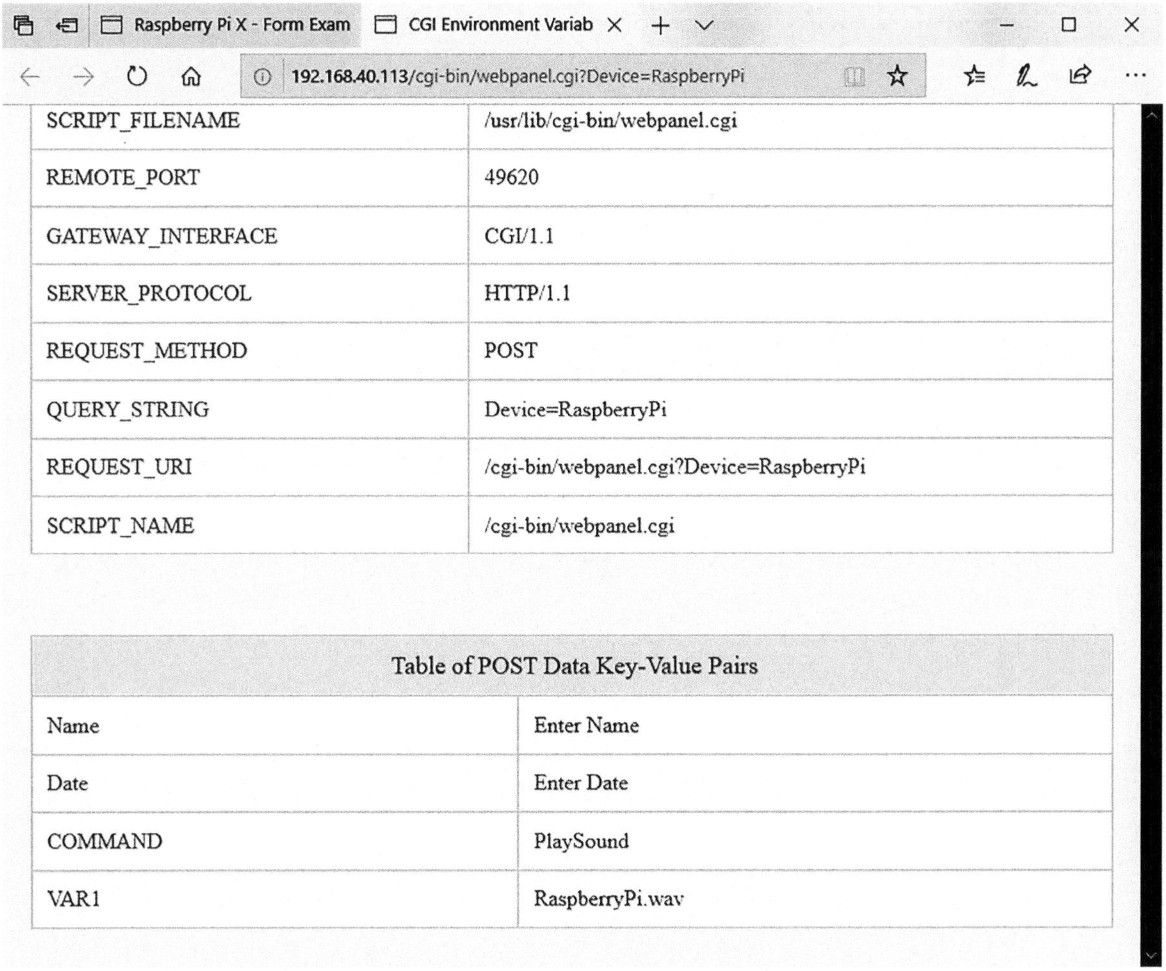

SCRIPT_FILENAME	/usr/lib/cgi-bin/webpanel.cgi
REMOTE_PORT	49620
GATEWAY_INTERFACE	CGI/1.1
SERVER_PROTOCOL	HTTP/1.1
REQUEST_METHOD	POST
QUERY_STRING	Device=RaspberryPi
REQUEST_URI	/cgi-bin/webpanel.cgi?Device=RaspberryPi
SCRIPT_NAME	/cgi-bin/webpanel.cgi

Table of POST Data Key-Value Pairs	
Name	Enter Name
Date	Enter Date
COMMAND	PlaySound
VAR1	RaspberryPi.wav

Figure 6.2 Web page results when running the Perl script with the debug command.

Normal CGI Mode

Now that the form has run in debug mode it's time to edit the webpanel.cgi Perl script to run in normal mode and hear some sound coming from the Raspberry Pi when submitting the web form.

Follow these steps to make the changes:

1. From a Terminal Prompt, change into the chapter6 project directory:

   cd /home/pi/webproj/chapter6

2. Using nano or a favorite text editor, edit the source file:

   nano webpanel.cgi

3. Edit webpanel.cgi comments to match the following:

   #my $retval = system("/var/www/webapp/cgimain", "CGI", "DEBUG", "ENV_NAME");

   #my $retval = system("/var/www/webapp/cgimain", "CGI", "DEBUG", "ENV_ALL");

   my $retval = system("/var/www/webapp/cgimain", "CGI");

4. When complete, press CTRL + O then ENTER to save then CTRL + X to exit nano.

5. Update the modified script in the cgi-bin directory: **sudo make install**

6. Execute the project as before; open a web browser on the Raspberry Pi Desktop and type the path to the chapt6form.html file in the URL box: **localhost/chapt6form.html**

7. The script can also be viewed on a remote computer by opening a web browser and typing the Raspberry Pi IP address followed by the path to the form:

   (IP Address)/chapt6form.html

8. Now, when the submit button is pressed, the Raspberry Pi should play the wav file previously downloaded and when the sound stops, the resulting web page should match that of Figure 6.3.

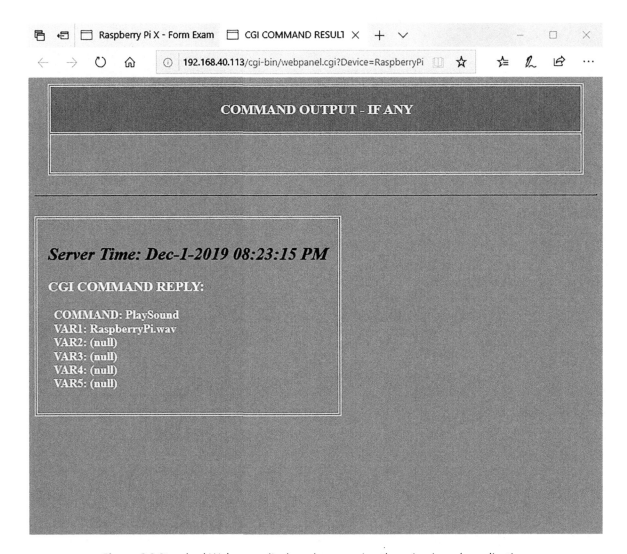

Figure 6.3 Standard Web page display when running the cgimain web application.

The resulting web page will normally be hidden once the framework is created for the static embedded web control panel environment that will be presented in a later chapter. Optionally, the hidden elements of the chapt6form.html can be edited to run the other drivespace command by changing the "PlaySound" text to "DriveSpace" and reloading the form. Be sure to run the **sudo make install** command to copy the changed file to the html directory. After pressing the submit button the **COMMAND OUTPUT - IF ANY** table in Figure 6.3 should display the results of the "df" command.

7

UNDERSTANDING DYNAMIC ELEMENTS

Dynamic Hypertext Markup Language, or DHTML, is a term used to describe dynamic elements on a web page. DHTML is really a description used to describe the processes of combining JavaScript, Cascading Styles, and HTML to create a dynamic effect on a web page without refreshing the page. The idea is that a static web page can use user input or timers to create dynamically changing elements. In subsequent chapters a new, dynamically changing process will be introduced that will allow page content to be updated based on changes in the Raspberry Pi hardware. For instance, the status of a GPIO input pin can be dynamically updated as the input changes from high to low or low to high.

This chapter is meant to provide a rudimentary understanding of the dynamic techniques that will be used in the final web control panel code. It is not meant to be a complete DHTML reference but simply a primer for moderate conception. The last example in this chapter will provide code that will serve as the basis for displaying a web control panel that will be used in subsequent chapters.

This chapter will provide code examples for the following:
- Understanding styles, the <div> tag, and the <span> tag
- A trick for centering content in <div> tags
- Using the <div> tag to create boxes and formatted text
- Using timers to update elements
- Moving elements around the screen
- Hiding and showing page elements by fading
- Creating button arrays
- Changing button state dynamically
- Create a responsive web page layout based on screen/device type

Using Styles

Styles are used to set attributes of an HTML tag or the underlying element the tag creates. Styles can be used to set any possible aspect of a web page element to include but not limited to: element or text color, text font, text size, element or text background color, element border size and color, element position on the screen, element shape, element visible or faded, element's tab stop position, change the element text, and even set new text strings or image file names. Styles can also be used to set a hyperlink URL. Using DHTML techniques, any style can be dynamically changed through code based on some type of event.

There are two primary methods for applying styles to web page elements. The first method is to create either a separate style sheet with predefined classes or define classes at the top of the web page code listing that can be applied to various elements on the page. The second method is to use Inline Styles that are defined within the element's HTML tag. The examples created in this chapter will make use of both styling methods.

DIV & SPAN Tags

The **<div>** and **<span>** tags are very similar in nature and purpose. Generally speaking, the <span> tag is normally used as a container to group other elements together when desiring to apply a common style to all child elements. It is applied inline with surrounding tags. A top level <span> tag's ID can be used to get any child element's reference ID dynamically.

The <div> tag can be thought of as a building block or block-level tag and is generally used to divide, style, and manipulate page elements. It can also be used to create graphical elements like points, lines, or boxes. The <div> tag can be nested within multiple levels of <div> tags where each tag will add additional styles or attributes to child elements—in other words, nested <div> tags build upon one another. The <div> tag is used when applying DHTML techniques to update or modify any style of a web page element.

A <div> tag or the element that it represents is identified by the tag "id" or "name" attribute. Some older web browsers used the "id" field and others used the "name" field to reference the element. Due to this issue it is always recommended to define both an "id" and "name" field with the same value for maximum browser support.

The case of a tag definition can be either uppercase or lowercase; however, in recent years HTML code checkers have tended to flag errors unless the tag and attribute fields are defined using all lowercase. Here is a basic <div> tag definition:

<div id = "Example1" name = "Example1" >Some Text or Page element</div>

Styles can be applied to almost any HTML tag and take the following syntax:

<tag style="property:value;">

Multiple property and value pairs can be used together. The next definition uses a few inline styles to format the textual element within a <div> tag:

<div id = "TxtLine1" name = "TxtLine1" style="color:blue; font-family:courier;

font-size:300%; font-weight:700;" >

  Formated Text

</div>

JavaScript can be used to dynamically change an attribute of an object by using the object's "ID". The first step is to get the object using the JavaScript function getElementById( ) and then the individual attributes of that object can be modified. Here is an example syntax to obtain the element's object: **var myObject = document. getElementById("TxtLine1")**

Using the newly created variable myObject, any of the object attributes can be modified as in the following:

```
myObject.style.color = "green";
myObject.style.fontFamily = "arial,sans-serif";
myObject.style.fontSize = "20px";
myObject.style.fontWeight = "1000";
```

Optionally, the attributes may be modified inline without first obtaining the object like the next code snippet:

```
document.getElementById("TxtLine1").style.color = "green";
document.getElementById("TxtLine1").style.fontFamily = "arial,sans-serif";
document.getElementById("TxtLine1").style.fontSize = "20px";
document.getElementById("TxtLine1").style.fontWeight = "1000";
```

There are a great number of attributes that can be modified and only a handful will be demonstrated in this chapter. Just about any attribute of an HTML tag can be changed using JavaScript, even if that attribute was not originally defined in the HTML code. For instance, a Hyperlink tag "<a>" can be created without the "href" attribute and then JavaScript can later be used to dynamically create the link. This comes in handy when desiring to change the hyperlink based on user input. Here is an example code snippet:

```
<a name="link1" id="link1" title="Hyperlink" target="_blank">Hyperlink</a>
```

Now to change, or in this case to add, the hyperlink:

```
document.getElementById("link1").href = "https://www.MSTMicro.com";
```

Using styles inline can sometimes add a lot of code to the HTML document if the same styles are used for multiple tags. It may be better to define a single class that contains all of the desired style definitions and then assign that class to any tags requiring those styles. There is also another reason to use classes versus inline styles. It is sometimes desirable to change the layout of a web page based on the device viewing the page. There are methods that can be used to reposition page elements to fit different screen sizes. These methods will require the use of classes that can be redefined relative to the screen size or the device viewing the page. This subject will be covered in more detail later.

The next example code will reside in the <head> section of a web page between <style> opening and closing tags. This class will be used to define the <div> tag styles:

```
<style>
.txtLineStyles
{
    display: inline-block;
    color: blue;
    font-family: courier;
    font-size:300%;
    font-weight:700;
}
</style>
```

Now the .txtLineStyles class can be applied to the <div> tag:

<div class="txtLineStyles" id = "TxtLine1" name = "TxtLine1">

JavaScript can still be used to modify the style attributes as in the previous examples. It does not matter if the original styles were defined by a class definition or by use of inline styles; JavaScript dynamic attribute modification can still be applied.

One point to note is that the inline styles, JavaScript styles, and class-defined styles don't always share the same style name. Always verify that the style names are valid and don't be surprised if an inline style requires a different spelling or formatting compared to a style defined in a class definition.

One last helpful tidbit before jumping into the programming examples. When defining <span> or <div> tags using styles, it is sometimes desirable to be able to visually see the physical space occupied by the tag. This can be done temporarily by enabling the tag's border style and later removing the border once the desired effect has been established. Here is an example of defining a <div> tag with both dimensions and a border:

<div id = "div1" name = "div1" style="height:40px; width:800px; border:2px solid black;">

Text in div1

</div>

Next are some real examples that can be created and viewed in a web browser. Alternatively, a*ll of the example text and graphics used in this book may be downloaded from the following URL:* **https://www.mstmicro. com/projects/webpanels.tgz** *if not already obtained previously.*

Trick for Centering Content in <div> Tags

One would think that centering content within a <div> tag would be straightforward, but that isn't always the case. While centering text within a <div> tag is relatively easy, centering an embedded <div> tag is not.

The following example will demonstrate a method that can be used to center embedded <div> content. This example also turns on element borders to help in determining element positioning. Notice that the first <div> tag uses the style: **text-align:center**. Even though the centering style is used, the subsequent <div> tags will not use this attribute by default. For the embedded <div> tags to pay attention to the outer tag centering attributes it must have the **display:inline-block** style defined, otherwise the inner <div> tag will most likely be left justified. Notice that the second embedded <div> tag does not use the **display:inline-block** style. To see how the two embedded <div> tags differ in position, create the example HTML document by following these steps:

1. To get started, a new folder must be created within the webproj directory for this chapter.

    a. At a Terminal Prompt, change into the project directory:

    cd /home/pi/webproj

    b. Create a new directory where the chapter 7 code will be stored:

    mkdir chapter7

    c. Change into the chapter7 directory: **cd chapter7**

2. Using either a favorite desktop editor or nano, create a file with the name centering.html:

    nano centering.html

3. Enter the script from Program Listing 7.1 below and then type CTRL + O then ENTER to save then CTRL + X to exit nano.

4. Copy the html file to: /var/www/html/ by typing the following at the Terminal Prompt:

   sudo cp centering.html /var/www/html/centering.html

5. Open a web browser on the Raspberry Pi Desktop and type the path to the html file:

   localhost/centering.html

6. The script can also be viewed on a remote computer by opening a web browser and typing the Raspberry Pi IP address followed by the path to the html file:

   (IP Address)/centering.html

Program Listing 7.1: centering.html

```
<!doctype html>

<html>
<head>
	<meta http-equiv="Content-Type" content="text/html; charset=iso-8859-1">
	<title>Centering &lt;div&gt; tags</title>
</head>

<body text="#220AF1" bgcolor="#FFFFFF" link="#0000FF" vlink="#666699"
alink="#FF0000" nosave>

<div style="text-align:center;font-size:32px;border:2px solid red;">
   <div id = "div1" name = "div1"
    style="display:inline-block;height:40px;width:800px;border:2px solid black;">
      Output div text line
   </div>

   <div id = "div2" name = "div2"
    style="height:50px;width:700px;border:2px solid black;">
      Output div text line 2
   </div>
</div>
</body>
</html>
```

Using the <div> Tag to Create Boxes and Formatted Text

In this next example the <div> tags are not embedded, but the desire is still to have the inner text centered both vertically and horizontally within the <div> element. Two <div> tags have text that will be centered using a combination of styles as follows: **display:flex; justify-content: center; align-items: center;**

The display:flex style allows the inline modification of the textual element in this case. The justify-content style is used for horizontal alignment of flexible items and the align-items style is used for vertical positioning of flexible items.

The following example will display boxes of various styles, borders, colors, and sizes as well as display formatted text and a partially opaque 30% visible element. Two textual elements will be overlaid to create a 3D or shadow effect. The overlaid elements are embedded into an outer <div> tag so that they can later be moved together by changing the outer tag's position. This example will be modified later to demonstrate moving objects around the screen. Figure 7.1 shows the resulting web page.

Follow these steps to create the example code:

1. At a Terminal Prompt, change into the project chapter7 directory:

    cd /home/pi/webproj/chapter7/

2. Using either a favorite desktop editor or nano, create a file with the name boxes.html:

    nano boxes.html

3. Enter the script from Program Listing 7.2 below and then type CTRL + O then ENTER to save then CTRL + X to exit nano.

4. Copy the html file to: /var/www/html/ by typing the following at the Terminal Prompt:

    sudo cp boxes.html /var/www/html/boxes.html

5. Open a web browser on the Raspberry Pi Desktop and type the path to the html file:

    localhost/boxes.html

6. The script can also be viewed on a remote computer by opening a web browser and typing the Raspberry Pi IP address followed by the path to the html file:

    (IP Address)/boxes.html

Program Listing 7.2: boxes.html

```
<!doctype html>

<html>
<head>

   <meta http-equiv="Content-Type" content="text/html; charset=iso-8859-1">
   <title>Creating &lt;div&gt; boxes</title>
</head>

<body text="#220AF1" bgcolor="#FFFFFF" link="#0000FF" vlink="#666699"
alink="#FF0000" nosave>

<!--- Display large background box without a border. --->
<div id = "div1" name = "div1" style="position:absolute; height:700px;
   width:900px; top:10px; left:20px; background-color:blueviolet; ">
```

```
</div>

<!--- Display a box with border and horizontally and vertically center text. --->
<div id = "div2" name = "div2"
    style="position:absolute; display:flex; height:75px; width:500px;
    top:50px; left:100px; border:20px solid #048B80;
    background-color:aqua; justify-content: center; align-items: center;">
      div2 text output
</div>


<!--- Display a box to appear as a bar. --->
<div id = "div3" name = "div3" style="position:absolute; height:20px;
    width:850px; top:200px; left:40px; background-color:brown; ">
</div>


<!--- Display a box to appear as a bar with a different position. --->
<div id = "div4" name = "div4" style="position:absolute; height:20px;
    width:850px; top:240px; left:40px; background-color:lightskyblue; ">
</div>


<!--- Formatted text container <div> tag. --->
<div id="fmtext" name="fmtext" style="position:absolute; top:313px;
    left:173px;" >
    <!--- Display formatted text  background shadow or 3D effect. --->
    <div id="fmt1" name="fmt1" style="position:relative; top:3px; left:5px;
      color: black; font-family:Segoe, 'Segoe UI', 'DejaVu Sans', 'Trebuchet MS',
      Verdana, 'sans-serif'; font-size: 75px;">
        Styled Text
    </div>

    <!--- Display formatted text. --->
    <div id="fmt2" name="fmt2" style="position:inherit; top:0px; left:0px;
     color:#09BD9F; font-family:Segoe, 'Segoe UI', 'DejaVu Sans', 'Trebuchet MS',
     Verdana, 'sans-serif'; font-size: 75px;">
        Styled Text
    </div>
</div>

<!--- Display a partially visable box that appears see-through. --->
<div id = "div5" name = "div5" style="position:absolute;  display:flex;
   height:100px; width:500px; top:370px; left:330px;
```

```
   background-color:chartreuse; opacity:0.3;
   justify-content: center; align-items: center;font-size: 50px;
   border:3px dashed #76E3F9; ">
      Opaque Color Box 30%
</div>

</body>
</html>
```

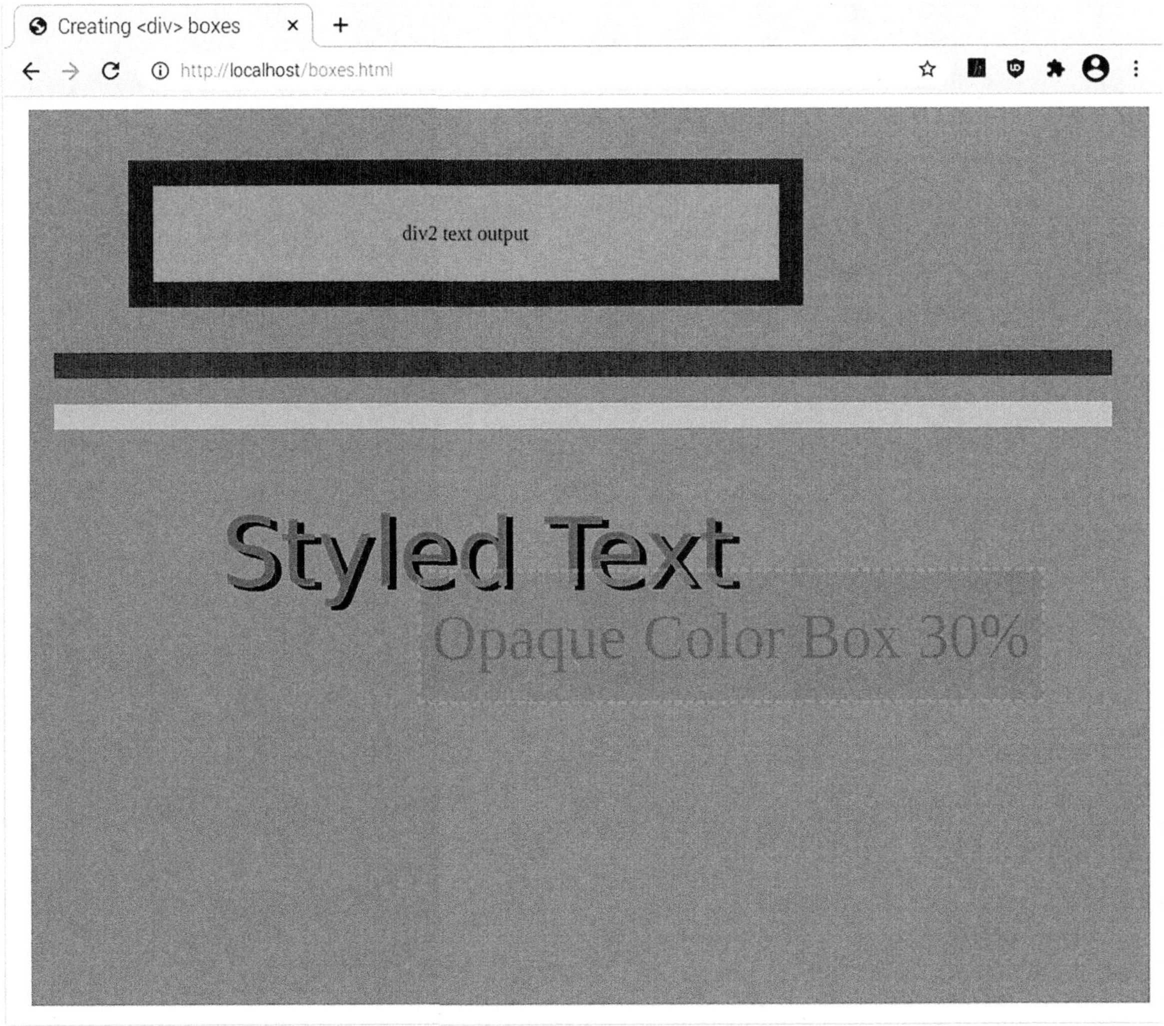

Figure 7.1 Display of the boxes.html web page.

Using Timers to Update Elements

The next example will make use of both inline styles and predefined style elements defined in the <head> section of the html code. In this case the <html> and <body> tags will be manipulated such that a gradient background will be created. Next, <div> tags will be used to create the look of a digital clock. The outer <div> tag is used for positioning and alignment. The inner "div3" <div> tag is used to create a clock border with rounded corners. The "clock" <div> is used to vertically align the clock text on top of the div3 element. JavaScript is then used within the <script> </script> tags to dynamically update the displayed time every second. The page output can been seen in Figure 7.2.

To create the digital web clock, follow these steps:

1. At a Terminal Prompt, change into the project chapter7 directory:

    cd /home/pi/webproj/chapter7/

2. Using either a favorite desktop editor or nano, create a file with the name clock.html:

    nano clock.html

3. Enter the script from Program Listing 7.3 below and then type CTRL + O then ENTER to save then CTRL + X to exit nano.

4. Copy the html file to: /var/www/html/ by typing the following at the Terminal Prompt:

    sudo cp clock.html /var/www/html/clock.html

5. Open a web browser on the Raspberry Pi Desktop and type the path to the html file:

    localhost/clock.html

6. The script can also be viewed on a remote computer by opening a web browser and typing the Raspberry Pi IP address followed by the path to the html file:

    (IP Address)/clock.html

Program Listing 7.3: clock.html

```
<!doctype html>

<html>
<head>

    <meta http-equiv="Content-Type" content="text/html; charset=iso-8859-1">
    <title>Digital Clock Example</title>

<!-- The following style definitions will automatically
be applied to the html and body tags. -->
<style>

    html {
        height: 100%;
    }
```

```
body {
    background: rgb(2,0,36);
    margin: 0;
    background:linear-gradient(342deg, rgba(2,0,36,1) 2%,
                        rgba(9,9,121,1) 37%,
                        rgba(0,212,255,1) 100%);
    background-repeat: no-repeat;
}
</style>

</head>

<body text="#220AF1" bgcolor="#80E6F7" link="#0000FF" vlink="#666699"
alink="#FF0000" nosave>

    <!-- Start of Javascript for dynamic clock update. -->
    <script>
        // Start initial timer on page load. Call the UpdateTime() function.
        setTimeout(UpdateTime, 1000);

        // Dynamically update the static web page with new time.
        function UpdateTime()
        {
            // 24 Hour clock data
            var date = new Date();
            var hours = date.getHours();  // returns 0 - 23
            var min = date.getMinutes();  // returns 0 - 59
            var sec = date.getSeconds();  // returns 0 - 59

            // Add leading zeros to keep double digits for each time field.
            if(hours < 10) hours = "0" + hours;
            if(min < 10) min = "0" + min;
            if(sec < 10) sec = "0" + sec;

            // Put the time values togather into a single string.
            var timestr = hours + ":" + min + ":" + sec;

            // Update the clock <div> text.
            document.getElementById("clock").innerText = timestr;

            // Reset the timer for one second update of the clock text.
            setTimeout(UpdateTime, 1000);
        }
    </script>
```

```html
<!-- <div> container to center and position the clock display. -->
<div style="position:absolute; width:100%; top:100px; text-align:center;
    align-items: center;">

        <!-- Draw a box with rounded corners and a black background. -->
        <div id = "div3" name = "div3" style="position:relative;
          display:inline-block; height:200px; width:550px;
          background-color:black; border-radius:15px;
          border: 4px solid white;">
        </div>

        <!-- Add formatted text to serve as the clock time display
        to be dynamically updated. -->
        <div id = "clock" name = "clock" style="position:relative;
                top:-170px; font-family: Gotham, 'Helvetica Neue',
                Helvetica, Arial, 'sans-serif'; font-size: 110px" >
            01:20:10
        </div>
  </div>
 </body>
</html>
```

Figure 7.2 Output of the clock.html web page.

Moving Elements around the Screen

Just about any object on a web page can be moved using DHTML. The following example will start with the **boxes.html** file previously created and JavaScript code will be added to dynamically move several of the boxes around the page. Remember the styled text <div> tags were created such that two copies of the text were overlaid to create a 3D or shadow effect. This example will use the outer <div> container to move the two text elements together in a diagonal movement across the page. The initial angle of movement will be will be 40°; however, feel free to change the variable **fmtextangle** to try out different angles of movement.

The two thin horizontal boxes will be moved back and forth at two different rates. The **UpdatePosition()** function is called when the **setTimeout()** timer reaches the set number of milliseconds.

Follow these steps to modify the boxes.html code:

1. At a Terminal Prompt, change into the project chapter7 directory:

    cd /home/pi/webproj/chapter7/

2. At the Terminal Prompt, make a copy of the boxes.html file by typing the following:

    cp boxes.html boxes2.html

3. Using either a favorite desktop editor or nano, modify the boxes2.html file to match Program Listing 7.4: **nano boxes2.html**

4. After updating the html code to match Program Listing 7.4 below, type CTRL + O then ENTER to save then CTRL + X to exit nano.

5. Copy the html file to: /var/www/html/ by typing the following at the Terminal Prompt:

    sudo cp boxes2.html /var/www/html/boxes2.html

6. Open a web browser on the Raspberry Pi Desktop and type the path to the html file:

    localhost/boxes2.html

7. The page can also be viewed on a remote computer by opening a web browser and typing the Raspberry Pi IP address followed by the path to the html file:

    (IP Address)/boxes2.html

Program Listing 7.4: boxes2.html

```
<!doctype html>
<html>
<head>
    <meta http-equiv="Content-Type" content="text/html; charset=iso-8859-1">
    <title>Moving Page Objects</title>
</head>

<body text="#220AF1" bgcolor="#FFFFFF"  nosave>

<!--- Display large background box without a border. --->
<div id = "div1" name = "div1" style="position:absolute; height:700px;
        width:900px; top:10px; left:20px; background-color:blueviolet; ">
</div>
```

```html
<!--- Display a box with a border and horizontally and
vertically center text. --->
<div id = "div2" name = "div2"
    style="position:absolute; display:flex; height:75px; width:500px;
          top:50px; left:100px; border:20px solid #048B80;
          background-color:aqua; justify-content: center; align-items: center;">
    div2 text output
</div>
<!--- Display a box to appear as a bar. --->
<div id = "div3" name = "div3" style="position:absolute; height:20px;
        width:850px; top:200px; left:40px; background-color:brown; ">
</div>

<!--- Display a box to appear as a bar with a different position. --->
<div id = "div4" name = "div4" style="position:absolute; height:20px;
        width:850px; top:240px; left:40px; background-color:lightskyblue; ">
</div>

<!--- Formatted text container <div> tag. --->
<div id="fmtext" name="fmtext" style="position:absolute; top:313px; left:173px;">
    <!--- Display formatted text  background shadow or 3D effect. --->
    <div id="fmt1" name="fmt1" style="position:relative; top:3px; left:5px;
          color: black; font-family:Segoe, 'Segoe UI', 'DejaVu Sans',
          'Trebuchet MS', Verdana, 'sans-serif'; font-size: 75px;">
      Styled Text
    </div>

    <!--- Display formatted text. --->
    <div id="fmt2" name="fmt2" style="position:inherit; top:0px; left:0px;
        color:#09BD9F; font-family:Segoe, 'Segoe UI', 'DejaVu Sans',
        'Trebuchet MS', Verdana, 'sans-serif'; font-size: 75px;">
        Styled Text
    </div>
</div>

<!--- Display a partially visable box that appears see through. --->
<div id = "div5" name = "div5" style="position:absolute;  display:flex;
        height:100px; width:500px; top:370px; left:330px;
        background-color:chartreuse; opacity:0.3; justify-content: center;
        align-items: center;font-size: 50px; border:3px dashed #76E3F9; ">
      Opec Color Box 30%
</div>
```

```
<!-- Start of Javascript for dynamic update. -->
<script>

    // Initialize variables.
    var fmtextX = window.innerWidth - 400;
    var fmtextY = window.innerHeight - 100;
    var fmtextangle = 40; // Angle of movement in degrees.
    // Change angle to radians
    var fmtextangleRad = fmtextangle * (Math.PI/180);
    var fmtextStep = -.5; // Step size of object movement.
    var fmtextDir = "up";

    var div3X = 40;
    var div3Dir = .4;
    var div4X = 40;
    var div4Dir = .2;

    // Start initial timer on page load. Call the UpdatePosition() function.
    setTimeout(UpdatePosition, 50);

    // Dynamically update page objects.
    function UpdatePosition()
    {
        UpdateStyledText();
        UpdateBars();

        // Reset the timer for next update.
        setTimeout(UpdatePosition, 10);
    }

    // Dynamically update the position of the two thin bars.
    function UpdateBars()
    {
        // Get the next X position for both bars.
        div3X = div3X + div3Dir;
        div4X = div4X + div4Dir;

        // Update the two bar positions.
        document.getElementById("div3").style.left = div3X + "px";
        document.getElementById("div4").style.left = div4X + "px";

        // Check for horizontal movment bounds for div3 bar.
        if(div3X >= 70) div3Dir = -.4;
        else if(div3X <= 20) div3Dir = .4;
```

```
            // Check for horizontal movment bounds for div4 bar.
            if(div4X >= 70) div4Dir = -.2;
            else if(div4X <= 20) div4Dir = .2;
        }

        // Dynamically update the styled text position moving at
        // an angle across the page.
        function UpdateStyledText()
        {
            // Update the styled text position on the page.
            document.getElementById("fmtext").style.top = fmtextY + "px";
            document.getElementById("fmtext").style.left = fmtextX + "px";

            // Set movement direction.
            if(fmtextDir == "down") fmtextStep = .5;
            else fmtextStep = -.5;

            // Calculate next styled text postion based on angle of movement.
            fmtextX = fmtextX + fmtextStep * Math.cos(fmtextangleRad);
            fmtextY = fmtextY + fmtextStep * Math.sin(fmtextangleRad);

            // Look for page edges.
            if(fmtextX <= 10) fmtextDir = "down";
            else if(fmtextX >= (window.innerWidth - 400)) fmtextDir = "up";
        }

    </script>

</body>
</html>
```

Hiding and Showing Page Elements by Fading

Objects on a web page can be hidden and then later shown by various techniques. An object can be hidden by simply setting its position off the page and then later moving its position to the desired location. Another method would be to use the **style.display** attribute. By setting the **style.display** parameter equal to **"none"** the page element will appear as if it didn't exist. Other page elements would simply occupy the element's position. When desiring to display the hidden element, simply change the **style.display** attribute equal to either **"block"** or **"inline"** to make it visible and automatically move subsequent objects further down the page when it appears.

Many times it's desirable to hide an object while keeping the page formatting as if the object was still present. This can be done by fading the object out or even making it partially opaque. To fully hide an element from view set the **style.opacity** value equal to **"0%"** and then **"100%"** to make it fully visible.

The following example hideshow.html creates three large bullet points on a page and then fades the bullets in and out sequentially by using a **setTimeout()** function to call the **Update()** function that gets the next opacity level and updates the currently selected bullet's opacity property. Notice in Program Listing 7.5 that two style classes are defined and reused for several <div> tags since they all use the same styles.

Follow these steps to create the hideshow.html code:

1. At a Terminal Prompt, change into the project chapter7 directory:

   cd /home/pi/webproj/chapter7/

2. Using either a favorite desktop editor or nano, create the hideshow.html file to match Program Listing 7.5: **nano hideshow.html**

3. After creating the html code to match Program Listing 7.5 below, type CTRL + O then ENTER to save then CTRL + X to exit nano.

4. Copy the html file to: /var/www/html/ by typing the following at the Terminal Prompt:

   sudo cp hideshow.html /var/www/html/hideshow.html

5. Open a web browser on the Raspberry Pi Desktop and type the path to the html file:

   localhost/hideshow.html

6. The page can also be viewed on a remote computer by opening a web browser and typing the Raspberry Pi IP address followed by the path to the html file:

   (IP Address)/hideshow.html

Program Listing 7.5: hideshow.html

```
<!doctype html>

<html>
<head>

    <meta http-equiv="Content-Type" content="text/html; charset=iso-8859-1">
    <title>Hiding Page Elements</title>

 <style>

.circle {
  position: relative;
  height: 75px;
  width: 75px;
  background-color: dodgerblue;
  border-radius: 50%;
  top: 0px;
  left: 0px;
}

.txt {
```

```
  position: relative;
  top: -70px;
  left: 100px;
  font-size: 48px;
  width: 700px;
  font-family: Segoe, 'DejaVu Sans', Verdana, 'sans-serif';
}

</style>


</head>

<body text="dodgerblue" bgcolor="#EEEEEE" nosave>

<!-- First bullet point. -->
<div style="position:absolute;top:100px;left:80px;">
    <div id="dot1" name="dot1" class="circle"></div>

    <div id="txt1" name="txt1" class="txt">
        Pick up Dry Cleaning
    </div>
</div>

<!-- Second bullet point. -->
<div style="position:absolute;top:220px;left:80px;">
    <div id="dot2" name="dot2" class="circle"></div>

    <div id="txt2" name="txt2" class="txt">
        Pack for fishing trip
    </div>
</div>

<!-- Thrird bullet point. -->
<div style="position:absolute;top:340px;left:80px;">
    <div id="dot3" name="dot3" class="circle"></div>

    <div id="txt3" name="txt3" class="txt">
        Relax and have fun
    </div>
</div>

    <!-- Javascript code for dynamic update. -->
    <script>
```

```javascript
var fadeish = 100;
var fadedir = "in";
var elementsel = "dot1";

// Start initial timer on page load. Call the Update() function.
setTimeout(Update, 500);

// Dynamically show and hide objects.
function Update()
{
    // Change the fade value.
    if(fadedir == "in") fadeish = fadeish + 5;
    else if(fadedir == "out") fadeish = fadeish - 5;

    // Fade in select
    if(fadeish <= 0)
    {
        fadeish = 10;
        fadedir = "in";

    }
    // Face out select
    else if(fadeish >= 100)
    {
        fadeish = 100;
        fadedir = "out"

        // Select next bullet point to fade.
        switch(elementsel)
        {
            case "dot1": elementsel = "dot2"; break;
            case "dot2": elementsel = "dot3"; break;
            case "dot3": elementsel = "dot1"; break;
        }
    }

    // Update the selected element in elementsel variable.
    document.getElementById(elementsel).style.opacity= fadeish + "%";

    // Reset the timer.
    setTimeout(Update, 20);
}
```

```
   </script>

</body>
</html>
```

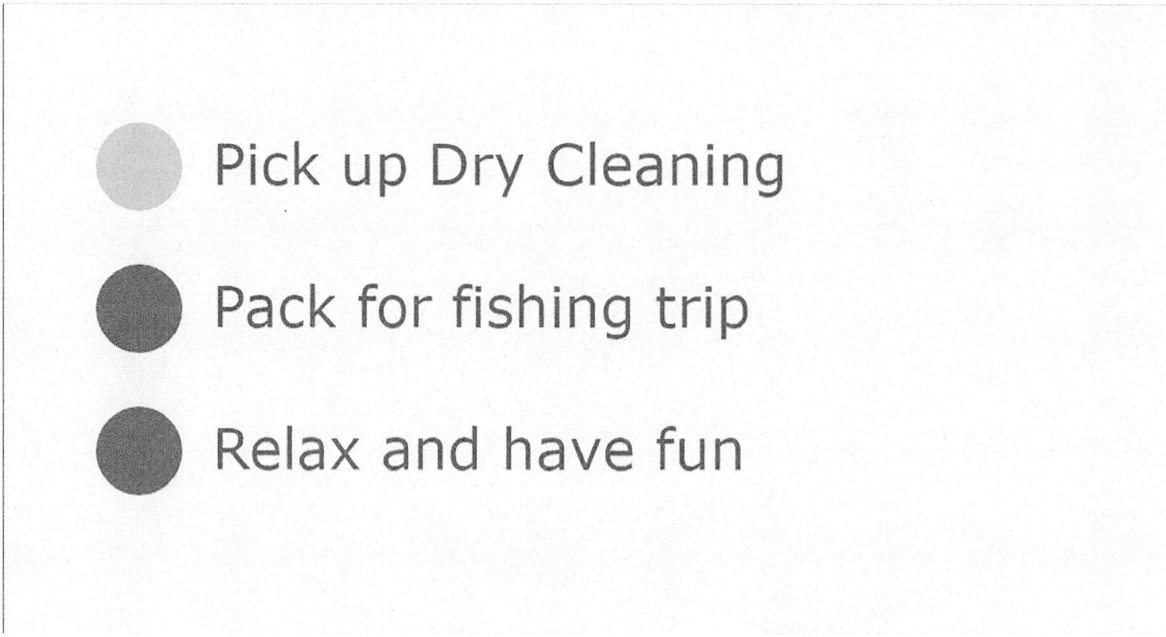

Figure 7.3 Bullet display from the hideshow.html web page.

Creating Button Arrays

This first button array example will demonstrate the use of CSS Classes in combination with <div> tags to create multiple rows of buttons. The button labels will match those of twenty-four of the GPIO pins on the Raspberry Pi 40-Pin expansion header. The button arrays are laid out in two groups representing both the left and right sides of the expansion header. Later chapters will also make use of similar arrangements.

A few centering tricks were used in this example. The main header <div> was placed in between <center> </center> tags to center the heading box. The two button arrays are centered by placing the contents into centered tables. This is a quick and easy way to keep relative-placed contents centered on the screen while applying individual or group positioning. See figure 7.4 for reference.

To create the button array example, follow these steps:

1. At a Terminal Prompt change into the project chapter7 directory:

   cd /home/pi/webproj/chapter7/

2. Using either a favorite desktop editor or nano, create the buttons.html file to match Program Listing 7.6: **nano buttons.html**

3. After creating the html code to match Program Listing 7.6 below, type CTRL + O then ENTER to save

then CTRL + X to exit nano.

4. Copy the html file to: /var/www/html/ by typing the following at the Terminal Prompt:

    sudo cp buttons.html /var/www/html/buttons.html

5. Open a web browser on the Raspberry Pi Desktop and type the path to the html file:

    localhost/buttons.html

6. The page can also be viewed on a remote computer by opening a web browser and typing the Raspberry Pi IP address followed by the path to the html file:

    (IP Address)/buttons.html

Program Listing 7.6: buttons.html

```html
<!doctype html>
<html>
<head>

    <meta http-equiv="Content-Type" content="text/html; charset=iso-8859-1">
    <title>Button Arrays</title>

<style>

.btn_grp {

  position:relative;
  text-align:center;
  width: 1150px;
  border:5px solid #5D5C61;
  border-radius:17px;
  background-color:#557A95;
  padding: 24px 0px;
}

.btn_row {
  padding: 4px 4px;
}

.btns {
  background-color: #938e94;
  color:#1E1A1A;
  cursor: pointer;
  width: 270px;
  height:70px;
  border-radius:12px;
  font-weight:600;
  font-family:Cambria, "Hoefler Text", "Liberation Serif",
```

```
      Times, "Times New Roman", "serif";
  font-size: 25px;
  padding: 6px 2px;
}


.btns:hover {
  color:beige;
  background-color:lightslategray;
}


</style>
</head>

<body bgcolor="#659DBD" text="beige"  nosave>

<br><br><br>
<center>
<div class="btn_grp" style="background:lightslategray;font-size:32px;">
    Button Arrays
</div>
</center>


<br><br><br>

<center>
<table border="0"><tbody>
    <tr><td>
        <div class="btn_grp">

            <div style="position: relative;top:-24px;background:lightslategray;
                    border-radius:12px;font-size: 25px;color:beige;">
            GPIO Header Odd Nubered Pins </div>

            <div class="btn_row">
              <button class="btns">GPIO 03: OFF</button>
              <button class="btns">GPIO 04: OFF</button>
              <button class="btns">GPIO 17: OFF</button>
              <button class="btns">GPIO 27: OFF</button>
            </div>


            <div class="btn_row">
              <button class="btns">GPIO 22: OFF</button>
              <button class="btns">GPIO 10: OFF</button>
```

```
            <button class="btns">GPIO 09: OFF</button>
            <button class="btns">GPIO 11: OFF</button>
        </div>

        <div class="btn_row">
            <button class="btns">GPIO 06: OFF</button>
            <button class="btns">GPIO 13: OFF</button>
            <button class="btns">GPIO 19: OFF</button>
            <button class="btns">GPIO 26: OFF</button>
        </div>
    </div>
  </td></tr>
</tbody></table>
</center>

<br>
<br>

<center>
<table border="0"><tbody>
    <tr><td>
        <div class="btn_grp">

            <div style="position: relative;top:-24px;background:lightslategray;
                    border-radius:12px;font-size: 25px;color:beige;">
            GPIO Header Even Nubered Pins </div>

            <div class="btn_row">
              <button class="btns">GPIO 14: OFF</button>
              <button class="btns">GPIO 15: OFF</button>
              <button class="btns">GPIO 18: OFF</button>
              <button class="btns">GPIO 23: OFF</button>
            </div>


            <div class="btn_row">
              <button class="btns">GPIO 24: OFF</button>
              <button class="btns">GPIO 25: OFF</button>
              <button class="btns">GPIO 08: OFF</button>
              <button class="btns">GPIO 07: OFF</button>
            </div>

            <div class="btn_row">
              <button class="btns">GPIO 12: OFF</button>
```

```
            <button class="btns">GPIO 16: OFF</button>
            <button class="btns">GPIO 20: OFF</button>
            <button class="btns">GPIO 21: OFF</button>
          </div>
        </div>
      </td></tr>
</tbody></table>
</center>

</body>
</html>
```

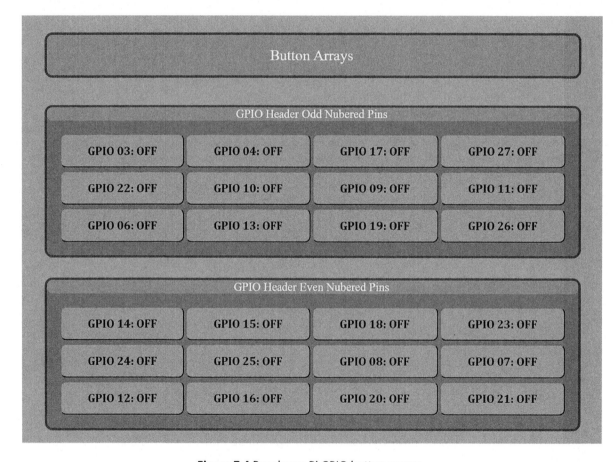

Figure 7.4 Raspberry Pi GPIO button arrays.

Notice that when the web browser width is narrowed, a scroll bar appears at the bottom of the browser such that the user has to scroll over to reach the buttons that are outside of the visible window. This issue will be corrected in a later example by creating a responsive web page that changes the layout based on screen size, making it much easer to view on a tablet or phone.

Changing Button State Dynamically

The idea of dynamically changing web page elements without refreshing the web page leads to many possibilities including creating web control panels. The previous example displayed arrays of buttons grouped together within a border box almost like a pushbutton panel. The panel is made even more realistic when used in conjunction with a touch screen. That truly constitutes a virtual control panel.

The next example will be a modification of the previous example. An onClick() action will be added to each button that will call a JavaScript function each time a button is pressed. The JavaScript function checks the button text looking for the current state by examining the last two characters. When the ending button text is "ON" and the button is pressed, then the button is turned "OFF". When in the "ON" state, the button will be highlighted with a highlight color and when turned "OFF", the button will return to normal state. Currently, this web control panel example does not actually turn the Raspberry Pi GPIO pins on or off; however, this feature will be added in a later chapter.

Follow the next steps to modify the button array example:

1. At a Terminal Prompt, change into the project chapter7 directory:

    cd /home/pi/webproj/chapter7/

2. Copy the previous example to a new file named actionbuttons.html:

    cp buttons.html actionbuttons.html

3. Using either a favorite desktop editor or nano, edit the actionbuttons.html file to match Program Listing 7.7:

    nano actionbuttons.html

4. After editing the html code to match Program Listing 7.7 below, type CTRL + O then ENTER to save then CTRL + X to exit nano.

5. Copy the html file to: /var/www/html/ by typing the following at the Terminal Prompt:

    sudo cp actionbuttons.html /var/www/html/actionbuttons.html

6. Open a web browser on the Raspberry Pi Desktop and type the path to the html file:

    localhost/actionbuttons.html

7. The page can also be viewed on a remote computer by opening a web browser and typing the Raspberry Pi IP address followed by the path to the html file:

    (IP Address)/actionbuttons.html

Program Listing 7.7: actionbuttons.html

```
<!doctype html>
<html>
<head>

    <meta http-equiv="Content-Type" content="text/html; charset=iso-8859-1">
    <title>Action Buttons</title>


<style>
```

```css
.btn_grp {

  position:relative;
  text-align:center;
  width: 1150px;
  border:5px solid #5D5C61;
  border-radius:17px;
  background-color:#557A95;
  padding: 24px 0px;
}

.btn_row {
  padding: 4px 4px;
}

.btns {
  background-color: #938e94;
  color:#1E1A1A;
  cursor: pointer;
  width: 270px;
  height:70px;
  border-radius:12px;
  font-weight:600;
  font-family:Cambria, "Hoefler Text", "Liberation Serif",
      Times, "Times New Roman", "serif";
  font-size: 25px;
  padding: 6px 2px;
}

.btns:hover {
  color:beige;
  background-color:lightslategray;
}

</style>
</head>

<body bgcolor="#659DBD" text="beige"  nosave>

<br><br><br>
<center>
<div class="btn_grp" style="background:lightslategray;font-size:32px;">
    Button Arrays
</div>
```

```
</center>

<br><br><br>

<center>
<table border="0"><tbody>
    <tr><td>
        <div class="btn_grp">

            <div style="position: relative;top:-24px;background:lightslategray;
                        border-radius:12px;font-size: 25px;color:beige;">
            GPIO Header Odd Numbered Pins
        </div>

        <div class="btn_row">
          <button class="btns" onClick="BtnToggle(this);">GPIO 03: OFF</button>
          <button class="btns" onClick="BtnToggle(this);">GPIO 04: OFF</button>
          <button class="btns" onClick="BtnToggle(this);">GPIO 17: OFF</button>
          <button class="btns" onClick="BtnToggle(this);">GPIO 27: OFF</button>
        </div>


        <div class="btn_row">
          <button class="btns" onClick="BtnToggle(this);">GPIO 22: OFF</button>
          <button class="btns" onClick="BtnToggle(this);">GPIO 10: OFF</button>
          <button class="btns" onClick="BtnToggle(this);">GPIO 09: OFF</button>
          <button class="btns" onClick="BtnToggle(this);">GPIO 11: OFF</button>
        </div>

          <div class="btn_row">
          <button class="btns" onClick="BtnToggle(this);">GPIO 06: OFF</button>
          <button class="btns" onClick="BtnToggle(this);">GPIO 13: OFF</button>
          <button class="btns" onClick="BtnToggle(this);">GPIO 19: OFF</button>
          <button class="btns" onClick="BtnToggle(this);">GPIO 26: OFF</button>
        </div>
      </div>
    </td></tr>
</tbody></table>
</center>

<br>
<br>

<center>
```

```
<table border="0"><tbody>
    <tr><td>
      <div class="btn_grp">

          <div style="position: relative;top:-24px;background:lightslategray;
                      border-radius:12px;font-size: 25px;color:beige;">
            GPIO Header Even Numbered Pins
          </div>

          <div class="btn_row">
            <button class="btns" onClick="BtnToggle(this);">GPIO 14: OFF</button>
            <button class="btns" onClick="BtnToggle(this);">GPIO 15: OFF</button>
            <button class="btns" onClick="BtnToggle(this);">GPIO 18: OFF</button>
            <button class="btns" onClick="BtnToggle(this);">GPIO 23: OFF</button>
          </div>

          <div class="btn_row">
            <button class="btns" onClick="BtnToggle(this);">GPIO 24: OFF</button>
            <button class="btns" onClick="BtnToggle(this);">GPIO 25: OFF</button>
            <button class="btns" onClick="BtnToggle(this);">GPIO 08: OFF</button>
            <button class="btns" onClick="BtnToggle(this);">GPIO 07: OFF</button>
          </div>

           <div class="btn_row">
            <button class="btns" onClick="BtnToggle(this);">GPIO 12: OFF</button>
            <button class="btns" onClick="BtnToggle(this);">GPIO 16: OFF</button>
            <button class="btns" onClick="BtnToggle(this);">GPIO 20: OFF</button>
            <button class="btns" onClick="BtnToggle(this);">GPIO 21: OFF</button>
          </div>
      </div>
    </td></tr>
</tbody></table>
</center>

<script>

    // Function to toggle the off/on button state.
    // Receives the button object to update.
    function BtnToggle(btnelement)
    {
        // Get the last two characters of the button text.
        var state = btnelement.innerHTML.slice(-2);
        var str = btnelement.innerHTML;
        // If the current state is "ON"
```

```
        if(state == "ON")
        {
            // Turn off button highligh color
            btnelement.style.backgroundColor = "#938e94";
            // Remove the "ON" from the button text.
            str = str.substring(0, str.length - 2);
            // Add "OFF" to the button text.
            btnelement.innerHTML = str + "OFF";
        }
        else
        {
            // Turn on button highlight color
            btnelement.style.backgroundColor = "#905B5D";
            // Remove the "OFF" from the button text.
            str = str.substring(0, str.length - 3);
            // Add "ON" to the button text.
            btnelement.innerHTML = str + "ON";
        }
    }

</script>

</body>
</html>
```

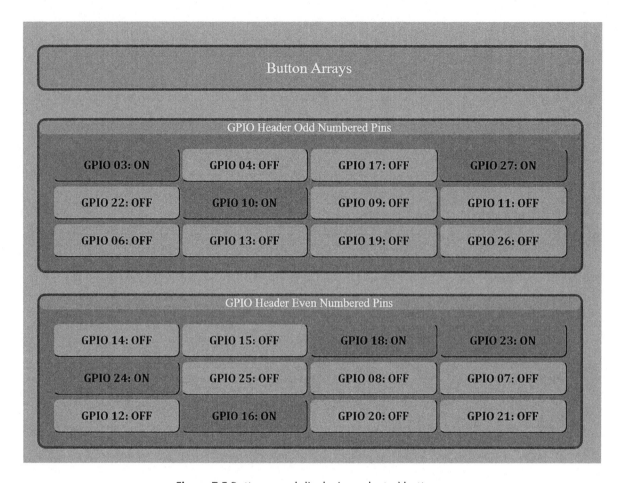

Figure 7.5 Button panel displaying selected buttons.

Create a Responsive Web Page Layout Based on Screen/Device Type

In earlier years, the personal computer was the primary platform for viewing web pages. One could create a fixed web page of a standard size, one size fits all. But obviously, in current years the hand held tablet or phone has gained ground considerably, quickly adding many various viewing platforms that need to be supported.

Early on, when many data devices were introduced, web page developers used environment variables to figure out the viewing device type then figure out how big the screen size should be. Multiple web pages would be created and a decision would be made as to which website to load. This approach can still be taken; however, the huge number of new devices and alternate browser names and types make it very hard to have a foolproof process in place to detect every type of device. This had led to a new type of web page, confusingly called a "Responsive Web Page." One's first thought would be that the web page is fast and responsive to input, but that is not the case here.

The Responsive Web Page is one that reacts to the browser media size. If the browser on a personal computer is resized, such that it is narrow, or the same web page is opened on a cell phone, the content of the web page is dynamically updated to look aesthetically pleasing at the more narrow size. In fact, the automatic update relative to media size can be performed at many different screen sizes for the same web page. The screen width at which a dynamic update is performed is called a breakpoint. A web developer can create as many breakpoints as is desired.

In the following example, three breakpoints will be set to change the appearance of the button arrays as the page width changes. When the page is 1250px or greater, then the page will display the GPIO buttons as before, having rows of four. When the screen width is 650px or less, the button display will change to only two buttons per row and when the screen reaches 369px or less, the buttons will be arranged onto a single column. In this case the arrangement is created simply by changing the .btn_grp class "width" value.

The following style text will be added in Program listing 7.8, which will cause the class definition to be updated at each breakpoint:

```
@media screen and (min-width: 369px)
{
    .btn_grp {
    width: 370px;
    }
}


@media screen and (min-width: 650px)
{
    .btn_grp {
    width: 600px;
    }
}


@media screen and (min-width: 1250px)
{
    .btn_grp {
    width: 1200px;
    }
}
```

To create the Responsive Web Page example, follow these steps:

1. At a Terminal Prompt, change into the project chapter7 directory:
    cd /home/pi/webproj/chapter7/

2. Copy the previous example to a new file named responsivedisplay.html:
    cp actionbuttons.html responsivedisplay.html

3. Using either a favorite desktop editor or nano, edit the responsivedisplay.html file to match Program Listing 7.8:
    nano responsivedisplay.html

4. After editing the html code to match Program Listing 7.8 below, type CTRL + O then ENTER to save then CTRL + X to exit nano.

5. Copy the html file to: /var/www/html/ by typing the following at the Terminal Prompt:

    sudo cp responsivedisplay.html /var/www/html/responsivedisplay.html

6. Open a web browser on the Raspberry Pi Desktop and type the path to the html file:

    localhost/responsivedisplay.html

7. The page can also be viewed on a remote computer by opening a web browser and typing the Raspberry Pi IP address followed by the path to the html file:

    (IP Address)/responsivedisplay.html

Program Listing 7.8: responsivedisplay.html

```html
<!doctype html>
<html>
<head>

    <meta http-equiv="Content-Type" content="text/html; charset=iso-8859-1">
    <title>Responsive Display</title>

<style>

.btn_grp {

  position:relative;
  text-align:center;
  border:5px solid #5D5C61;
  border-radius:17px;
  background-color:#557A95;
  padding: 24px 0px;
}

.btn_row {
  padding: 4px 4px;
}

.btns {
  background-color: #938e94;
  color:#1E1A1A;
  cursor: pointer;
  width: 270px;
  height:70px;
  border-radius:12px;
  font-weight:600;
```

```
  font-family:Cambria, "Hoefler Text", "Liberation Serif",
      Times, "Times New Roman", "serif";
  font-size: 25px;
  padding: 6px 2px;
}

.btns:hover {
  color:beige;
  background-color:lightslategray;
}


@media screen and (min-width: 369px)
{
    .btn_grp {
        width: 370px;
    }
}

@media screen and (min-width: 650px)
{
    .btn_grp {
        width: 600px;
    }
}

@media screen and (min-width: 1250px)
{
    .btn_grp {
        width: 1200px;
    }
}

</style>
</head>

<body bgcolor="#659DBD" text="beige"  nosave>

<br><br><br>
<center>
<div class="btn_grp" style="background:lightslategray;font-size:32px;">
    Button Arrays
</div>
</center>
```

```
<br><br><br>

<center>
<table border="0"><tbody>
    <tr><td>
      <div class="btn_grp">

          <div style="position: relative;top:-24px;background:lightslategray;
                      border-radius:12px;font-size: 25px;color:beige;">
            GPIO Header Odd Numbered Pins
          </div>

          <div class="btn_row">
            <button class="btns" onClick="BtnToggle(this);">GPIO 03: OFF</button>
            <button class="btns" onClick="BtnToggle(this);">GPIO 04: OFF</button>
            <button class="btns" onClick="BtnToggle(this);">GPIO 17: OFF</button>
            <button class="btns" onClick="BtnToggle(this);">GPIO 27: OFF</button>
          </div>

          <div class="btn_row">
            <button class="btns" onClick="BtnToggle(this);">GPIO 22: OFF</button>
            <button class="btns" onClick="BtnToggle(this);">GPIO 10: OFF</button>
            <button class="btns" onClick="BtnToggle(this);">GPIO 09: OFF</button>
            <button class="btns" onClick="BtnToggle(this);">GPIO 11: OFF</button>
          </div>

           <div class="btn_row">
            <button class="btns" onClick="BtnToggle(this);">GPIO 06: OFF</button>
            <button class="btns" onClick="BtnToggle(this);">GPIO 13: OFF</button>
            <button class="btns" onClick="BtnToggle(this);">GPIO 19: OFF</button>
            <button class="btns" onClick="BtnToggle(this);">GPIO 26: OFF</button>
          </div>
      </div>
    </td></tr>
</tbody></table>
</center>

<br>
<br>

<center>
<table border="0"><tbody>
    <tr><td>
```

```html
    <div class="btn_grp">

        <div style="position: relative;top:-24px;background:lightslategray;
                    border-radius:12px;font-size: 25px;color:beige;">
            GPIO Header Even Numbered Pins
        </div>

        <div class="btn_row">
          <button class="btns" onClick="BtnToggle(this);">GPIO 14: OFF</button>
          <button class="btns" onClick="BtnToggle(this);">GPIO 15: OFF</button>
          <button class="btns" onClick="BtnToggle(this);">GPIO 18: OFF</button>
          <button class="btns" onClick="BtnToggle(this);">GPIO 23: OFF</button>
        </div>

        <div class="btn_row">
          <button class="btns" onClick="BtnToggle(this);">GPIO 24: OFF</button>
          <button class="btns" onClick="BtnToggle(this);">GPIO 25: OFF</button>
          <button class="btns" onClick="BtnToggle(this);">GPIO 08: OFF</button>
          <button class="btns" onClick="BtnToggle(this);">GPIO 07: OFF</button>
        </div>

         <div class="btn_row">
          <button class="btns" onClick="BtnToggle(this);">GPIO 12: OFF</button>
          <button class="btns" onClick="BtnToggle(this);">GPIO 16: OFF</button>
          <button class="btns" onClick="BtnToggle(this);">GPIO 20: OFF</button>
          <button class="btns" onClick="BtnToggle(this);">GPIO 21: OFF</button>
        </div>
    </div>
  </td></tr>
</tbody></table>
</center>

<script>

    // Function to toggle the off/on button state.
    // Receives the button object to update.
    function BtnToggle(btnelement)
    {
        // Get the last two characters of the button text.
        var state = btnelement.innerHTML.slice(-2);
        var str = btnelement.innerHTML;
        // If the current state is "ON"
        if(state == "ON")
        {
```

```
                // Turn off button highligh color
                btnelement.style.backgroundColor = "#938e94";
                // Remove the "ON" from the button text.
                str = str.substring(0, str.length - 2);
                // Add "OFF" to the button text.
                btnelement.innerHTML = str + "OFF";
            }
        else
            {
                // Turn on button highlight color
                btnelement.style.backgroundColor = "#905B5D";
                // Remove the "OFF" from the button text.
                str = str.substring(0, str.length - 3);
                // Add "ON" to the button text.
                btnelement.innerHTML = str + "ON";
            }
        }

</script>

</body>
</html>
```

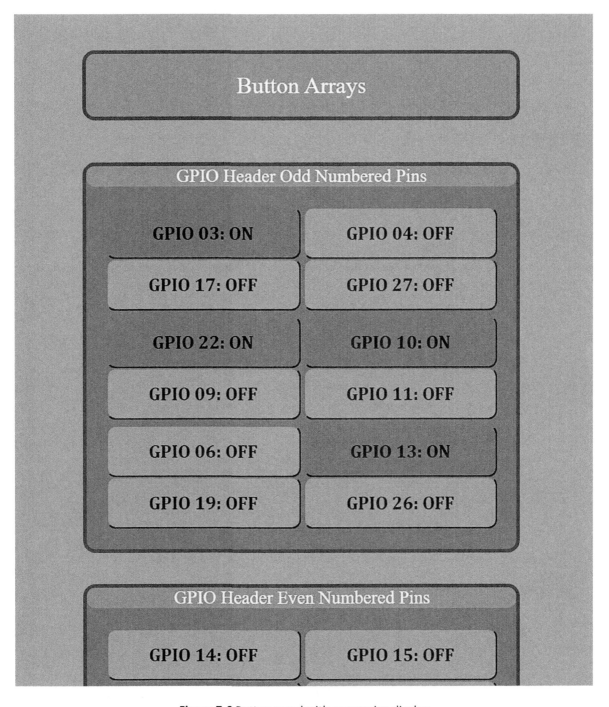

Figure 7.6 Button panel with responsive display.

Try changing the width of the web browser and watch how the layout changes as the screen width changes. Optionally, use a cell phone or tablet connected to Wi-Fi to view the web page by opening a web browser and typing the following into the address bar:

(IP Address)/responsivedisplay.html

Be sure to replace the IP Address with the IP address of your Raspberry Pi.

Extra Notes about CSS and <div> Tags

Multiple CSS classes can be applied to the same tag. Simply list each class name separated by a space in the class definition as in the following:

<div class = "firstclass secondclass thirdclass">Some Object</div>

Normally a class attribute is used to apply a CSS class to an HTML tag; however, that can also be accomplished by using a "#" sign that matches the ID attribute of a tag. This is similar to how class attributes are denoted in CSS with a period (.) before the class name; however, ID attributes are **prefixed with a #** sign. Code is applied to the tag that uses that ID versus the class definition. See the following example.

CSS:

```
.btn_row {
  padding: 4px 4px;
}


#btn_id_name {
  color:#1E1A1A;
}
```

HTML:

<div id="btn_id_name" class="btn_row" >Text</div>

Both CSS definitions are applied to the <div> tag, one relative to the tag ID and the other defined by the class attribute.

8

GPIO Control

One very desirable use of the Raspberry Pi single board computer is the ability to control things externally. For instance, turning lights on and off in the house remotely while on vacation or turning on a sprinkler system based on preprogrammed times throughout the day. Imagine being able to create your own Drag Racing Christmas Tree with colored flood lights to start races at the local race track. Sometimes it's just fun to have some LEDs hooked up to the GPIO pins for a visual indication that your software program is operating as expected. Advanced users may wish to create incredible light shows with music for various celebrations or holidays. The GPIO pins can also be used in conjunction with transistors and relays to control all kinds of external devices. Basic designs with LEDs, Transistors, and Relays will be explained in this chapter. Using the GPIO pins on a single board computer for control opens up so many possibilities limited only by one's imagination.

This chapter will cover the following topics:

1. GPIO description and basics
2. How to safely hook up an LED to the Raspberry Pi GPIO pins
3. Using Python to control the GPIO pins
4. Using a transistor to control an LED with a higher voltage
5. Using a transistor to operate a relay for controlling external devices
6. How to create Python scripts that can be used to Set and Get GPIO pin states

GPIO Description and Basics

GPIO stands for **General Purpose Input Output**, many times abbreviated simply as **IO Pins**. The idea is that a processor has the ability to read and write IO pins for monitoring and control of external devices. The board designer does not necessarily know how the IO Pins will be used because that is up to the end user to decide; however, certain rules have to be followed when using the IO Pins to prevent damage to the processor or peripheral device that drives the IO interface. For example, an LED cannot be connected directly to the IO Pins without risk of damaging the single board computer. An LED needs to have a resistor of the correct value connected in series with the LED to limit current and protect both the LED and the IO Pin from being damaged.

When used as an output, the Raspberry Pi IO Pins switch between 0.2V (logic low) and 3.3V (logic high). The actual logic low and logic high voltages will vary slightly from board to board. The documentation specifies that if all IO pins are used at the same time, each pin is designed to operate safely at a maximum of 3mA, which is to say 0.003 Amps. Individually, a single IO pin can be set up to operate at up to 16mA; however, this limits how many IO pins can be used as outputs as there is a maximum current limit for the combination of all IO pins. Another note about IO on the Raspberry Pi is that the expansion header does not contain all of the IO signals supported by the Raspberry Pi. The single board computer itself uses some of the IO signals internally and thus those signals are not routed to the expansion header. For instance, one of the internal signals is connected to an LED on the circuit board that is driven by the low-level device drivers for certain activities. The user does not specifically have access to this LED and should avoid accessing the internal registers that control the on-board LED or other internal IO.

The IO Pins can individually be configured as either inputs or outputs. If configured as an input, the pin state can be read in software and will show that the pin state is either "1", logic high, or "0", logic low. The physical signal connected to the IO pin configured as an input should either be 3.3V (high) or 0V (low). Connecting a signal higher than 3.3V can damage the single board computer.

The Raspberry Pi expansion header is a two-row connector with Pin 1 designated by a square pad on the Printed Circuit Board (PCB). The pin numbers alternate from side to side such that all odd pin numbers are on one side and all even pin numbers on the other side. When accessing the IO pins in software, they are normally referenced by a GPIO numeric designation that does not match the pin numbers on the 40-Pin header. For example, the expansion header Pin 3 is designated as GPIO 2 and expansion header Pin 40 is designated as GPIO 21. The following illustration shows the GPIO numbers versus the pin numbers:

Raspberry Pi PINOUTS

NAME	PIN #	NAME
3V3	1 2	5V
GPIO02	3 4	5V
GPIO03	5 6	GND
GPIO04	7 8	GPIO14
GND	9 10	GPIO15
GPIO17	11 12	GPIO18
GPIO27	13 14	GND
GPIO22	15 16	GPIO23
3V3	17 18	GPIO24
GPIO10	19 20	GND
GPIO09	21 22	GPIO25
GPIO11	23 24	GPIO08
GND	25 26	GPIO07
GPIO00	27 28	GPIO01
GPIO05	29 30	GND
GPIO06	31 32	GPIO12
GPIO13	33 34	GND
GPIO19	35 36	GPIO16
GPIO26	37 38	GPIO20
GND	39 40	GPIO21

Figure 8.1 Raspberry Pi GPIO pins on the 40-Pin expansion header.

How to Safely Hook Up an LED to the Raspberry Pi GPIO Pins

It is quite common to use an LED as an indicator when developing code for a single board computer. This makes it easy to have a visual indicator that the software program is performing as desired. At times it can be exciting for a software programmer to see an LED blinking on and off. A spectator may not quite understand all that is involved in getting to that point and think, *Big Deal,* but ignorance is not always bliss! If you are able to get an LED blinking on and off successfully without damaging the physical hardware then that is quite an accomplishment, especially if this is your first time.

Before moving on to designing some LED circuits, here are some basic facts about electronics. Electricity is basically the flow of electrons. Electrons are negatively charged, thus they flow from negative to positive. This is called the Electron Flow concept. There is another concept called Conventional Current where circuits are analyzed by considering electronics flowing from positive to negative. The examples shown here will be using the Electron Flow version where electrons are considered to flow from negative to positive.

A basic electronics circuit can be described as "creating a path for electrons to flow." If this path is interrupted or disconnected, then the path is broken and electrons have nowhere to go; this is described as an Open Circuit. A Short Circuit is created when current has an alternate path to take that bypasses one or more devices in the current path or a component has failed, thus shorting its input to its output.

To design a simple LED circuit some rules have to be applied. These rules are known as Ohm's law. Ohm's law provides some simple math that will allow us to calculate the appropriate resistor to connect in series with an LED to create a functional circuit. The following illustration in Figure 8.2 shows the simplified Ohm's Law Equation Triangle.

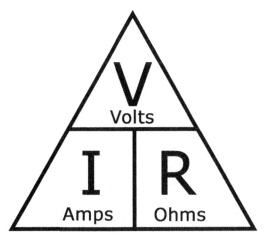

Figure 8.2 Ohm's Law Equation Triangle.

Ohm's law provides the following simple equations:

$$V = I * R$$
$$I = V/R$$
$$R = V/I$$

"V" stands for Voltage expressed in Volts, "I" stands for Current expressed in Amps, and "R" stands for resistance expressed in Ohms. These equations are easier to remember using the equation triangle in Figure 8.2 and will be used in the next few sections. Examine the Ohm's Law Triangle to see how the three equations are derived. Voltage is always divided by either Current or Resistance to find the needed value for the remaining variable. Current and Resistance are multiplied to find the Voltage.

Figure 8.3 presents a simple Light Emitting Diode (LED) circuit using GPIO 21, Header Pin 40 for the Positive Voltage and Header Pin 39 for the Ground or Negative connection. When the IO pin is set low, the LED will be off and when the IO Pin is set high, the LED will be illuminated.

The LED, labeled D1, has two pins labeled K and A. The K stands for Cathode and the A stands for Anode. For an LED to light, the cathode must be more negative than the anode. In other words, if the LED is inserted into a circuit backwards it will not conduct current, thus it will not illuminate. Normally the cathode on an LED is always marked. The following example uses a two pin through hole LED that has a flat spot on the side of the plastics that indicates the cathode or negative connection. That pin is also the shorter of the two pins. In the circuit in Figure 8.4 the resistor, R1, and LED, D1, can be exchanged where the resistor is drawn on top and the LED on the bottom and the circuit will still work properly.

Now the value of the Resistor needs to be determined; however, details about the LED must be known before the Resistor can be calculated. Electronic components will normally have a Datasheet available that provides extensive information about the part. In this case we need to know a value known as the **Forward Voltage (FV)**, commonly called the LED voltage. Since the circuit will be powered by 3.3 Volts it's best to select an LED with a Forward Voltage between 1.6V and 2.2V.

> **Note:** *GPIO pins on a single board computer, like the Raspberry Pi, will not always be exactly 3.3V. Depending on how accurate the power supply is and how heavily loaded the supply is, the voltage could vary by a couple tenths of a volt.*

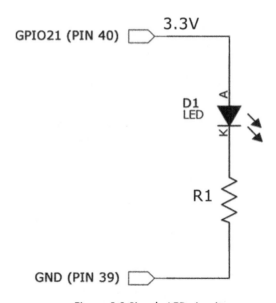

Figure 8.3 Simple LED circuit.

In this example we will use a red LED with a forward voltage of 1.8V. The LED part number is TLLK4401. This LED was selected because it will illuminate brightly at only 2mA of current. Keep in mind that it is ideal to keep the GPIO pin current under 3mA, if possible. So now we know the following about this circuit:

GPIO Pin Supply Voltage: 3.3V

LED Forward Voltage: 1.8V

Desired LED Current: 2mA

The next step is to figure out the voltage drop across resistor R1. To get the R1 Voltage simply subtract the LED forward voltage from the power supply voltage:

3.3V - 1.8V = 1.5V Across Resistor R1

Ohm's law can now be used to calculate the size of the resistor using the following equation: (R = V / I) Resistance = Voltage / Current

1.5V / 2mA = 750 Ohm

Resistor Value: 750 Ohm   Part# RNF14FTD750R or CFR-25JB-52-750R

Based on the calculations, a 750 Ohm resistor is needed to limit the current through the LED to 2mA. The updated circuit with part numbers is displayed in Figure 8.4.

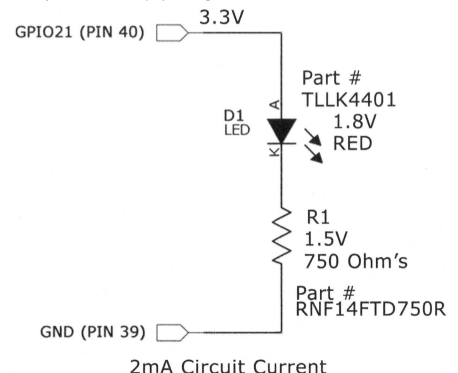

Figure 8.4 Finalized LED circuit.

Below is a short worksheet that can be used to determine a resistor value for an LED with a different forward voltage or different power supply voltage level:

Supply Voltage: _____ Desired LED Current:_____

LED Forward Voltage:_____

Resistor Voltage = Supply Voltage - LED Forward Voltage

Resistor Voltage = _____ - _____ = _____

Resistor Value = Resistor Voltage / Desired LED Current

Resistor Value = _____ / _____ = _____

Here is another LED current-limiting resistor example using the worksheet:

Supply Voltage: 3.3V Desired LED Current: 3mA

LED Forward Voltage: 2.2V (LED Voltage)

Resistor Voltage = Supply Voltage - LED Forward Voltage

Resistor Voltage = 3.3V - 2.2V = 1.1V

Resistor Value = Resistor Voltage / Desired LED Current

Resistor Value = 1.1V / 3mA = 367 Ohm

When purchasing a resistor, the exact value may not be available. In this case, selecting a resistor that is close should work well. For instance, a 370 ohm or a 365 ohm resistor can be used in place of a 367 Ohm resistor. Other types of circuits may not work when substituting different values; however, for an LED current-limiting resistor a few ohms in either direction won't make much of a difference in current or illumination.

If your eyes are glossing over right about now and selecting LED components and wiring them to the expansion header just isn't your cup of tea, you're in luck. Fortunately, an LED HAT was designed specifically for use with this book and testing of the Web Control Panel framework. The part number is **RPI-LED** and details are available through the following publisher site: **https://www.mstmicro.com/projects**

Figure 8.5 RPI-LED HAT for the Raspberry Pi.

The RPI-LED board has the GPIO pin designations printed on the top side to make it easy to identify the desired GPIO pin and verify that pin's ON/OFF state. The board is available with either Green, Bright Blue, or Bright Red LEDs. There are twenty-four LEDs connected to GPIO pins and two control inputs with on-board pull-ups for monitoring or control purposes.

Using Python to Control the GPIO Pins

This example Python script will turn on and off GPIO 21, pin 40, on the expansion connector based on the circuit depicted in Figure 8.4. Two additional GPIO pins will also be toggled on and off for reference as well. There are three ways to verify the code is changing the state of the GPIO pins:

1. Plug in the RPI-LED HAT and watch the GPIO pins toggle the LEDs on and off.

2. Hook up an LED as shown in Figure 8.4 to verify GPIO 21, Pin 40 is changing state.

3. Use a multimeter to measure the voltage between Pin 40 and Pin 39. Be careful not to touch any other pins with the leads so as not to short out any of the outputs.

The following Python script will be written to make use of the RPi.GPIO functionality on the Raspberry Pi to turn on and off GPIO pins on the board's 40-pin expansion header. The RPi.GPIO module is normally installed with the Raspbian or Raspberry Pi OS distribution. Verify Python and RPi.GPIO installation by typing the following highlighted lines at the Terminal Prompt. Be sure the case is correct or it will not succeed since it is case sensitive. Notice the lowercase 'i' in RPi.

sudo python3

Python 3.7.3 (default, Apr 3 2019, 05:39:12)

[GCC 8.2.0] on linux

Type "help", "copyright", "credits" or "license" for more information.

>>>import RPi.GPIO as IO

>>>ver = IO.VERSION

>>>print(ver)

0.6.5

>>>exit()

These Python commands should have returned the RPi.GPIO version. Note that the version may not match the version listed here. If the module is not found then it will need to be installed to use the example script. The module can be installed with the following Terminal command:

sudo apt-get install python-rpi.gpio python3-rpi.gpio

Create the Python GPIO Control Script

Follow the steps below to create an example Python script that will be used to toggle three GPIO pins on and off twenty times and then read the state of the three output pins and the state of two input pins. If using the RPI-LED board depicted in Figure 8.5 the two input pins will read a logic '1' since the two pins are pulled high by a resistor on the RPI-LED board. For a logic low, connect the two input pins to ground (GND). Follow these steps to enter the Python script:

1. To get started, a new folder must be created within the webproj directory for this chapter. At a

Terminal Prompt, change into the project directory: **cd /home/pi/webproj**

2. Create a new directory where the chapter eight code will be stored:

    mkdir chapter8

3. Change into the chapter8 directory: **cd chapter8**

4. Using either a favorite desktop editor or nano, create a file with the name gpioctl.py:

    nano gpioctl.py

5. Enter the script from Program Listing 8.1 below. The first line of the script should start with a "#" character. Make sure to keep the indent spacing the same as the example for the start of each line so that Python can interpret which lines of code are part of the loop that repeats twenty times.

6. When finished entering Program Listing 8.1, type CTRL + O then ENTER to save then CTRL + X to exit nano.

7. Next, the script must be set to be executable so it can be run. At the Terminal Prompt, type the following: **chmod +x+r gpioctl.py**

8. Now the script can be run from a Terminal Prompt. If you are using an RPI-LED board or have hooked up an LED to connect to any of the three pins gpio21 on pin 40, gpio20 on pin 38, or gpio16 on pin 36 then the LEDs should blink twenty times before exiting the application. Type the following to run the script: **./gpioctl.py** (Be sure to type the dot at the beginning).

9. The script can be run as many times as desired. If different pins need to be accessed then simply change the script to use the GPIO values that match the desired pins. Reference Figure 8.1 for the GPIO number to associate with each pin on the 40-pin expansion header.

Program Listing 8.1: gpioctl.py

```
#!/usr/bin/python3


# Warning, those sensitive to flashing lights should not use this Python Script.


import RPi.GPIO as GPIO
import time


# Define GPIO output pin numbers.
gpio21_pin40 = 21
gpio20_pin38 = 20
gpio16_pin36 = 16


# Define GPIO input pin numbers.
gpio2_pin3 = 2
gpio5_pin29 = 5


# I want to use GPIO reference numbers.
GPIO.setmode(GPIO.BCM)


# Setup GPIO outputs for the three pins.
```

```python
GPIO.setup(gpio21_pin40, GPIO.OUT)
GPIO.setup(gpio20_pin38, GPIO.OUT)
GPIO.setup(gpio16_pin36, GPIO.OUT)

# Setup GPIO inputs for the two input pins
GPIO.setup(gpio2_pin3 , GPIO.IN)
GPIO.setup(gpio5_pin29 , GPIO.IN)

print('\nStart of gpio program.')
# repeat 20 times
for loop in range(20):
    GPIO.output(gpio21_pin40, GPIO.HIGH)
    GPIO.output(gpio20_pin38, GPIO.HIGH)
    GPIO.output(gpio16_pin36, GPIO.HIGH)
    # take a break, have a coffee, for 200mS
    time.sleep(0.2)
    GPIO.output(gpio21_pin40, GPIO.LOW)
    GPIO.output(gpio20_pin38, GPIO.LOW)
    GPIO.output(gpio16_pin36, GPIO.LOW)
    time.sleep(0.2)

# Read and print the current value of the three output pins
# The outputs should all be low or logic '0' at this point.
gpiostate = GPIO.input(gpio21_pin40)
print("\nGPIO 21, pin 40 state: ", gpiostate)

gpiostate = GPIO.input(gpio20_pin38)
print("GPIO 20, pin 38 state: ", gpiostate)

gpiostate = GPIO.input(gpio16_pin36)
print("GPIO 16, pin 36 state: ", gpiostate)

# Read and print the current value of the two input pins.
gpiostate = GPIO.input(gpio2_pin3)
print("GPIO  2, pin  3 state: ", gpiostate)

gpiostate = GPIO.input(gpio5_pin29)
print("GPIO  5, pin 29 state: ", gpiostate)

GPIO.cleanup()
print('\nFinished pulsing GPIO Output Pins on the expansion header!')
```

Using a Transistor to Control an LED with a Higher Voltage

In the previous section, an LED with a current limiting resistor was connected in series to a GPIO pin on the Raspberry Pi. This worked well for the LED with a 1.8 Volt forward voltage drop, but what if it is desirable to hook up an LED that requires a much higher forward voltage drop or requires greater than 16mA of current? Since the GPIO pin only supplies approximately 3.3 Volts when set to a logic high, it would not be possible to properly power an LED with a forward voltage drop of 3.4 Volts. Even a 1.8V diode that requires 20mA to operate would not be able to be powered directly by a GPIO signal. In either case a bipolar transistor can be used like an electrically powered switch allowing a higher voltage level to power the LED. In the following instance, depicted in Figure 8.6, the +5V power on Pin 2 of the Raspberry Pi expansion header may be used for the LED power supply. GPIO21, Pin 40, will still be used but will serve as the switch control input.

Bipolar transistors are current-controlled devices, meaning that the higher the current through the emitter to the base the higher the amplified current between the emitter and collector. The DC Current Gain of a transistor is known as the hfe value or the Beta of the transistor. The hfe for a 2N3904 NPN transistor is normally between 60 and 300. With proper biasing the emitter-to-collector current will be equal to the emitter-to-base current multiplied by the hfe value. A transistor datasheet provides the hfe and several additional values that need to be examined to be able to properly bias the transistor as a switch. When being used as a switch, the transistor is either in a state of saturation, which is the full on state, or is turned off. To reach the saturation state (transistor full on state) the base (B) current must be high enough that the voltage between the emitter (E) and the collector (C) is at the minimum value called VCE(sat), which provides the least amount of resistance and lowest voltage drop between the emitter (E) and the collector (C). There are other values that must be examined as well so that the transistor is not used in a manner that will cause it to fail. For instance, the 2N3904 NPN transistor has the following maximum values:

Collector-to-Emitter Voltage (VCEO) = 40V DC Max

Collector-to-Base Voltage (VCBO) = 60V DC Max

Emitter-to-Base Voltage (VEBO) = 6V DC Max

Continuous Collector Current (Ic max) = 200mA DC Max

Total Power Dissipation: 625mW

Operational Parameters:

Collector-to-Emitter Saturation VCE(sat) = 0.2 to 0.3 Volts

Base-to-Emitter Saturation VBE(sat) = 0.65 Volts

hfe (Beta) = 60 to 300

If the 2N3904 transistor's maximum values are exceeded then it could damage the part so it is important to make sure any transistor design stays within proper operating conditions. In the following transistor circuit example the LED has the following attributes:

Color = Blue, 470nm

Forward Voltage drop (Vf) = 3.4V

Nominal Current: 20mA or 0.020 Amps, 25mA continuous recommended maximum.

Part Number: OVLFB3C7

Brightness: 5200mcd

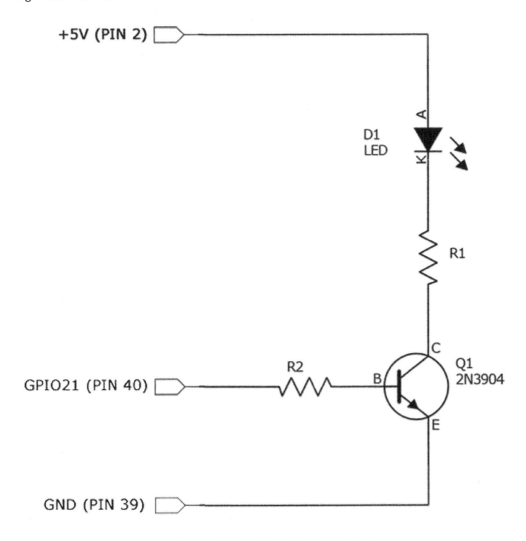

Figure 8.6 Transistor-driven LED circuit.

In the circuit of Figure 8.6 GPIO21, Pin 40, is used to control the transistor switch. The Ground (GND) is picked up by Pin 39 on the 40-Pin expansion header and Pin 2 will be used to supply +5V DC to the circuit to power the LED.

WARNING: The LED used in this circuit is very bright. Do not stare directly into the LED when lit.

The first step in determining the resistor values for R1 and R2 is to determine the amount of base (b) current that will be needed to keep the transistor in saturation when turned on. It is also important to make sure the GPIO pin is kept under 3mA to keep the total GPIO current of the Raspberry Pi down to a minimum. In this case

2mA or less will be the target base current. As long as the VBE(sat) voltage is reached and the resulting collector current (Ic) can support at least 20mA the transistor will operate in saturation; however, it's always best to provide a greater amount of available current than what will be needed to be sure to keep the transistor well into saturation mode. This extra current destination is called the overdrive factor (ODF). An ODF value of at least two is desirable but could be made anything between 2 and 10 times the desired collector current. It should be noted that the maximum continuous collector current of the 2N3904 transistor is 200mA so the final value of ODF times the desired current should be below 200mA. In this example the target LED current will be 15mA.

The following equation can be used to determine the amount of base current (Ib) required to be sure the transistor stays in saturation when supplying the desired collector current (Ic) to the LED:

Ib = (Ic * ODF) / hfe (min)

Ib = Base current

Ic = Collector current = 15mA for the LED

ODF = Overdrive factor = 8 (for a max of 120mA collector current)

hfe = Minimum transistor gain = 60

Base current: Ib = (15mA * 8) / 60 = 2mA

Based on the equation result above it can be seen that the transistor can supply up to 120mA of current to the LED with 2mA of base current. The next step is to calculate the value of R2, the current limiting resistor connected to the transistor base. Since the GPIO logic high value is approximately 3.3V and the Base-Emitter Saturation, VBE(sat), is approximately 0.65 Volts the following equation can be used to calculate R2:

R2 = (3.3V - VBE(sat)) / Base current

R2 = (3.3V - 0.65) / 2mA = 1,325 Ohms

R2 = 1,325 Ohms or 1.3K Ohm rounded down to the nearest available resistor value

R2 Voltage Drop = VCC - VBE(sat) = 3.3V - 0.65 = 2.65V

Next, the value of the current limiting resistor R1 needs to be calculated using the following equation:

R1 = (VCC - LED (Vf) - VCE(sat)) / IC

R1 = LED Current limiting resistor value in Ohms

VCC = Supply voltage = +5V

LED (Vf) = LED forward voltage = 3.4V

VCE(sat) = Saturation voltage from collector (C) to emitter (E) = 0.3 Volts worst case

IC = Collector current = 15mA

R1 = (+5V - 3.4V - 0.3V) / 15mA

R1 = 86.6 Ohms

The voltage drop across R1 = VCC - LED (Vf) - VCE(sat) = +5V - 3.4V - 0.3V = 1.3V

The data sheet shows the typical voltage drop for the selected LED as 3.4V; however, the minimum voltage drop is specified to be as low as 2.6V. This means the maximum LED current can be higher than 15mA and is calculated as follows: Voltage across R1 = VCC - LED (Vf) - VCE(sat) = +5V - 2.6V - 0.3V = 2.1V. Current = 2.1V / 86.6 Ohms = 24mA. The LED current can also be affected by the +5V power supply that can verify by several tenths of a volt and can change the current slightly outside of the range of 15mA - 24mA.

The last step in designing a transistor switch is to make sure that all of the components in the design will operate within the specified maximum power designated by the component manufacturers. Power equals heat and it's always best to operate components under their maximum power capability so the circuit will endure the test of time. The bottom line is that heat degrades or destroys electronic components so keeping the power dissipation down to a minimum is always desirable. Normally the power dissipation for a component should be 80% or less than the maximum power rating of the part.

The following are the part numbers and maximum power ratings for each of the four components used in the final design displayed in Figure 8.8:

Resistor R1: MFR-25FBF52-86R6 , 86.6 OHM, 1%, **250mW**

Resistor R2: CF14JT1K30, RES 1.3K OHM, 5%, **250mW**

Transistor Q1: 2N3904, Transistor, **625mW**

Blue Light Emitting Diode (LED) D1: OVLFB3C7, **100mW**

Ohm's Law can be used to calculate the total power dissipation of the components used in this design. The following power triangle provides some of the power equations for calculating power:

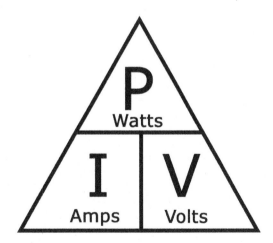

Figure 8.7 Ohm's Law power equation triangle.

The power triangle provides the following simple equations:

P = I * V

I = P/V

V = P/I

"P" stands for Power expressed in Watts. "V" stands for Voltage expressed in Volts. "I" stands for Current expressed in Amps. These equations are easier to remember using the Ohm's law power equation triangle in Figure 8.7 and will be used to calculate the approximate power dissipation for each component in the final circuit of Figure 8.8 below.

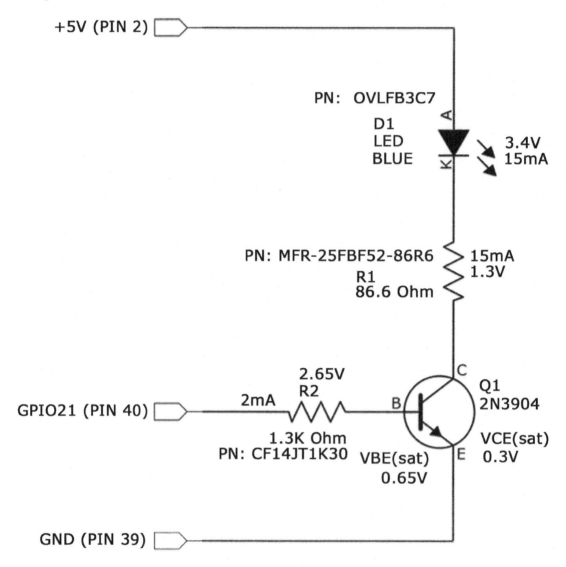

Figure 8.8 Transistor used as a switch circuit with values.

P (Power) = I (Current) * V (Voltage)

Approximate Power dissipated by Resistor R1 = 15mA * 1.3V = 0.0195 Watts = **19.5mW**

Approximate Power dissipated by Resistor R2 = 2mA * 2.65V = 0.0053 Watts = **5.3mW**

Approximate LED Power dissipation = 15mA * 3.4V = 0.051 Watts = **51mW**

The power calculations for the two resistors and the LED are straightforward; however, the Transistor requires the addition of the combined power of both the Base-Emitter Junction and the Emitter-Collector Junction using the following equation:

Q1 Transistor Power = VBE(sat) * Ib + VCE(sat) * Ic

VBE(sat) = Saturation Base - Emitter Voltage = 0.65V

Ib = Base Current = 2mA

VCE(sat) = Saturation Collector - Emitter Voltage = 0.3 Volts Max

Ic = Collector Current = 15mA

Q1 Transistor Power = (0.65V * 2mA) + (0.3V * 15mA) = (0.0013 Watts) + (0.0045 Watts) = 5.8mW

Notice that the total power dissipation of the transistor when turned on in saturation mode is minimal at 5.8mW. This is because the transistor resistance when in saturation mode is very small. The saturation impedance (Resistance) of the transistor from Emitter to Collector can be calculated using the following equation:

Q1 Saturation Impedance = VCE(sat) / Ic = 0.3V / 15mA = 20 Ohms

Based on the manufacturer power ratings this circuit should operate for a very long time since all of the operating power levels are less than 80% of the rated power:

R1 Max power = 1/4 Watt = 250mW, actual power used = 19.5mW

R2 Max power = 1/4 Watt = 250mW, actual power used = 5.3mW

LED Max power = 100mW, actual power used = 51mW

Q1 Max power = 625mW, actual power used = 5.8mW

Total Circuit Power = 19.5mW + 5.3mW + 51mW + 5.8mW = 81.6mW

Below is a worksheet that can be used to determine the values of the transistor circuit of Figure 8.6 with a different LED forward voltage, a different transistor, or a different power supply voltage level:

Transistor parameters from the datasheet:

hfe (Beta) minimum: _____

Max Collector-to-Emitter Voltage (VCEO): _____

Max Collector-to-Base Voltage (VCBO): _____

Max Emitter-to-Base Voltage (VEBO): _____

Max Continuous Collector Current (Ic max): _____

Max Continuous Power Dissipation: _____

Collector-to-Emitter Saturation VCE(sat): _____

Base-to-Emitter Saturation VBE(sat): _____

LED parameters from the datasheet:

Forward Voltage drop (Vf): _____

Nominal Current: _____ **(Ic)** This will be the collector current **(Ic)** and is the desired LED steady state current normally listed as the test current in the LED datasheet but must not be more than the maximum continuous current. Quite often this value is between 2mA and 20mA.

Power supply values:

Power Supply for the LED (VCC): _____ Volts

Power Supply to the base of the transistor (VB): _____ Volts

Circuit calculations:

Desired current overdrive (ODF) value (2 to 10): _____

Base current (Ib) = (Ic * ODF) / hfe (min)

Base current (Ib) = (_____ * _____) / _____ = _____ Amps

R2, Base Resistor Value = (VB - VBE(sat)) / Ib

R2, Base Resistor Value = (_____ - _____) / _____ = _____ Ohms

R2 Voltage Drop = VB - VBE(sat)

R2 Voltage Drop = _____ - _____ = _____ Volts

R2 Current = Ib (Same as the base current)

R2 Power = R2 Voltage Drop * Ib

R2 Power = _____ * _____ = _____ Watts

R1, LED Current-limiting Resistor Value =

    R1 Value = (VCC - LED (Vf) - VCE(sat)) / Ic

    R1 Value = (_____ - _____ - _____) / _____ = _____ Ohms

R1 Voltage Drop = VCC - LED (Vf) - VCE(sat)

R1 Voltage Drop = _____ - _____ - _____ = _____ Volts

R1 Current = Ic (Same as the current through the LED)

R1 Power = R1 Voltage Drop * Ic

R1 Power = _____ * _____ = _____ Watts

Q1 Transistor Power = VBE(sat) * Ib + VCE(sat) * Ic

Q1 Transistor Power = (_____ * _____) + (_____ * _____) = _____ Watts

Note: *Parentheses were added above to help clarify the order of mathematical operations.*

Q1 Saturation Impedance = VCE(sat) / Ic

Q1 Saturation Impedance = _____ / _____ = _____ Ohms

Caution must be taken to be sure that VCC is less than the Max Collector-to-Emitter Voltage (VCEO) and that VB is less than the Max Emitter-to-Base Voltage (VEBO) specified in the datasheet. The calculated Ic should be less than or equal to (Ic max). The calculated power values of each of the components used in the circuit of Figure 8.6 should be at least 20% lower than the specified max power levels in the corresponding datasheets.

Using a Transistor to Operate a Relay for Controlling External Devices

In the previous section, a 2N3904 transistor was used to turn an LED on and off because the LED had a forward voltage higher than the 3.3V that the GPIO pin could supply. This section will also make use of a 2N3904 transistor so that a GPIO pin can be used to turn on and off a relay. A relay is an electromechanical device. It has an internal electro magnet by way of a coil of wire. When electric current flows through the coil, the core becomes magnetic and pulls the relay contacts together just as if someone toggled a switch. When the relay coil is de-energized, the magnetic field is lost and a spring separates the relay output contacts leaving them in the normally open (off) state. It is very useful to be able to control a relay because its contacts can normally switch much higher voltage and current levels. Think of a relay like a toggle switch similar to a light switch in a home. Rather than toggling the power on and off by flipping the switch it is controlled by the Raspberry Pi GPIO Pin by energizing the relay coil. Some examples of devices that can be controlled by relays are sprinkler systems, electric motors, house lighting, camera power, automatic gate or door, electric fence, and much more. In any of the above cases the correct relay must be used so that it does not fail or cause damage to equipment.

CAUTION: *Any time a relay is used with high current or high voltage a fuse or circuit breaker should be in line with the device being powered. When using 120V or 240V power, it is best to use a GFCI plug to help in preventing electric shock.*

WARNING: Only qualified personnel should attempt to wire a relay with high voltage AC or DC power to prevent the chance of electrical shock, damage to equipment, or fire. Do not attempt to wire a high-voltage circuit unless you are qualified to do so or you could create an electrical shock hazard or fire.

The relay control example provided below demonstrates the use of a transistor to turn on and off a relay. When the relay changes state, an audible click can be heard. The relay is a Single Post, Single Throw (SPST) type and is normally open, meaning that the two relay contact pins are not normally connected until the relay is energized; then they will connect as if the switch was turned on. When the relay is turned back off, the two relay contact pins will open again. An ohmmeter can be used to measure the relay contacts on relay pins 3 and 4. When unpowered, the contacts should read "infinity" or "open circuit." When the relay is powered, the contact pins 3 and 4 should measure zero ohms or short circuit.

The relay selected for this example is a PCB mount relay that can be used with a prototype circuit board or wire wrap circuit board. When used with high current, it's best to solder the connections with large enough wire to carry the current or the wires can overheat or burn up. The relay circuit is depicted in Figure 8.9 and the relay specifications are as follows:

Relay Part Number: G5CA-1A-E-DC5

Relay Coil Specifications:

Normal Coil Voltage: 5V DC

Max Coil Voltage: 130% of 5V = 6.5V

Min Coil Voltage: 75% of 5V to activate = 3.75V

Coil Release Voltage: 10% of 5V = 0.5V

Max Coil Power Consumption: 200mW

Normal Coil Current: 40mA

Coil Resistance: 125 Ohms, 10% Tolerance

Relay Contact Ratings:

Single Post, Single Throw (SPST), Normally Open

Max Voltage: 250V AC, 125V DC

Max Current, Resistive load: 15A @ 110V AC or 10A @ 30V DC

Max Current Inductive load: 5A @ 110V AC or 3A @ 30V DC

Ambient Operating Temperature: -25°C to 70°C

Ambient Operating Humidity: 5% to 85%

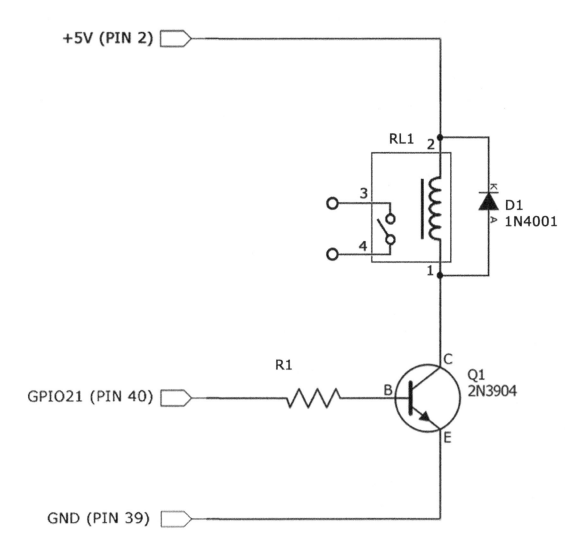

Figure 8.9 Transistor controlled relay circuit.

Note: The relay contact specifications mention the current and the voltage ratings for both resistive and inductive loads. Inductive loads refer to electric motors, electro magnets or any other device that uses a large coil of wire including some welders. An example of a resistive load would be a light bulb, LED lighting or other devices that do not rely on a coil of wire or a transformer. Some home appliances use a power supply that can be considered to be inductive so the type of load should be verified prior to hooking up any device to the relay contacts. If the type of load is not known then it's best to use the lower rating specified for the inductive load with a maximum of: 5A @ 110V AC or 3A @ 30V DC.

Using the relay specifications and the previous 2N3904 transistor specifications the relay circuit parameters can be calculated. The transistor will be used as a switch to turn on and off the relay by energizing the relay coil. As in the previous transistor circuit example, the transistor will need to operate in saturation mode when switched on so most of the same calculations will be used; however, the relay does not require a current limiting resistor and has an impedance (resistance) of 125 Ohms with a tolerance of + or - 10%. The 2N3904 transistor specifications were previously listed but will be listed here again for convenience:

2N3904 specifications:

Collector-to-Emitter Voltage (VCEO) = 40V DC Max

Collector-to-Base Voltage (VCBO) = 60V DC Max

Emitter-to-Base Voltage (VEBO) = 6V DC Max

Continuous Collector Current (Ic max) = 200mA DC Max

Total Power Dissipation: 625mW

Operational Parameters:

Collector-to-Emitter Saturation VCE(sat) = 0.2 to 0.3 Volts

Base-to-Emitter Saturation VBE(sat) = 0.65 Volts

hfe (Beta) = 60 to 300

The relay coil needs approximately 40mA of current and requires a voltage drop between 3.75V and 6.5V to turn on. The first step is to find the required transistor base current so that the value or R1 can be calculated.

Circuit calculations:

Desired current overdrive (ODF) value (2 to 10) = 4

Base current (Ib) = (Ic * ODF) / hfe (min)

Base current (Ib) = (40mA * 4) / 60 = 2.67mA

R1, Base Resistor Value = (VB - VBE(sat)) / Ib

R1, Base Resistor Value = (3.3V - 0.65V) / 2.67mA = 993 Ohms (Round up to **1K**)

The 993 Ohm resistor will be rounded up to a 1K resistor because it's a common value that is easy to find in stock and the value is very close to the calculated value.

R1 Voltage Drop = VB - VBE(sat)

R1 Voltage Drop = 3.3V - 0.65 = 2.65V

R1 Current = Ib (Same as the base current) 2.67mA

R1 Power = R2 Voltage Drop * Ib

R1 Power = 2.65V * 2.67mA = 7.1mW

Relay RL1 Voltage Drop = VCC - VCE(sat) = +5V - 0.3 = 4.7V

Q1 Saturation Impedance = VCE(sat) / Ic = 0.3V / 40mA = 7.5 Ohms

Q1 Transistor Power = VBE(sat) * Ib + VCE(sat) * Ic

Q1 Transistor Power = 0.65V * 2.67mA + 0.3V * 40mA = 1.74mW + 12mW = .01374 Watts = **13.74mW**

The final relay circuit showing the resulting values and component part numbers is depicted in Figure 8.10 below. The normally open contacts on relay pins 3 and 4 are basically the connections that can be used as a switch. Figure 8.11 provides one example of how the relay contacts can be used.

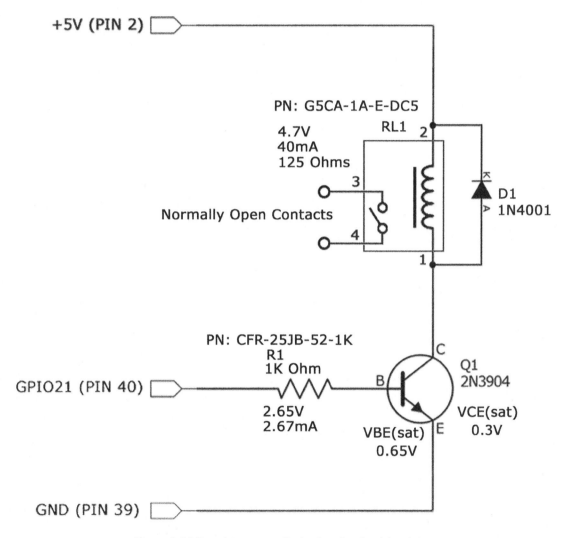

Figure 8.10 Transistor controlled relay circuit with values.

Notice the 1N4001 Diode, D1, in the circuit of Figure 8.10. This diode is for circuit protection. When a relay coil is de-energized, the existing magnetic field will try to force the current through the coil to continue to conduct and that energy needs a way to be dissipated. Diode D1 provides a path for the built-up energy to be released or shorted. Failure to use a reversed biased diode like the 1N4001 across a relay coil will result in large voltage spikes within the circuit and could cause damage to the Raspberry Pi. Care must be taken to make sure the diode is hooked up properly. If wired incorrectly (incorrect polarity) the diode will short out the relay and prevent it from operating. In other words, the diode has to be hooked up in the correct direction. The Cathode (K) of a diode is normally marked in some manner to make it easier to know how to hook it up in a circuit. This mark is normally a line, arrow, dot, or some other marking.

If using a higher voltage relay or desiring to hook up multiple relays an external power supply will be required. The Raspberry Pi +5V supply is limited. To use an external power supply simply replace the +5V Pin2 (VCC) with an external power source and connect the external power source GND (return) to a ground pin on the Raspberry Pi. Be careful not to reverse the polarity or it could damage the Raspberry Pi.

Figure 8.11 below shows an example where the relay contacts on relay pins 3 and 4 are used as a switch to turn on and off landscape lighting. The battery ground terminal is connected directly to the lighting ground and the battery positive terminal is connected to the lighting through the relay contacts (switch) such that when the relay is activated, the positive lighting power is applied, turning on the lights.

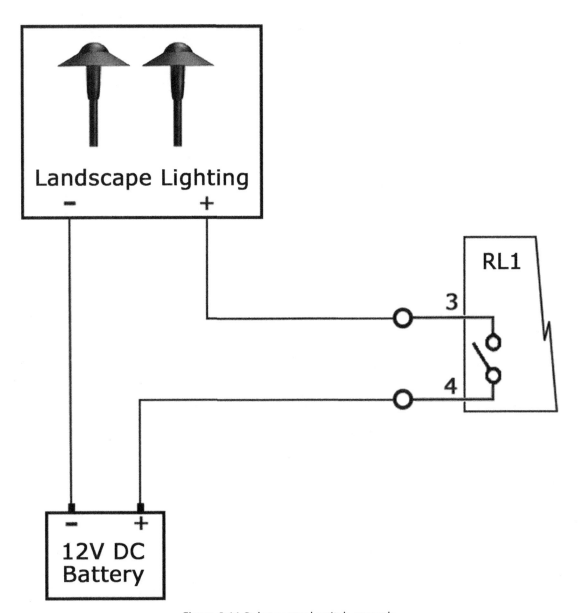

Figure 8.11 Relay control switch example.

Create Python Scripts That Can Be Used to Set and Get GPIO Pin States

It can be very handy to create some generic scripts to both Set and Get the GPIO pin states. These Python scripts will be created to accept command line arguments that allow the specific selection of a GPIO pin for reading or writing. Once created, these scripts will come in handy when trying to test or debug an external device connected to a GPIO pin. These scripts can also be used with an Embedded Web Control Panel to change the GPIO pin states from a web page, as will be seen in the next chapter. Follow the steps below to create and test the first script named **ioSet.py**:

1.   At a Terminal Prompt, change into the chapter8 directory:

     cd /home/pi/webproj/chapter8

2.   Using either a favorite desktop editor or nano, create a file with the name ioSet.py:

     nano ioSet.py

3.   Enter the script from Program Listing 8.2 below. The first line of the script should start with a "#" character. Make sure to keep the indent spacing the same as the example for the start of each line so that Python can properly interpret the script.

4.   When finished entering Program Listing 8.2, type CTRL + O then ENTER to save then CTRL + X to exit nano.

5.   Next, the script must be set to be executable and readable so it can be run. At the Terminal Prompt, type the following: **chmod +x+r ioSet.py**

6.   Now the script can be run by typing:

     ./ioSet.py <GPIO #> <State 0|1>

7.   Try typing the following example to turn on GPIO 21:

     ./ioSet.py 21 1

8.   Next try turning off GPIO 21:

     ./ioSet.py 21 0

When the ioSet.py script completes, it returns the new state of the GPIO pin. This value can be read by an application calling the script or by typing **echo $?** at the Terminal Prompt just after running the script. It should return either 0 or 1 depending on the new state fo the GPIO pin.

The ioSet.py script can be used to change the state of any GPIO pin simply by changing the command line arguments.

Program Listing 8.2: ioSet.py

```
#!/usr/bin/python3
# Python program to set GPIO output state.
# Syntax ./pySet.py <GPIO #> <State 0|1>
# Exits with -1 (255) on error else new output state.
import sys
import RPi.GPIO as GPIO

# Check for two command line arguments.
# Do nothing if incorrect input.
numArgv = len(sys.argv)
if numArgv < 3:
    print("Syntax: pySet.py <GPIO> <0|1>")
    sys.exit(-1)

ioNum = int(sys.argv[1])
```

```python
state = int(sys.argv[2])

# Check input
if (ioNum < 1) or (ioNum > 30):
    print ("Invalid <GPIO> number:", ioNum)
    sys.exit(-1)
if (state < 0) or (state > 1):
    print ("Invalid state, must be 0 or 1")
    sys.exit(-1)

# Use GPIO reference numbers.
GPIO.setmode(GPIO.BCM)

# Disable GPIO warnings due to resetting as output
GPIO.setwarnings(False)
# Configure GPIO and set output value.
GPIO.setup(ioNum, GPIO.OUT)

# Set GPIO output value.
if state == 1:
    GPIO.output(ioNum, GPIO.HIGH)
else:
    GPIO.output(ioNum, GPIO.LOW)

# Get new value of the GPIO output.
newstate = GPIO.input(ioNum)

# Exit with newstate value.
sys.exit(newstate)
```

The next script file name is ioGet.py. This script will read the state of the GPIO pin specified on the command line and print the value in the terminal. This script also returns the value of the GPIO pin on exit and can be read by typing **echo $?** at the Terminal Prompt just after running the script.

Follow these steps to create and test the **ioGet.py** Python script:

1. At a Terminal Prompt, change into the chapter8 directory:

   cd /home/pi/webproj/chapter8

2. Using either a favorite desktop editor or nano, create a file with the name ioGet.py:

   nano ioGet.py

3. Enter the script from Program Listing 8.3 below. The first line of the script should start with a "#" character. Make sure to keep the indent spacing the same as the example for the start of each line so that Python can properly interpret the script.

4. When finished entering Program Listing 8.3, type CTRL + O then ENTER to save then CTRL + X to exit nano.

5. Next, the script must be set to be executable so it can be run. At the Terminal Prompt, type the following:

    chmod +x+r ioGet.py

6. Now the script can be run by typing: **./ioGet.py** <GPIO #>

7. Try typing the following example to read the state of GPIO 21:

    ./ioGet.py 21

8. Verify the return value by typing the following:

    echo $?

The script ioGet.py returns the GPIO state on exit such that the value can be read by another calling application programmatically.

Program Listing 8.3: ioGet.py

```
#!/usr/bin/python3
# Python program to get the GPIO state.
# Syntax ./pyGet.py <GPIO #>
# Exits with -1 (255) on error else new output state 0|1.
import sys
import RPi.GPIO as GPIO

# Check for one command line argument.
numArgv = len(sys.argv)
if numArgv < 2:
    print("Syntax: pyGet.py <GPIO>")
    sys.exit(-1)


ioNum = int(sys.argv[1])

# Check input
if (ioNum < 1) or (ioNum > 30):
    print ("Invalid <GPIO> number:", ioNum)
    sys.exit(-1)

# Use GPIO reference numbers.
GPIO.setmode(GPIO.BCM)

# Disable GPIO warnings due to resetting GPIO setup.
GPIO.setwarnings(False)
```

```python
# Verify current GPIO configuration
cfg = GPIO.gpio_function(ioNum)
if cfg == 0:      # Output
   GPIO.setup(ioNum, GPIO.OUT)
elif cfg == 1:   # Input
   GPIO.setup(ioNum, GPIO.IN)
elif cfg == -1:  # Unknown
   GPIO.setup(ioNum, GPIO.IN)
else: # If GPIO is set to another function, just exit.
   sys.exit(-1)

# Get value of the GPIO pin.
newstate = GPIO.input(ioNum)

print("GPIO{}:{}".format(ioNum, newstate))

# Exit with newstate value.
sys.exit(newstate)
```

The idea of calling the ioSet.py and ioGet.py scripts from another application is to provide a quick way to add GPIO support to an application written in other languages like 'C'. The application can call the scripts and then read the return value to know if the action was successful. One issue with this approach is that the Python GPIO module is not considered to be real-time, meaning it could take various lengths of time to execute the scripts and in some cases be very time consuming. In fact, using the ioGet.py script to sequentially read the state of twenty-six GPIO pins would require repetitive calls that could result in several seconds of time to complete. Desiring to update a web page at a one-second interval when the overhead of reading the GPIO pin states takes several seconds to complete simply won't do. A later chapter will demonstrate how to use 'C' code to access the GPIO pins from within the Web Control Panel Framework, which will provide a much faster solution. For now, a new Python script will be created that can read twenty-six GPIO pins in a single pass that will take less than a second to complete. The output will be printed to the terminal and can be read and parsed by the control panel framework as will be seen in the next chapter.

Use these steps to create and test the new ioGetAll.py script:

1. At a Terminal Prompt, change into the chapter8 directory:

   cd /home/pi/webproj/chapter8

2. Using either a favorite desktop editor or nano, create a file with the name ioGetAll.py:

   nano ioGetAll.py

3. Enter the script from Program Listing 8.4 below. The first line of the script should start with a "#" character. Make sure to keep the indent spacing the same as the example for the start of each line so that Python can properly interpret the script.

4. When finished entering Program Listing 8.4, type CTRL + O then ENTER to save then CTRL + X to exit nano.

5. Next, the script must be set to be executable so it can be run. At the Terminal Prompt, type the following:

    chmod +x+r ioGetAll.py

6. Now the script can be run by typing:

    ./ioGetAll.py

If successful, the output of ioGetAll.py should look like the following:

```
pi@raspberrypi:~/webproj/chapter8 $ ./ioGetAll.py
P2:1
P3:0
P4:0
P5:1
P17:0
P27:0
P22:0
P10:0
P9:0
P11:0
P6:0
P13:0
P19:0
P26:0
P14:0
P15:0
P18:0
P23:0
P24:0
P25:0
P8:0
P7:0
P12:0
P16:0
P20:0
P21:0
pi@raspberrypi:~/webproj/chapter8 $
```

The resulting output shows the GPIO number next to the "P" then the current state after the ":" character. This output will be used by the web control panel example in the next chapter.

Program Listing 8.4: ioGetAll.py

```
#!/usr/bin/python3
import sys
import RPi.GPIO as GPIO
```

```python
# Use GPIO reference numbers.
GPIO.setmode(GPIO.BCM)
# Disable GPIO warnings due to resetting GPIO setup.
GPIO.setwarnings(False)

BCMArray = [2, 3, 4, 5, 17, 27, 22, 10, 9, 11, 6, 13, 19, 26,
        14, 15, 18, 23, 24, 25, 8, 7, 12, 16, 20, 21]

for ioNum in BCMArray:
    # Verify current GPIO configuration
    cfg = GPIO.gpio_function(ioNum)
    if cfg == 0:     # Output
        GPIO.setup(ioNum, GPIO.OUT)
    elif cfg == 1:  # Input
        GPIO.setup(ioNum, GPIO.IN)
    elif cfg == -1: # Unknown
        GPIO.setup(ioNum, GPIO.IN)
    else: # If GPIO is set to another function, just exit.
        sys.exit(-1)

    # Get value of the GPIO pin.
    newstate = GPIO.input(ioNum)

    # Prints the GPIO BCM Number : State 0|1.
    print('P{}:{}'.format(ioNum, newstate))
```

9

WEB CONTROL PANEL FRAMEWORK

Having covered multiple technologies in the previous chapters it's time to pull everything together and create a fully functional embedded web control panel that is statically displayed with dynamically updated content, just as if it were a physical electronic control panel. This virtual control panel will use a framework that will allow background access to the embedded target over CGI while keeping the main user interface static. As an example, a user can press a button to turn on a GPIO pin and watch the state of that pin change. The button state on the web page will then be automatically updated to match the state of the GPIO pin based on information returned by the physical hardware without having to refresh or reload the web page.

The feeling of an actual control panel is even more genuine if a tough screen is used to display the webpage. For instance, using a cell phone connected to the local Wi-Fi allowing the user to physically touch the buttons as in a real physical control panel provides a great user experience and feeling of realism. The control panel web page can be accessed by any computer that has access to the Raspberry Pi over the network or over the internet if the Raspberry Pi is set up in a router DMZ or if port forwarding is used for Port 80. Port 80 is the normal internet communications port for the Hypertext Transfer Protocol (HTTP), although alternate ports can be used to provide additional security if so desired.

> **Note:** *Placing the Raspberry Pi in a router DMZ for external internet access may leave the device open to attack from external sources or via port scanners. It is best to set up a username and password using the Apache HTTP Server that will prevent anyone from external access unless they know the credentials to access the device. An example of such settings will be provided in a later chapter.*

This exciting chapter will cover the code required to create an interactive static control panel with some great features:

- Display the time of day from the internal time of the Raspberry Pi.
- Display the CPU temperature.
- Buttons to individually turn on and off twenty-four of the GPIO pins.
- Read the state of two GPIO pins set up as inputs.
- Use several buttons to play sound files.
- Demonstrate the use of an HTML framework that will create a hidden page to send and receive dynamic data.
- Create a timer used to automatically update control panel information and status.

The topmost part of the Embedded Web Control Panel can be viewed in Figure 9.1 below. If viewed in printed form the image will be in grayscale. The color version of the control panel is very pleasing to the eye; however, the color scheme can be changed simply by updating the CSS color values at the top of the main.html document.

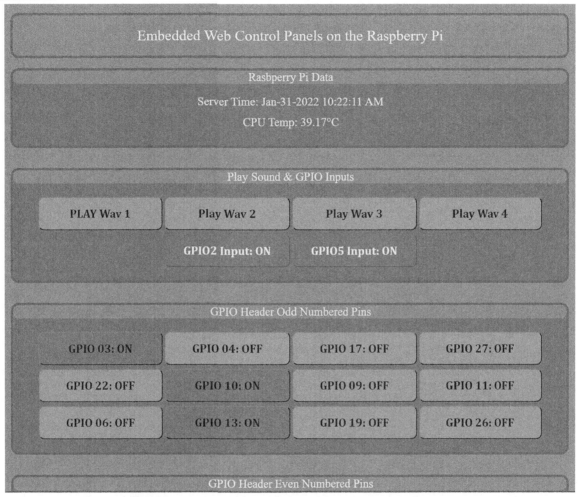

Figure 9.1: Topmost part of the Embedded Web Control Panel.

The Embedded Web Control Panel makes use of an HTML Frameset that creates a unique method for sending and receiving embedded information between the static web page and the embedded target. The frameset code is located within the <head> section of the frameset parent document named index.html and is coded as follows:

```
<frameset ROWS="100%,*" BORDER="0" FRAMEBORDER="0" BORDERCOLOR="#FFFFFF">
    <frame SRC="main.html" name="main_frame" scrolling="auto" NORESIZE MARGINWIDTH="0"
        MARGINHEIGHT="0">
    <frame SRC=" " name="hidden_frame" scrolling="auto" NORESIZE MARGINWIDTH="0"
        MARGINHEIGHT="0">
</frameset>
```

The frameset code basically divides the web page into three main parts:

- The parent index.html file that holds the Frameset and top-level code.
- The main.html static web control panel source page.
- A hidden page that is dynamically created each time a CGI call needs to be made.

The frameset HTML code is used to create two page frames. The first is set up to fill 100% of the screen area and the second, using the " * ", means to use whatever space is left, basically keeping the second frame hidden from view. Changing the 100% to 50% means that the second frame will no longer be hidden and both pages will share 50% of the screen area. This is helpful for debugging because the hidden page will display return information from the CGI call that can be viewed to verify proper operation.

The first frame, named "main_frame", is configured to load main.html by default. Once this page is loaded it will be kept static and not be reloaded. The second frame, with the name "hidden_frame", is configured to be hidden and will be used for all CGI access to the hardware.

The parent index.html file is loaded once and remains static. It serves as the container or parent for all interactions to and from the embedded target. This file contains the HTML Frameset, JavaScript functions to send CGI post data to the embedded target through the hidden page, and JavaScript functions that can be called from the embedded target to update the control panel objects displayed by the main.html page.

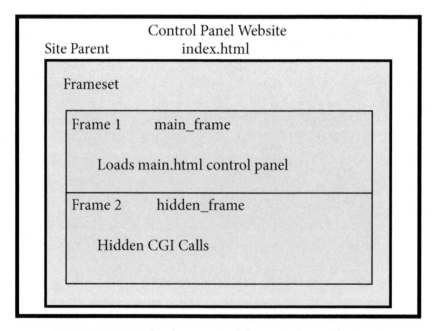

Figure 9.2: Depicts the three parts of the control panel frameset.

Figure 9.2 shows the division of the three main parts of the web control panel framework defined in the index.html file. Control panel operation is event driven, being triggered by either a button press or a background update based on an interval timer that is set up in the index.html file. When an event is triggered, a JavaScript function in the parent index.html file is called that creates a new hidden form on the hidden page. The hidden form is then submitted as a CGI Post to the target hardware. The CGI call invokes the cgimain application, which handles the request and then creates a web page reply that will appear on the hidden frame. If the hidden frame is made visible then the return content may be viewed. Part of the return content will be JavaScript function calls that will cause a dynamic update of the main_frame (main.html) page elements reflecting the current GPIO status, date, time, and CPU temperature. Figure 9.3 below shows the relationship between the individual components that make up the data Post and Reply operations.

The framework process only requires the hidden frame to change when a CGI call is invoked so the main control panel frame can remain static while the individual objects are dynamically updated with the latest status providing the look and feel of an actual physical control panel. Any type of control can be added and monitored using these concepts.

It's time to create the files required to build the fully functional Embedded Web Control Panel. Alternatively, the files can be downloaded, as explained in Chapter 3, to save time, but the instructions should still be followed to make sure all the background configuration requirements are set up properly. Otherwise, some features may not work including playing sound files and exercising the Python GPIO module over a web interface to change the GPIO pin states. If using the downloaded files from chapter 3 then the chapter9 directory should already contain two sound files, RaspberryPi.wav and test.wav, which will need to be copied to the /var/www/html directory.

The www-data user must be added to the audio group to be able to play a sound from a web page. If not already completed from chapter 6, follow these steps to update the Raspberry Pi to allow the web user, www-data, to access audio services:

1. From a Terminal Prompt, add the web user to the audio group:

   sudo usermod -a -G audio www-data

2. This next step is very important. For the new change to take effect the web server must be restarted:

   sudo service apache2 restart

Note: When attempting to play the sound files, it's best to set up both speakers connected to the speaker jack on the Raspberry Pi and to have a monitor or TV set up with HDMI since the OS could be configured to use either sound interface. Failing to do so may cause no sound to be heard.

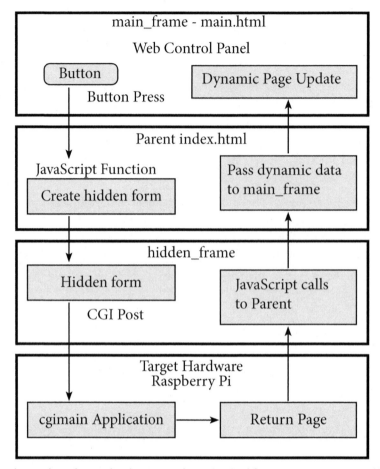

Figure 9.3: Shows the relationship between the individual frame components and hardware.

Many of the files for this chapter are built upon the code created in previous chapters. Those files will be copied to a new chapter 9 folder and will be the starting point for the web control panel. To get started, a new folder must be created within the webproj directory for this chapter.

1. At a Terminal Prompt, change into the project directory: **cd /home/pi/webproj**

2. Create a new directory where the chapter9 code will be stored:

   mkdir chapter9

3. Change into the chapter9 directory: **cd chapter9**

4. The responsive button code from chapter 7 will be used as a starting point for the main user interface html file, but it needs to be renamed. Copy the HTML code and rename the file by typing the following command at the Terminal Prompt:

   cp ../chapter7/responsivedisplay.html main.html

5. By typing "**ls -als**" at the Terminal Prompt while in the chapter9 directory, the main.html file should be seen in the directory listing.

6. For the next step the full contents of the code created in chapter 6 need to be copied to the chapter9 directory. While in the chapter9 folder type the following:

cp ../chapter6/* ./

7. Next, the Python scripts created in chapter 8 will be needed. Copy the scripts by typing the following at the Terminal Prompt:

   cp ../chapter8/*.py ./

8. Clean up the old object files by typing the following at the Terminal Prompt:

   make clean

9. Verify the full list of files now in the chapter 9 folder by typing: **ls -als**

10. The output should look like the following:

    pi@raspberrypi:~/webproj/chapter9 $ ls -als

    ```
    4 drwxr-xr-x  2 pi pi   4096 Feb  1 09:54 .
    4 drwxr-xr-x 12 pi pi   4096 Jan 26 17:23 ..
    12 -rw-r--r--  1 pi pi   8792 Jan 28 11:24 cgidebug.c
    4 -rw-r--r--  1 pi pi    389 Jan 22 11:41 cgidebug.h
    16 -rw-r--r--  1 pi pi  13724 Jan 28 11:22 cgimain.c
    4 -rw-r--r--  1 pi pi    496 Jan 28 11:23 cgimain.h
    16 -rw-r--r--  1 pi pi  13701 Jan 26 13:30 cgitools.c
    4 -rw-r--r--  1 pi pi   1570 Jan 26 13:31 cgitools.h
    4 -rw-r--r--  1 pi pi   1739 Jan 22 11:41 chapt6form.html
    4 -rwxr-xr-x  1 pi pi   1700 Jan 28 14:07 gpioctl.py
    4 -rwxr-xr-x  1 pi pi    837 Jan 28 14:07 ioGetAll.py
    4 -rwxr-xr-x  1 pi pi   1043 Jan 28 14:07 ioGet.py
    4 -rwxr-xr-x  1 pi pi   1042 Jan 28 14:07 ioSet.py
    12 -rw-r--r--  1 pi pi  10395 Jan 27 08:58 main.html
    4 -rw-r--r--  1 pi pi    881 Jan 28 11:25 makefile
    4 -rw-r--r--  1 pi pi    547 Jan 28 11:25 webpanel.cgi
    ```

The Web Control Panel will make use of two sound files. If the previous chapters were followed then the file **RaspberryPi.wav** should already exist in the /var/www/html directory. If not then it will need to be added along with the new wav file test.wav by entering these terminal commands:

1. Change to the /var/www/html directory:

   cd /var/www/html

2. Next, download the new wav file by typing the following at the terminal:

   sudo wget https://www.mstmicro.com/projects/test.wav

3. If the RaspberryPi.wav is not already in the /var/www.html directory then type the following:

   sudo wget https://www.mstmicro.com/projects/RaspberryPi.wav

The following is a list of twelve files that will be used to create the interactive Embedded Web Control Panel:

index.html
main.html
ioGetAll.py, ioSet.py
cgimain.c, cgimain.h
cgidebug.c, cgidebug.h
cgitools.c, cgitools.h
makefile
webpanel.cgi

The code for each of the source files that were added or modified for the control panel will be provided along with details of the purpose of each file. Many of the source files have not changed from the previous chapters. The new file index.html and any files that have been changed will be listed first. The following files are not required for chapter 9 and can be deleted from the chapter9 directory if so desired:

gpioctl.py
ioGet.py
chapt6form.html

The Web Control Panel framework is set up in a new file named index.html found in Program Listing 9.1 and is called the parent document when referenced by either the main_frame or the hidden_frame. A JavaScript function in the parent document can be called from a child frame simply by preceding the function call with the "parent." identifier. Example, parent.function_name(). This will allow the two child frames to access any function created in the parent document, index.html. The index.html file provides four different functions; it creates the frameset, provides several JavaScript functions for posting CGI content, provides several JavaScript functions for the returning page to dynamically update the main web page content, and provides an interval timer to allow background updates of the web page objects at a timed interval. The interval timer is defined as such: setInterval(DynamicUpdate, 2000). The "DynamicUpdate" points to the DynamicUpdate() function and the 2000 sets the interval of two seconds. The interval timer can be commented out if desired to help in initial debugging when making a change to the control panel or the time interval can be modified to run faster or slower as desired. Be sure to slow down the interval timer when using a slow connection to allow time for the background update to finish. This can be an issue if accessing the target device over the internet with a slow connection. When this occurs, the timer interval should be set to a higher number providing a slower update rate.

When debugging the Web Control Panel, it may be necessary to make the hidden_frame visible to see the results of a CGI call. The first line in the frameset is as follows:

<frameset ROWS="100%,*" BORDER="0" FRAMEBORDER="0" BORDERCOLOR="#FFFFFF">

Notice the ROWS="100%, * ", this means that the first frame will cover 100% of the screen area and the second frame will cover the remaining area. Since the first frame covers 100% the second frame is hidden from view. For debugging purposes the first frame can be changed to a different percentage so that the second frame is visible. This way, the resulting hidden page can be seen. Follow these next steps to create the index.html parent document:

1. At the Terminal Prompt, change into the chapter9 directory:

   cd /home/pi/webproj/chapter9

2. Using either a favorite desktop editor or nano, create a file with the name index.html:

   nano index.html

3. Enter the script from Program Listing 9.1 below.

4. When finished entering Program Listing 9.1, type CTRL + O then ENTER to save then CTRL + X to exit nano.

5. The index.html file will be installed in the appropriate directory once the makefile is updated later in this chapter.

Program Listing 9.1: index.html

```html
<!DOCTYPE doctype PUBLIC "-//w3c//dtd html 4.0 transitional//en">
<html>
<head>
   <meta http-equiv="Content-Type" content="text/html; charset=iso-8859-1">
   <title>Raspberry Pi CTRL</title>

   <script language="javascript">

   // On startup turn on the background update timer for 2 Seconds.
   setInterval(DynamicUpdate, 2000);


   // ********* Section of hidden forms used to send CGI Post data. **********

   // Function used to play a sound file on the Raspberry Pi.
   function ButtonSound(SndFileNumber)
   {
     var URL1 = document.URL;
     URL1 = URL1.slice(0, URL1.lastIndexOf("/")+1) + "cgi-bin/webpanel.cgi";

     // Verify there are at least two frames present.
     if(window.frames.length >= 2)
     {
       // Open the hidden frame (web page) for sending background CGI
       // Create a hidden form for posting data.
       hidden_frame.document.open();
       SndFrm = hidden_frame.document;
       SndFrm.write("<html><body nosave>");
       SndFrm.write("<form name='BtnSound' method='POST' ");
       SndFrm.write("target='hidden_frame' ACTION='" + URL1 + "' >");
```

```javascript
      SndFrm.write("<input name='COMMAND' type='hidden' value='PlaySound'>");
      SndFrm.write("<input name='VAR1' type='hidden' ");
      SndFrm.write("value='"+ SndFileNumber +"'>");
      SndFrm.write("</form></body></html>");
      SndFrm.close();
      SndFrm.BtnSound.submit();
   }
}


// Function used to change the output state of a GPIO pin.
function GPIOSet(gpioNum, state)
{
   var URL1 = document.URL;
   URL1 = URL1.slice(0, URL1.lastIndexOf("/")+1) + "cgi-bin/webpanel.cgi";

   if(window.frames.length >= 2)
   {
      // Open the hidden frame (web page) for sending background CGI
      hidden_frame.document.open();
      GPIOFrm = hidden_frame.document;
      GPIOFrm.write("<html><body nosave>");
      GPIOFrm.write("<form name='GPIOctl' method='POST' ");
      GPIOFrm.write("target='hidden_frame' ACTION='" + URL1 + "' >");
      GPIOFrm.write("<input name='COMMAND' type='hidden' value='GPIOSet'>");
      GPIOFrm.write("<input name='VAR1' type='hidden' value='"+ gpioNum +"'>");
      GPIOFrm.write("<input name='VAR2' type='hidden' value='" + state + "'>");
      GPIOFrm.write("</form></body></html>");
      GPIOFrm.close();
      GPIOFrm.GPIOctl.submit();
   }
}


// Function used to get updated informaiotn from the target device.
function DynamicUpdate()
{
   var URL1 = document.URL;
   URL1 = URL1.slice(0, URL1.lastIndexOf("/")+1) + "cgi-bin/webpanel.cgi";

   if(window.frames.length >= 2)
   {
      // Open the hidden frame (web page) for sending background CGI
```

```
    hidden_frame.document.open();
    UpdateFrm = hidden_frame.document;
    UpdateFrm.write("<html><body nosave>");
    UpdateFrm.write("<form name='UpdateReq' method='POST' ");
    UpdateFrm.write("target='hidden_frame' ACTION='" + URL1 + "' >");
    UpdateFrm.write("<input name='COMMAND' type='hidden' ");
    UpdateFrm.write(" value='DynamicUpdate'>");
    UpdateFrm.write("</form></body></html>");
    UpdateFrm.close();
    UpdateFrm.UpdateReq.submit();
  }
}


// ****** END Section of hidden forms used to send CGI Post data. *********

// Section of return handler functions for dynamic update of the main page.

// Function used to dynamically update a button state.
function DoBtnUpdate(gpioName, state)
{
   // Call the main page (frame) button update function in main.html.
   main_frame.BtnUpdate(gpioName, state)
}


// Function used to update the server time on the main_frame page.
function UpdateTime(timestr)
{
   main_frame.UpdateTime(timestr);
}


// Function used to update the CPU temperature.
function UpdateTemp(tempstr)
{
   main_frame.UpdateTemp(tempstr);
}


// END Section of return handler functions.


</script>
```

```
    <frameset ROWS="100%,*" BORDER="0" FRAMEBORDER="0" BORDERCOLOR="#FFFFFF">
        <frame SRC="main.html" name="main_frame" scrolling="auto"
                    NORESIZE MARGINWIDTH="0" MARGINHEIGHT="0">
        <frame SRC=" " name="hidden_frame" scrolling="auto"
                    NORESIZE MARGINWIDTH="0" MARGINHEIGHT="0">
        <noframes>
        <body>Please upgrade browser to support frames to view this site.</body>
        </noframes>
    </frameset>

</head>
<body>
</body>
</html>
```

The next file that needs to be updated is the main.html, main_frame, HTML source code. This file contains all of the Graphical User Interface (GUI) elements and will remain static after loading. The main.html file was originally created back in chapter 7 and was called responsivedisplay.html. The file was renamed to main.html when the chapter9 directory structure was created. This file will now be modified to add additional graphical elements, addition of names and IDs for the buttons, JavaScript functions will be added, and existing functions edited to provide an interface to the parent document based on events created by the user, like clicking on a button. The file will retain the responsive code that will allow the web page to scale to different devices including cell phones. The following are the steps to modify the main.html file to add the new content. The updated main.html file needs to exactly match the program listing 9.2 including the addition of the button names:

1. At the Terminal Prompt, change into the chapter9 directory:

    cd /home/pi/webproj/chapter9

2. Using either a favorite desktop editor or nano, edit the file main.html:

    nano main.html

3. Edit the main.html file to match Program Listing 9.2 below.

4. When finished editing, type CTRL + O then ENTER to save then CTRL + X to exit nano.

5. The main.html file will be installed in the appropriate directory once the makefile is updated later in this chapter.

Program Listing 9.2: main.html

```
<!doctype html>
<html>
<head>

    <meta http-equiv="Content-Type" content="text/html; charset=iso-8859-1">
    <title>Responsive Display</title>
```

```
<style>

.btn_grp {

  position:relative;
  text-align:center;
  border:5px solid #5D5C61;
  border-radius:17px;
  background-color:#557A95;
  padding: 24px 0px;
}

.btn_row {
  padding: 4px 4px;
}

.btns {
  background-color: #938e94;
  color:#1E1A1A;
  cursor: pointer;
  width: 270px;
  height:70px;
  border-radius:12px;
  font-weight:600;
  font-family: "Cambria", "Hoefler Text", "Liberation Serif",
      "Times", "Times New Roman", "serif";
  font-size: 25px;
  padding: 6px 2px;
}


.btns:hover {
  color:beige;
  background-color:lightslategray;
}

.inbtn {
  background-color: lightslategray;
  color:beige;
  cursor: not-allowed;
  width: 270px;
```

```
  height:70px;
  border-radius:12px;
  font-weight:600;
  font-family:"Cambria", "Hoefler Text", "Liberation Serif",
      "Times", "Times New Roman", "serif";
  font-size: 25px;
  padding: 6px 2px;
  outline: none;
}


@media screen and (min-width: 369px)
{
    .btn_grp {
        width: 370px;
    }
}

@media screen and (min-width: 650px)
{
    .btn_grp {
        width: 600px;
    }
}

@media screen and (min-width: 1250px)
{
    .btn_grp {
        width: 1200px;
    }
}

</style>
</head>

<body bgcolor="#659DBD" text="beige"  nosave>

<br>

<center>
<div class="btn_grp" style="background:lightslategray;
```

```
            font-size:32px;color:beige;">
    Embedded Web Control Panels on the Raspberry Pi
</div>
</center>

<br>
<center>
<table border="0"><tbody>
    <tr><td>
        <div class="btn_grp" style="height:110px;">

            <div style="position: relative;top:-24px;background:lightslategray;
                        border-radius:12px;font-size: 25px;color:beige;">
            Raspberry Pi Data</div>

            <div name="ServerTime" id="ServerTime"
                style="font-size:25px;color:beige;">
                Server Time:
            </div>

            <div name="CPUTemp" id="CPUTemp"
                style="position:relative;color:beige;top:15px;font-size:25px;">
                CPU Temp:
            </div>

        </div>
    </td></tr>
</tbody></table>
</center>

<br><br>

<center>
<table border="0"><tbody>
    <tr><td>
        <div class="btn_grp">

            <div style="position: relative;top:-24px;background:lightslategray;
                        border-radius:12px;font-size: 25px;color:beige;">
            Play Sound &#38; GPIO Inputs </div>
```

```html
            <div class="btn_row">
              <button class="btns" onClick="PlaySound(this, 1);">PLAY Wav 1
              </button>
              <button class="btns" onClick="PlaySound(this, 2);">Play Wav 2
              </button>
              <button class="btns" onClick="PlaySound(this, 3);">Play Wav 3
              </button>
              <button class="btns" onClick="PlaySound(this, 4);">Play Wav 4
              </button>
            </div>


            <div class="btn_row">
              <button name="gpio2" id="gpio2" class="inbtn"
                    onClick="BtnToggle(this);" disabled>
                GPIO2 Input: OFF</button>
              <button name="gpio5" id="gpio5" class="inbtn"
                    onClick="BtnToggle(this);" disabled>
                GPIO5 Input: OFF</button>
            </div>

        </div>
    </td></tr>
</tbody></table>
</center>

<br>
<br>

<center>
<table border="0"><tbody>
    <tr><td>
        <div class="btn_grp">

            <div style="position: relative;top:-24px;background:lightslategray;
                    border-radius:12px;font-size: 25px;color:beige;">
            GPIO Header Odd Numbered Pins </div>

            <div class="btn_row">
              <button name="gpio3" id="gpio3" class="btns"
                    onClick="BtnToggle(this);">GPIO 03: OFF</button>
```

```
            <button name="gpio4" id="gpio4" class="btns"
                  onClick="BtnToggle(this);">GPIO 04: OFF</button>
            <button name="gpio17" id="gpio17" class="btns"
                  onClick="BtnToggle(this);">GPIO 17: OFF</button>
            <button name="gpio27" id="gpio27" class="btns"
                  onClick="BtnToggle(this);">GPIO 27: OFF</button>
          </div>

          <div class="btn_row">
            <button name="gpio22" id="gpio22" class="btns"
                  onClick="BtnToggle(this);">GPIO 22: OFF</button>
            <button name="gpio10" id="gpio10" class="btns"
                  onClick="BtnToggle(this);">GPIO 10: OFF</button>
            <button name="gpio9" id="gpio9" class="btns"
                  onClick="BtnToggle(this);">GPIO 09: OFF</button>
            <button name="gpio11" id="gpio11" class="btns"
                  onClick="BtnToggle(this);">GPIO 11: OFF</button>
          </div>

           <div class="btn_row">
            <button name="gpio6" id="gpio6" class="btns"
                  onClick="BtnToggle(this);">GPIO 06: OFF</button>
            <button name="gpio13" id="gpio13" class="btns"
                  onClick="BtnToggle(this);">GPIO 13: OFF</button>
            <button name="gpio19" id="gpio19" class="btns"
                  onClick="BtnToggle(this);">GPIO 19: OFF</button>
            <button name="gpio26" id="gpio26" class="btns"
                  onClick="BtnToggle(this);">GPIO 26: OFF</button>
          </div>
        </div>
    </td></tr>
</tbody></table>
</center>

<br>
<br>

<center>
<table border="0"><tbody>
    <tr><td>
        <div class="btn_grp">
```

```
            <div style="position: relative;top:-24px;background:lightslategray;
                    border-radius:12px;font-size: 25px;color:beige;">
            GPIO Header Even Numbered Pins </div>

             <div class="btn_row">
              <button name="gpio14" id="gpio14" class="btns"
                    onClick="BtnToggle(this);">GPIO 14: OFF</button>
              <button name="gpio15" id="gpio15" class="btns"
                    onClick="BtnToggle(this);">GPIO 15: OFF</button>
              <button name="gpio18" id="gpio18" class="btns"
                    onClick="BtnToggle(this);">GPIO 18: OFF</button>
              <button name="gpio23" id="gpio23" class="btns"
                    onClick="BtnToggle(this);">GPIO 23: OFF</button>
            </div>


            <div class="btn_row">
              <button name="gpio24" id="gpio24" class="btns"
                    onClick="BtnToggle(this);">GPIO 24: OFF</button>
              <button name="gpio25" id="gpio25" class="btns"
                    onClick="BtnToggle(this);">GPIO 25: OFF</button>
              <button name="gpio8" id="gpio8" class="btns"
                    onClick="BtnToggle(this);">GPIO 08: OFF</button>
              <button name="gpio7" id="gpio7" class="btns"
                    onClick="BtnToggle(this);">GPIO 07: OFF</button>
            </div>

             <div class="btn_row">
              <button name="gpio12" id="gpio12" class="btns"
                    onClick="BtnToggle(this);">GPIO 12: OFF</button>
              <button name="gpio16" id="gpio16" class="btns"
                    onClick="BtnToggle(this);">GPIO 16: OFF</button>
              <button name="gpio20" id="gpio20" class="btns"
                    onClick="BtnToggle(this);">GPIO 20: OFF</button>
              <button name="gpio21" id="gpio21" class="btns"
                    onClick="BtnToggle(this);">GPIO 21: OFF</button>
            </div>
          </div>
        </td></tr>
</tbody></table>
```

```
</center>

<br><br><br>

<script>

    // Function to toggle the off/on button state.
    // Receives the button object to update.
    function BtnToggle(btnelement)
    {
        // Get the last two characters of the button text.
        var state = btnelement.innerHTML.slice(-2);

        // Find the ":" in the button text string.
        var loc1 = btnelement.innerHTML.indexOf(":");

        // Get the button number.
        var gpioNum = btnelement.innerHTML.slice(loc1 - 2, loc1);

        // If the current state is "ON"
        if(state == "ON")
        {
            parent.GPIOSet(gpioNum, 0); // Turn off
        }
        else
        {
            parent.GPIOSet(gpioNum, 1); // Turn on
        }
    }


    // Update button status.
    // Receives the button name and new state 0|1.
    function BtnUpdate(gpioName, state)
    {
        // Get the button object.
        var btnelement = document.getElementById(gpioName);

        // Find the ":" in the button text string.
        var loc1 = btnelement.innerHTML.indexOf(":");
```

```javascript
        // Get the string up to the ':'
        var str = btnelement.innerHTML.substring(0, loc1+1);

        // If the new state is off
        if(state == 0)
        {
            // Turn off button highlight color
            btnelement.style.backgroundColor = "#938e94";

            // Add "OFF" to the button text.
            btnelement.innerHTML = str + " OFF";
        }
        else
        {
            // Turn on button highlight color
            btnelement.style.backgroundColor = "#905B5D";

            // Add " ON" to the button text.
            btnelement.innerHTML = str + " ON";
        }
}

// Function to play a sound file through the web page.
function PlaySound(btnelement, btnnum)
{
    // Call the ButtonSound function in the parent frame.
    parent.ButtonSound(btnnum);
}

// Function used to update the server time on the main_frame page.
 function UpdateTime(timestr)
 {
    // Get the server time object.
    var serverTimeStr = document.getElementById("ServerTime");
    serverTimeStr.innerHTML = timestr;
 }

// Function used to update the CPU temperature.
function UpdateTemp(tempstr)
{
    // Get the server time object.
```

```
        var cputempStr = document.getElementById("CPUTemp");
        cputempStr.innerHTML = tempstr;
    }

</script>

</body>
</html>
```

The next file that needs to be modified is cgimain.c shown in Program Listing 9.3 below. Processing for several new CGI commands have been added to the PostDataOperations() function. Also the existing "PlaySound" command has been modified to accept a second parameter that allows the selection of four different sound files to be played. Currently there are only two sound files used out of four possible. Simply change the sound file names to play different sound files. Any new sound file must be placed into the /var/www/html directory.

A new CGI command named "DynamicUpdate" was added that calls a new function named DynamicUpdate(). This new function gets all of the data required to update the status of all elements on the main web page. It also uses the new ioGetAll.py created in chapter 8 as the interface to read the state of the GPIO pins.

Another new CGI command named "GPIOSet" was added that calls a new function named SetGPIO(). This command will make use of the ioSet.py script as the backend mechanism to change the GPIO pin states. Note that the GPIO module is not real-time and can take various amounts of time to complete the script calls. At the time of the writing of this book the GPIO pin states stay set between Python script calls. If the GPIO pin is turned on it stays on, if turned off it stays off after the Python script exits. If this changes in the future then using the Python GPIO module may not be a viable backend interface for web-based control. Fortunately, the next few chapters will provide another method of changing the GPIO pins using 'C' code to control the GPIO pins through a standard Linux device driver. Follow these steps to update the cgimain.c file based on listing 9.3:

1. At the Terminal Prompt, change into the chapter9 directory:

   cd /home/pi/webproj/chapter9

2. Using either a favorite desktop editor or nano, edit the file cgimain.c:

   nano cgimain.c

3. Update cgimain.c to match Program Listing 9.3 below.

4. When finished editing, type CTRL + O then ENTER to save then CTRL + X to exit nano.

5. To use the Python GPIO module over a web page requires that the www-data user be a member of the gpio group. Type the following three commands at the Terminal Prompt to enable use of the GPIO module over the web interface:

   sudo adduser www-data gpio

   sudo usermod -a -G gpio www-data

   sudo service apache2 restart

6. The cgimain.c file will be compiled in a later step.

Program Listing 9.3: cgimain.c

```c
/******************************************************************************
* File: cgimain.c
* Purpose: Program to control various Raspberry Pi operations from the web.
*
******************************************************************************/
#include <stdio.h>
#include <string.h>
#include <stdlib.h>
#include <time.h>

#include "cgimain.h"
#include "cgitools.h"
#include "cgidebug.h"

/* Global Post data linked list variable. */
CGIPostData CGIData;


/******************************************************************************
* Function: main()
* Receives: int argc - Number of command line arguments.
*           char *argv[] - Command line argument strings.
*           char *env[]  - Optionally add for systems that support
*                          environment variables passed to the main function.
*
* Returns 0 = OK or ERROR CODE
******************************************************************************/
int main(int argc, char *argv[], char *env[])
{
   int retval = 0;
   CGIPostData *CGIDataPtr = &CGIData;

   /* Preinitialize the linked list to prevent unallocation errors. */
   CGIData.ListHead = NULL;
   CGIData.Count = 0;

   /* Start of web page. */
   printf("%s%c%c","Content-Type:text/html;charset=iso-8859-1",10,10);
   printf("<!DOCTYPE html>\n");
```

```c
    /* Verify the application is called by the CGI script. If the argument
     * text "CGI" is not found then don't run anything. */
    if(argc > 1 && strncmp(argv[1], "CGI", 3) == 0)
    {
        /* Load CGI POST data, if any. */
        ReadCGIPostData(CGIDataPtr);

        /* If debug operations specified. */
        if(argc >= 3 && strncmp(argv[2], "DEBUG", 5) == 0)
        {
            retval = DebugOperations(argc, argv, env);
        }

        /* Act on control panel POST data, if any. */
        else
        {
            retval = PostDataOperations(argc, argv, env);
        }

    }
    else
    {
        printf("<html>\n<head>\n\n<title>Execution Error</title>\n\n</head>\n\n");
        printf("<body bgcolor=\"#669999\" text=\"#FFFFFF\">\n\n");
        printf("<br/><br/><center>\n<h1>Application Error!</h1>\n</center>\n");
        printf("<br/><br/>\n</body></html>\n");
        retval = 0;
    }

    /* Free CGI POST data allocated memory, if any. */
    DeleteLinkedList(CGIDataPtr);

    return retval;
}


/*****************************************************************************
* Function: PostDataOperations()
* Purpose: Act on POST data form information to perform various control
*          panel operations.
```

```c
*
* Receives: int argc - Number of script command line arguments.
*           char *argv[] - Command line argument strings.
*           char *env[]  - Environment variables passed to the main function,
*                          only on supported operating systems.
*
* Returns 0 on success
******************************************************************************/
int PostDataOperations(int argc, char *argv[], char *env[])
{
    int retval = 0;
    int val1 = 0;
    char *COMMAND = NULL;
    char *VAR1 = NULL, *VAR2 = NULL, *VAR3 = NULL, *VAR4 = NULL, *VAR5 = NULL;
    char buf[512];

    printf("<html>\n<head>\n\n<title>CGI COMMAND RESULTS</title>\n\n</head>\n");
    printf("<body bgcolor=\"#559BC7\" text=\"#0E1923\">\n\n");

    /* Get the POST command string. */
    COMMAND = GetKeyValue(&CGIData, "COMMAND", 0);

    /* Act on POST data submission. */
    if(strncmp(COMMAND, "PlaySound", 9) == 0)
    {
        /* POST Data command to play a wav file. */
        /* Get the sound file number from the web form data named 'VAR1'. */
        VAR1 = GetKeyValue(&CGIData, "VAR1", 0);

        /* Get the numeric value for the selected sound file. */
        val1 = atoi(VAR1);

        // Modify the file names below to play different sound files.
        // Put any new sound files in the /var/www/html directory.
        // This will play from either HDMI or through the speaker
        // jack on the board depending on the OS settings. Try listening
        // to both sound channels to be sure it is working. See chapter 9
        // details for more information.

        /* Prepare to play the wav file. */
        sprintf(buf, "aplay /var/www/html/");
```

```c
    // Play the correct sound file based on the button number.
    switch(val1)
    {
        case 1:
            strncat(buf, "RaspberryPi.wav",  16);
        break;

        case 2:
            strncat(buf, "RaspberryPi.wav",  16);
        break;

        case 3:
            strncat(buf, "RaspberryPi.wav",  16);
        break;

        case 4:
            strncat(buf, "test.wav",  9);
        break;
    }

    /* Make a system call to play the wav file.        */
    /* Be sure the www-data user is in the audio group  */
    /* and the Apache HTTP Server has been restarted.    */
    /* If command fails see the apache error log.       */
    GenericSystemCall(buf);
}

else if(strncmp(COMMAND, "DriveSpace", 10) == 0)
{
    GenericSystemCall("df");
}

/* Received command to set the output state of a GPIO pin. */
else if(strncmp(COMMAND, "GPIOSet", 7) == 0)
{
    /* Get the BCM GPIO number from the web form. */
    VAR1 = GetKeyValue(&CGIData, "VAR1", 0);
    /* Get the new output state either "0" or "1". */
    VAR2 = GetKeyValue(&CGIData, "VAR2", 0);
```

```c
        /* Call function to handle the GPIO set command. */
        SetGPIO(VAR1, VAR2);
    }
    else if(strncmp(COMMAND, "DynamicUpdate", 13) == 0)
    {
        DynamicUpdate();
    }


    /* Display CGI command information. */
    printf("\n<br><table border='1' cellspacing='2' cellpadding='15px'>\n");
    printf("\n<tr align='left'>\n<th>\n");
    serverTime();
    printf("\n<h3>CGI COMMAND REPLY:</h3><p>");
    printf("\n  COMMAND: %s<br>", COMMAND);
    printf("\n  VAR1: %s<br>", VAR1);
    printf("\n  VAR2: %s<br>", VAR2);
    printf("\n  VAR3: %s<br>", VAR3);
    printf("\n  VAR4: %s<br>", VAR4);
    printf("\n  VAR5: %s\n</p>", VAR5);
    printf("\n</th>\n</tr>");
    printf("\n</table><br><br>");
    printf("\n</body>\n</html>\n");


    return retval;
}



/*****************************************************************************
* Function: DebugOperations()
* Purpose: Call various debug functions relative to the script command line
*          options.
*
* Receives: int argc - Number of script command line arguments.
*           char *argv[] - Command line argument strings.
*           char *env[]  - Environment variables passed to the main function,
*                          only on supported operating systems.
*
* Returns 0 on success
*****************************************************************************/
int DebugOperations(int argc, char *argv[], char *env[])
{
```

```c
   int retval = 0;

   /* Request ENV variables by name. */
   if(argc >= 4 && strncmp(argv[3], "ENV_NAME", 8) == 0)
   {
      retval = CGIDebugByName(argc, argv);
   }

   /* If environment variable debug information requested.
    * Request variables by name. */
   else if(argc >= 4 && strncmp(argv[3], "ENV_ALL", 7) == 0)
   {
      retval = CGIDebugAll(argc, argv);
   }

   return retval;
}


/*****************************************************************************
* Function: GenericSystemCall()
* Purpose: Executes and displays the results of a Raspberry Pi system call.
*
* Receives: char *sysComand - Command line for system call.
*
* Returns: 0 on success else ERROR.
*****************************************************************************/
int GenericSystemCall(char *sysComand)
{
   FILE *fp;
   char buf[1024];
   int strpos;
   int retval = ERROR;

   /* Make a system call based on the sysCommand string. */
   fp = popen(sysComand, "r");

   /* Create a table to hold any command line output. */
   printf("<center><table width='95%' border='1' cellspacing='2' ");
   printf("cellpadding='1'> <tr bgcolor=\"#65ABD7\">\n\t<th>\n\t\t<h3>");
   printf("COMMAND OUTPUT - IF ANY</h3>\n\t</th>\n</tr>\n");
```

```c
printf("<tr align='left'>\n\t<th>\n");

if(fp == NULL)
{
   printf("<br/><h1>ERROR: Could not execute command! bye...</h1>\n");
}
else
{
   retval = 0;

   printf("\n\t<div style='color:#00134F;font:14pt,courier, arial;'>\n");
   printf("\t<strong><font face='FreeMono, Lucida Console, Consolas'><p>");
   printf("\n\t ");

   /* Display command output on the web page, if any. */
   while(fgets(buf, sizeof(buf), fp))
   {
      /* For each character in text string. */
      for(strpos = 0; strpos < strlen(buf); strpos++)
      {
         switch(buf[strpos])
         {
            case '\n': printf("\n<br>");
            break;

            case ' ': printf(" ");
            break;

            case '\t': printf("    ");
            break;

            default: putchar(buf[strpos]);
            break;
         }
      }
   }

   printf("\n\t</P>\n\t</font>");
   printf("\n\t</strong>\n\t</div>");
   /* Close the file pointer to the command. */
   pclose(fp);
```

```c
    }

    /* Close the table. */
    printf("</th>\n\t</tr>\n");
    printf("\n</table></center>\n<br><hr>\n\n");
}



/*****************************************************************************
 * Function: SetGPIO()
 * Purpose: Sets the output value of a Raspberry Pi GPIO pin based on BCM value.
 *
 * Receives: char ioNumStr - Char string holding the GPIO number.
 *           char ioStateStr - Char string of either "0" or "1".
 *
 * Returns: 0 on success else ERROR.
 *****************************************************************************/
int SetGPIO(char *ioNumStr, char *ioStateStr)
{
    int exitcode = 0;
    int ioNum = atoi(ioNumStr);
    int ioState = atoi(ioStateStr);
    char cmd[256];

    sprintf(cmd, "/var/www/webapp/./ioSet.py %d %d", ioNum, ioState);

    /* Get the ioSet.py command exit value with the new button state. */
    exitcode = system(cmd) / 256;   // Should be either 0 or 1 if success.

    printf("<p><h3>GPIO (BCM): %d", ioNum);
    printf("<br/>Desired State: %d", ioState);
    printf("<br/>System call exit code: %d</h3></p>", exitcode);

    if(exitcode == 1 || exitcode == 0)
        /* This javascript command executed in the hidden_frame will dynamically
           update the button state and color on the static main_frame. */
        printf("<script>parent.DoBtnUpdate('gpio%d', %d);</script>", ioNum,
exitcode);

    /* NOTE: If the GPIO state is not changing or an error occures see the
     * book text about setting up www-data user in the GPIO group.
```

```
     */

   return 0;
}



/******************************************************************************
* Function: DynamicUpdate()
* Purpose: Gets the following information to update the main_frame web page:
* 1. Gets the server time and date.
* 2. Gets the current CPU temperature.
* 3. Gets the current GPIO pin state for all pins.
*
* Returns: 0 on success else ERROR.
******************************************************************************/
int DynamicUpdate(void)
{
   const int DATA_SZ = 256;
   const int DATA_TMP = 50;

   double cputemp;
   double gputemp;
   char *token;
   int bcmNum = 0;
   int state = 0;
   char cmd[DATA_SZ];
   char tempStr[DATA_TMP];

   time_t timeval;
   struct tm *timeinfo;
   FILE *fp;

   printf("\n\r <script>");

   /* Dynamically update the main_frame server time text. */
   if(time(&timeval) != ERROR)
   {
      timeinfo = localtime(&timeval);
      strftime(cmd,100,"Server Time: %h-%-d-%Y %I:%M:%S %p",timeinfo);
      printf("\n\r parent.UpdateTime('%s'); ", cmd);
   }
```

```
/* Dynamically update the main_frame CPU temperature text. */
cputemp = cpu_temp();

if(cputemp != -255)
   sprintf(cmd, "CPU Temp: %.2f&#176;C", cputemp);
else
   sprintf(cmd, "CPU Temp: Error");
/* Call JavaScript function to update the CPU temp on the main_frame page.*/
printf("\n\r parent.UpdateTemp('%s'); ", cmd);

 /* Run system command to open the ioGetAll script. */
 fp = popen("/var/www/webapp/./ioGetAll.py", "r");
 if(fp != NULL)
 {
     memset(cmd, 0, DATA_SZ);  /* Zero memory buffer. */
     while(fgets(tempStr, DATA_TMP, fp))
     {
        strncat(cmd, tempStr, (DATA_SZ - strlen(cmd)));
     }
     fclose(fp);

     /* Extract the GPIO numbers and the GPIO state from the
      * return buffer after running the ioGetAll.py script. */
     token = strtok(cmd, ":\n");

     /* walk through all GPIO states. */
     while(token != NULL)
     {
        if(token[0] == 'P')
           bcmNum = atoi(&token[1]);
        else
        {
           state = atoi(token);
           //printf("\nBCM:%d State:%d", bcmNum, state);
           /* Create JavaScript to update the main_frame button objects. */
           printf("\n\r parent.DoBtnUpdate('gpio%d', %d); ", bcmNum, state);
        }
        token = strtok(NULL, ":\n");
     }
 }
}
```

```c
    printf("\n\r </script>");
}



/****************************************************************************
* Function: cpu_temp()
* Purpose: Open the CPU temperature file and read the current CPU temp.
* *
* Returns: CPU Temperature in Deg. C or -250 on error.
****************************************************************************/
double cpu_temp(void)
{
    const int DATA_SZ = 200;
    char tempStr[DATA_SZ];
    double temperature = -250;
    FILE *fp;

    /* Open the cpu temperature file for reading. */
    fp = fopen("/sys/class/thermal/thermal_zone0/temp","r");

    /* Read temperature data and convert to Deg. C */
    if(fp != NULL)
    {
        memset(tempStr, 0, DATA_SZ);  /* Zero memory buffer. */
        fread(tempStr, DATA_SZ, 1, fp);
        fclose(fp);

        temperature = atoi(tempStr);
        temperature /= 1000;

        if(temperature > 140 || temperature < -60)
          temperature = -250;
    }
    return temperature;
}
```

The supporting file cgimain.h was changed to add three new function prototypes. Follow these steps to update the cgimain.h source code:

1. At the Terminal Prompt, change into the chapter9 directory:

    cd /home/pi/webproj/chapter9

2. Using either a favorite desktop editor or nano, edit the file cgimain.h:

   nano cgimain.h

3. Update cgimain.h to match Program Listing 9.4 below.

4. When finished editing, type CTRL + O then ENTER to save then CTRL + X to exit nano.

Program Listing 9.4: cgimain.h

```
/*****************************************************************************
* File: cgimain.h
* Purpose: Header file for the cgimain CGI application.
*
*****************************************************************************/


/* Function prototypes. */
int DebugOperations(int argc, char *argv[], char *env[]);
int PostDataOperations(int argc, char *argv[], char *env[]);
int GenericSystemCall(char *);
int SetGPIO(char *, char *);
int DynamicUpdate(void);
double cpu_temp(void);
```

The makefile for the Web Control Panel project has changed to add a few additional install options. First, the two Python scripts ioGetAll.py and ioSet.py are configured to be copied to the webapp directory. Secondly, the makefile was changed to copy both .html files to the /var/www/html directory. The last change was made to allow the web page to be accessed without specifying a html or script file. After the Apache HTTP Server is installed it includes a default index.html page that opens if the IP address of the device is entered in a web page. In this case it is desirable that the new index.html file be loaded with the Web Control Panel. If desiring to save the Apache defined index.html file for later, it should be backed up with a different name for later use by typing:

sudo cp /var/www/html/index.html /var/www/html/org_index.html

This will allow the original Apache default index.html file to be restored if desired. The last edit to the makefile will set the permission so that the new index.html file will be opened when the IP address is entered into a web page for the Raspberry Pi. Edit the makefile by following these next steps:

1. At the Terminal Prompt, change into the chapter9 directory:

   cd /home/pi/webproj/chapter9

2. Using either a favorite desktop editor or nano, edit the file named makefile:

   nano makefile

3. Update the makefile to match Program Listing 9.5 below.

4. When finished editing, type CTRL + O then ENTER to save then CTRL + X to exit nano.

Program Listing 9.5: makefile

```
# type 'make cgimain' to build the project.
cgimain:     cgimain.o cgitools.o cgidebug.o
      gcc -lm -o cgimain cgimain.o cgitools.o cgidebug.o

cgimain.o:   cgimain.c
      gcc -c cgimain.c

cgitools.o:  cgitools.c
      gcc -c cgitools.c

cgidebug.o:  cgidebug.c
      gcc -c cgidebug.c

# type 'sudo make install' to copy files and change their attributes.
install:
      if test -d /var/www/webapp; then echo -n;  else mkdir /var/www/webapp/; fi
      cp cgimain /var/www/webapp
      cp webpanel.cgi /usr/lib/cgi-bin
      cp *.py /var/www/webapp
      chmod 755 /var/www/webapp/cgimain
      chmod 755 /usr/lib/cgi-bin/webpanel.cgi
      cp *.html /var/www/html
      # Allow permissions such that the index.html file can be accessed.
      sudo chown -R `whoami` /var/www/html

# type 'make clean 'to remove objects for a fresh build.
clean:
      rm cgitools.o cgimain.o cgidebug.o cgimain
```

The webpanel.cgi perl script in Program Listing 9.6 did not change from the last edit but will be listed here to make sure the correct use is configured so the Web Control Panel page can be viewed. There are three lines of code in the script that allow the CGI call to be accomplished with different results. The two lines that use the keyword "DEBUG" should be commented out and the system call without the debug statement should not be commented out as in the Programing Listing 9.6. If desirable, the debug lines can be used in place of the normal CGI call to provide debugging information about the different actions that can take place on the main web panel. Just remember to change the script back to match the code below so that the Web Control Panel can be loaded. Only one of the three system calls should be selected.

Program Listing 9.6: webpanel.cgi

```perl
#!/usr/bin/perl -w

#my $retval = system("/var/www/webapp/cgimain", "CGI", "DEBUG", "ENV_NAME");
#my $retval = system("/var/www/webapp/cgimain", "CGI", "DEBUG", "ENV_ALL");
my $retval = system("/var/www/webapp/cgimain", "CGI");
if($retval != 0)
{
    print "Content-Type: text/html\n\n";
    print "<!DOCTYPE html>\n\n<html>\n<head>\n";
    print "<title>ERROR PAGE</title></head>\n";
    print "<body>\n";
    print "<h1>Error! \'cgimain\' failed.\n";
    print "<br />See Apache error log...</h1>\n";
    print "</body>\n</html>\n";


}
```

The file named "ioGetAll.py" did not change from the code entered in chapter 8. If this file is not present then reference Program Listing 8.4 and make sure this file exists in the chapter9 directory.

The file named "ioSet.py" did not change from the code entered in chapter 8. If this file is not present then reference Program Listing 8.3 and make sure the file exists in the chapter9 directory.

The file named "cgidebug.c" did not change from the code entered in chapter 6. If this file is not present then reference Program Listing 6.6 and make sure the file exists in the chapter9 directory.

The file named "cgidebug.h" did not change from the code entered in chapter 5. If the file does not exist then reference Program Listing 5.6 and make sure the file is present in the chapter9 directory.

The file named "cgitools.c" did not change from the code entered in chapter 6. If the file does not exist then reference Program Listing 6.4 and make sure the file is present in the chapter9 directory.

The file named "cgitools.h" did not change from the code entered in chapter 6. If the file does not exist then reference Program Listing 6.5 and make sure the file is present in the chapter9 directory.

The last step in preparing the Embedded Web Control Panel is to compile and install the source code. Follow these steps:

1. At the Terminal Prompt, change into the chapter9 directory:

   cd /home/pi/webproj/chapter9

2. Type in the following to compile the source code:

   make

   The output should look like the following:

   pi@raspberrypi:~/webproj/chapter9 $ make

```
gcc -c cgimain.c

gcc -c cgitools.c

gcc -c cgidebug.c

gcc -lm -o cgimain cgimain.o cgitools.o cgidebug.o

pi@raspberrypi:~/webproj/chapter9 $
```

3. If there are any errors they will need to be fixed and the project remade again until all errors have been resolved. If the code was entered correctly there shouldn't be any errors.

4. Now install the files by typing the following:

```
sudo make install
```

The output should look like the following:

```
pi@raspberrypi:~/webproj/chapter9 $ sudo make install
if test -d /var/www/webapp; then echo -n;  else mkdir /var/www/webapp/; fi
cp cgimain /var/www/webapp
cp webpanel.cgi /usr/lib/cgi-bin
cp *.py /var/www/webapp
chmod 755 /var/www/webapp/cgimain
chmod 755 /usr/lib/cgi-bin/webpanel.cgi
cp *.html /var/www/html
# Allow permissions such that the index.html file can be accessed.
sudo chown -R `whoami` /var/www/html
pi@raspberrypi:~/webproj/chapter9 $
```

Now the Embedded Web Control Panel should be able to be accessed by either opening a web browser on the Raspberry Pi desktop and typing "**localhost**" in the address bar or by opening a web browser on another computer and typing the **<IP Address>** of the Raspberry Pi into the address bar. No additional path information is needed since the main web page file is named index.html and is the default http page name loaded automatically by the Apache HTTP Server for any directory when no specific file name is specified.

If desiring to use a tablet or cell phone to access the web page, connect the device to the local wireless network then open a web browser with the <IP Address> of the Raspberry Pi entered into the address bar.

If the Raspberry Pi has been set up in a router DMZ that connects to the Internet then the IP address of the router on the Internet can be entered to access the web control panel on the Raspberry Pi.

If desiring to make any changes to the web control panel simply repeat the build steps above to compile and install the desired changes. Remember that if there are any issues with the web control panel, several debugging options exist that can be used to help pinpoint the problem:

1. Always check the apache2 error log by typing:

```
sudo cat /var/log/apache2/error.log
```

2. The webpanel.cgi script can be changed to use one of the system calls with the "DEBUG" option.

3. The index.html frameset can be modified to be able to view the hidden_frame by changing the main_frame ROW from 100% to 50%.

4. If sound files are not playing then check to make sure the www-data user is in the audio group by typing **getent group** at the Terminal Prompt.

5. If the GPIO pins are not chaning state or do not turn off then make sure the www-data user is in the gpio group using the command **getent group** at the Terminal Prompt.

One neat feature of the Embedded Web Control Panel is the page can be opened on two web browsers at the same time, like from a computer and a cell phone. If a button state is changed from one control panel the state will update on both browsers. Be careful not to open the panel on too many browsers at the same time as it can slow down the background update for the pages.

10

GPIO CHARACTER DEVICE DRIVER

There are multiple methods of accessing the Raspberry Pi General Purpose Input/Output (GPIO) pins on the Raspberry Pi Expansion Header. Many of the methods are custom to the Raspberry Pi hardware exclusively and thus are not directly portable to other single board computers running a Linux Operating System. The most portable and standardized method of accessing embedded hardware peripherals is to use Linux device drivers. Code that uses standard device drivers can be ported to various computing hardware without requiring a complete rewrite of the code to perform the same actions. This makes it a lot easier to get code up and running on a new platform without spending a lot of effort trying to learn or write custom algorithms specific only to the new hardware.

Up until recent years, one of the standardized methods of accessing GPIO pins was to use the sysfs driver interface; however, this interface is being deprecated and is being replaced by GPIO character device drivers. Due to portability this will be the interface of choice for the next Embedded Control Panel Example. The character device driver will replace the backend interface used to control the GPIO pins on the Raspberry Pi expansion header through web page control.

The previous sysfs GPIO interface was deprecated by Linux Kernel version 4.8. To use the newer character device driver requires Raspbian version 4.11 or greater. To check the version of the Raspbian image installed on the Raspberry Pi enter either **uname -a** or **hostnamectl** at a Terminal Prompt:

pi@raspberrypi:/ $ **uname -a**

Linux raspberrypi 4.19.57-v7+ #1244 SMP Thu Jul 4 18:45:25 BST 2019 armv7l GNU/Linux

pi@raspberrypi:/ $ **hostnamectl**

　Static hostname: raspberrypi

　Icon name: computer

　Machine ID: 2c7da437dc014854802b1549645245a6

　Boot ID: ba71c75a9e3b4af7af513ef8da43cb92

　Operating System: Raspbian GNU/Linux 10 (buster)

　Kernel: Linux 4.19.57-v7+

Architecture: arm

The Kernel version must be at least 4.11 or the GPIO character device driver source code will not work and the Raspbian image will require an update. Another method to verify that the GPIO character device is supported is to look for the actual GPIO device. To do so, open to a Terminal Prompt and type the following:

cd /dev

ls gpio*

The result should look similar to the following:

gpiochip0 gpiochip1 gpiochip2 gpiomem

The available GPIO character devices should be displayed in the form of gpiochipX where X stands for the GPIO chip number. As seen in the output above there are three devices found for this version of the OS, listed as gpiochip0, gpiochip1, and gpiochip2. Other versions of the OS may only have two devices. These are the names of the devices that will be referenced in the example code in this chapter. The gpiomem device is not part of the GPIO character device interface but can be used to directly access GPIO pins and alternate functions like setting the current drive capability of the port pin; however, the gpiomem device is not a standard method and may not exist on other target hardware.

Each GPIO device is associated with particular hardware and GPIO signals. Many of the signals are used internally on the Raspberry Pi hardware. Out of the listed device drivers only one controls the GPIO pins connected to the 40-pin header. Each device driver can be accessed to get details about the individual signals and the number of signals it supports.

The GPIO character device driver can be opened for access using the standard open() function. After obtaining an open handle to the GPIO device the GPIO pins can be manipulated using standard ioctl commands. The header file gpio.h contains the ioctl definitions and data structures required to access the GPIO device drivers.

Program Listing 10.1 provides a way to open and read the details for all signals controlled by the specified GPIO device driver. This application is useful when desiring to get an overview of the number of GPIO pins controlled by the driver and return the chip information string. If a pin happens to be configured it will show the owner of that pin. The Flags attribute provides a way of viewing the current configuration state. The GPIO detail is read in the dispPin() function. The IO signals on the Raspberry Pi 40-pin GPIO header are controlled by gpiochip0 and uses the greatest number of pins. The gpiolist.c application will display the information for the other two GPIO drivers first because they both only have a few signals to display.

Follow these steps to create the gpiolist application:

1. At a Terminal Prompt, change into the project directory: **cd /home/pi/webproj**
2. Create a new directory where the Chapter 10 code will be stored:
   mkdir chapter10
3. Change into the chapter10 directory: **cd chapter10**
4. Using either a favorite desktop editor or nano, create a file with the name gpiolist.c:
   nano gpiolist.c
5. Enter the code from Program Listing 10.1 below.

6. When finished entering Program Listing 10.1, type CTRL + O then ENTER to save then CTRL + X to exit nano.

7. Compile the program by typing the following at the Terminal Prompt:

   gcc gpiolist.c -o gpiolist

8. Make sure the program is executable: **chmod +x+r gpiolist**

9. To run the application from the Terminal Prompt type: **./gpiolist**

10. To display one screen at a time the following can be typed at the Terminal Prompt:

    ./gpiolist | more

Note: If any of the devices are not present on the current OS then it will be reported as a file not found error.

Program Listing 10.1: gpiolist.c

```c
/****************************************************************************
 * File: gpiolist.c
 * Purpose: Display GPIO information and port pin status.
 *
 ****************************************************************************/
#include <unistd.h>
#include <dirent.h>
#include <stdio.h>
#include <stdlib.h>
#include <string.h>
#include <fcntl.h>
#include <errno.h>
#include <sys/ioctl.h>
#include <linux/gpio.h>

/* Function prototypes. */
int dispDevice(char *gpiodevice);
int dispPin(int openfd, int pin);
void dispError(char *Msg, char *Name, int errorid);

#define ERROR -1

/* Definitions */
#define MAX_DEVICE_NAME 24

/****************************************************************************
 * Function: main()
 * Purpose: Main function entry point for the GPIO list application.
 *
```

```
 * Returns: 0 = OKAY, or ERROR
 ************************************************************************/
int main(void)
{
    int retval;

    /* Get the GPIO chip information through driver IOCTL calls. */
    retval = dispDevice("gpiochip1");
    if(retval == ERROR) printf("\nCould not display gpiochip1 information!");
    retval = dispDevice("gpiochip2");
    if(retval == ERROR) printf("\nCould not display gpiochip2 information!");
    retval = dispDevice("gpiochip0");
    if(retval == ERROR) printf("\nCould not display gpiochip0 information!");

    return 0;
}



/*************************************************************************
 * Function: dispDevice()
 * Purpose: To read a GPIO chip's information and its current port pin
 *          states. The resulting output will be sent to STDOUT.
 *
 * Receives: char *gpiodevice - The name of the device to access.
 *
 * Returns: 0 = OKAY, or ERROR if something goes wrong.
 ************************************************************************/
int dispDevice(char *gpiodevice)
{
    int fd, errorid, cnt;
    int retval = 0, result = 0;
    char deviceName[MAX_DEVICE_NAME];

    struct gpiochip_info gpioInfoStruct;

    /* Create full textual path to device up to MAX_DEVICE_NAME length. */
    snprintf(deviceName, MAX_DEVICE_NAME, "/dev/%s", gpiodevice);

    printf("\nOpen device: %s", deviceName);

    /* Open the character device for access. */
```

```c
fd = open(deviceName, O_RDONLY);

if (fd != ERROR)
{
   /* Clear information structure memory. */
   memset(&gpioInfoStruct, 0, sizeof(gpioInfoStruct));

   /* Get the GPIO chip information using a IOCTL call. */
   /* Header file <linux/gpio.h> has the definitions for the   */
   /* various IOCTL options for GPIO. */
   result = ioctl(fd, GPIO_GET_CHIPINFO_IOCTL, &gpioInfoStruct);
   if (result != ERROR)
   {
      printf("\nDevice: %s, Label: %s, Num IO: %u\n",
         gpioInfoStruct.name, gpioInfoStruct.label, gpioInfoStruct.lines);

      /* Display individual GPIO information and current value for each. */
      for(cnt = 0; cnt < gpioInfoStruct.lines; cnt++)
      {
         /* Get pin information and status. Break on error. */
         if(dispPin(fd, cnt) != 0)
         {
            retval = ERROR;
            break;
         }
      }
   }
   else
   {
      /* Failed to access the GPIO device so print error message. */
      dispError("IOCTL Error for device: ", deviceName, errno);
      retval = ERROR;
   }

   close(fd);
}
else
{
   /* Failed to open device so print error message. */
   dispError("Error opening device: ", deviceName, errno);
   retval  = ERROR;
}
```

```
      return retval;
}


/*************************************************************************
* Function: dispPin()
* Purpose: To read line info about a specific GPIO pin and display the
*          resulting output to STDOUT.
* Receives:
*          int openfd - The current open file descriptor of the device.
*          int pin - The BCM pin number (offset) within the GPIO device.
*
* Returns: 0 = OKAY, or ERROR if something goes wrong.
*************************************************************************/
int dispPin(int openfd, int pin)
{
   int retval = 0, result = 0;
   char buf[7];
   struct gpioline_info signal;

   /* Clear the line information structure. */
   memset(&signal, 0, sizeof(signal));

   /* Set the pin number to query. */
   signal.line_offset = pin;

   /* Get the pin's current information. */
   result = ioctl(openfd, GPIO_GET_LINEINFO_IOCTL, &signal);

   if (result != ERROR)
   {
      /* Display the pin's current information. */
      printf("BCM:%02d Name:'%s' Consumer:'%s' Flags:", signal.line_offset,
         ((signal.name[0] == '\0') ? "none" : signal.name),
         ((signal.consumer[0] == '\0') ? "none" : signal.consumer));

      /* Display the pin's active flags. */
      if (signal.flags == 0) printf("'none'");
      else
      {
```

```c
            if (signal.flags & GPIOLINE_FLAG_KERNEL)
                printf("KERNEL, ");
            if (signal.flags & GPIOLINE_FLAG_IS_OUT)
                printf("IS_OUT, ");
            if (signal.flags & GPIOLINE_FLAG_ACTIVE_LOW)
                printf("ACTIVE_LOW, ");
            if (signal.flags & GPIOLINE_FLAG_OPEN_DRAIN)
                printf("OPEN_DRAIN, ");
            if (signal.flags & GPIOLINE_FLAG_OPEN_SOURCE)
                printf("OPEN_SOURCE");
        }
        printf("\n");
    }
    else
    {
        /* Failed to access the GPIO pin; print error message. */
        snprintf(buf, 7, "%d", pin); // Current max pin count is 64.
        dispError("IOCTL Error, pin ", buf, errno);
        retval = ERROR;
    }

    return retval;
}


/****************************************************************************
* Function: dispError()
* Purpose: Function to display error based on the setting of errno.
*
* Receives:
*         char *Msg1 - Message to display with the error information.
*         char *Name - Name associated with message or NULL.
*         int errorid - The system errno for the fault.
*
* Returns: void
****************************************************************************/
void dispError(char *Msg, char *Name, int errorid)
{
    printf("\n%s%s, Error number:%d, %s\n",
        Msg, Name, errorid, strerror(errorid));
}
```

The output of the gpiolist application should look similar to the following:

Open device: /dev/gpiochip1
Device: gpiochip1, Label: brcmvirt-gpio, Num IO: 2
BCM:00 Name:'none' Consumer:'led0' Flags:KERNEL, IS_OUT,
BCM:01 Name:'none' Consumer:'none' Flags:'none'

Open device: /dev/gpiochip2
Device: gpiochip2, Label: raspberrypi-exp-gpio, Num IO: 8
BCM:00 Name:'none' Consumer:'none' Flags:IS_OUT,
BCM:01 Name:'none' Consumer:'none' Flags:IS_OUT,
BCM:02 Name:'none' Consumer:'none' Flags:IS_OUT,
BCM:03 Name:'none' Consumer:'none' Flags:IS_OUT,
BCM:04 Name:'none' Consumer:'none' Flags:'none'
BCM:05 Name:'none' Consumer:'none' Flags:IS_OUT,
BCM:06 Name:'none' Consumer:'none' Flags:IS_OUT,
BCM:07 Name:'none' Consumer:'led1' Flags:KERNEL,

Open device: /dev/gpiochip0
Device: gpiochip0, Label: pinctrl-bcm2835, Num IO: 54
BCM:00 Name:'none' Consumer:'none' Flags:'none'
BCM:01 Name:'none' Consumer:'none' Flags:'none'
BCM:02 Name:'none' Consumer:'none' Flags:'none'
BCM:03 Name:'none' Consumer:'none' Flags:IS_OUT,
BCM:04 Name:'none' Consumer:'none' Flags:IS_OUT,
BCM:05 Name:'none' Consumer:'none' Flags:'none'
BCM:06 Name:'none' Consumer:'none' Flags:'none'
BCM:07 Name:'none' Consumer:'none' Flags:'none'
BCM:08 Name:'none' Consumer:'none' Flags:'none'
BCM:09 Name:'none' Consumer:'none' Flags:'none'
BCM:10 Name:'none' Consumer:'none' Flags:IS_OUT,
BCM:11 Name:'none' Consumer:'none' Flags:'none'
BCM:12 Name:'none' Consumer:'none' Flags:'none'
BCM:13 Name:'none' Consumer:'none' Flags:IS_OUT,
BCM:14 Name:'none' Consumer:'none' Flags:'none'
BCM:15 Name:'none' Consumer:'none' Flags:'none'

. . .

The next GPIO driver example in Program Listing 10.2 will implement a way to view the GPIO pins connected to the 40-pin header along with the GPIO status and ownership for each pin. This application is very useful because it displays a snapshot of the current state of all the GPIO pins on the 40-pin header. The program output of the gpiodisp application should look similar to the following:

```
pi@raspberrypi:~/webproj/chapter10 $ ./gpiodisp

Device: gpiochip0, Label: pinctrl-bcm2835, Num IO: 54
DIR Values: POW(Power), GND(Ground), IN, or OUT.
V Values: 1 (3.3V), 0 (GND 0V), or X(busy or kernel owned)


._____.
| Consumer      |BCM|  Name   |V|DIR|  Pins   |DIR|V|  Name   |BCM| Consumer   |
|_____|___|_____|_|___|_____|___|_|_____|___|_____|
|               |   |   3.3V| |POW|[ 1](2 )|POW| |5V     |   |            |
|          None| 2| GPIO02|1| IN|( 3)(4 )|POW| |5V     |   |            |
|          None| 3| GPIO03|1|OUT|( 5)(6 )|GND| |GND    |   |            |
|          None| 4| GPIO04|1|OUT|( 7)(8 )|IN |0|GPIO14 |14 |None        |
|               |   |   GND| |GND|( 9)(10)|IN |0|GPIO15 |15 |None        |
|          None|17| GPIO17|0|OUT|(11)(12)|IN |0|GPIO18 |18 |None        |
|          None|27| GPIO27|0| IN|(13)(14)|GND| |GND    |   |            |
|          None|22| GPIO22|0| IN|(15)(16)|IN |0|GPIO23 |23 |None        |
|               |   |   3.3V| |POW|(17)(18)|IN |0|GPIO24 |24 |None        |
|          None|10| GPIO10|1|OUT|(19)(20)|GND| |GND    |   |            |
|          None| 9| GPIO09|0| IN|(21)(22)|IN |0|GPIO25 |25 |None        |
|          None|11| GPIO11|0| IN|(23)(24)|IN |0|GPIO08 |8  |None        |
|               |   |   GND| |GND|(25)(26)|IN |0|GPIO07 |7  |None        |
|          None| 0| GPIO00|1| IN|(27)(28)|IN |1|GPIO01 |1  |None        |
|          None| 5| GPIO05|1| IN|(29)(30)|GND| |GND    |   |            |
|          None| 6| GPIO06|0| IN|(31)(32)|IN |0|GPIO12 |12 |None        |
|          None|13| GPIO13|1|OUT|(33)(34)|GND| |GND    |   |            |
|          None|19| GPIO19|0| IN|(35)(36)|IN |0|GPIO16 |16 |None        |
|          None|26| GPIO26|0| IN|(37)(38)|IN |0|GPIO20 |20 |None        |
|               |   |   GND| |GND|(39)(40)|OUT|1|GPIO21 |21 |None        |
|_____|
```

To create the gpiodisp application, follow these steps:

1. At a Terminal Prompt, change into the chapter10 directory: **cd /home/pi/webproj/chapter10**

2. Using either a favorite desktop editor or nano, create a file with the name gpiodisp.c:

    nano gpiodisp.c

3. Enter the code from Program Listing 10.2 below.

4. When finished entering Program Listing 10.2, type CTRL + O then ENTER to save then CTRL + X to exit nano.

5. Compile the program by typing the following at the Terminal Prompt:

   gcc gpiodisp.c -o gpiodisp

6. Make sure the program is executable: **chmod +x+r gpiodisp**

7. To run the application from the Terminal Prompt type: **./gpiodisp**

Program Listing 10.2: gpiodisp.c

```c
/*****************************************************************************
* File: gpiodisp.c
* Purpose: Application to read the current state of the Raspberry Pi GPIO port
*          pins and report the ones currently in use. Requires a Raspberry Pi
*     with the 40-Pin header.
*
* Build with the following command line: gcc gpiodisp.c -o gpiodisp
*****************************************************************************/
#include <unistd.h>
#include <dirent.h>
#include <stdio.h>
#include <stdlib.h>
#include <string.h>
#include <fcntl.h>
#include <errno.h>
#include <sys/ioctl.h>
#include <linux/gpio.h>


#define ERROR -1
#define NUM_HDR_PINS    40
#define MAX_LINE_NAME   32
#define MAX_CONSUMER    32


/* Array map of pins versus GPIO BCM numbers.  */
/* -1 = 3.3V, -2 = 5V, -3 = Ground.            */
int iPin[NUM_HDR_PINS] =
{
    -1, /*    3V3  [1] (2)  5V      */ -2,
     2, /*  GPIO2  (3) (4)  5V      */ -2,
     3, /*  GPIO3  (5) (6)  GROUND  */ -3,
     4, /*  GPIO4  (7) (8)  GPIO14  */ 14,
    -3, /* GROUND  (9) (10) GPIO15  */ 15,
    17, /* GPIO17 (11) (12) GPIO18  */ 18,
```

```
    27, /* GPIO27 (13) (14) GROUND */ -3,
    22, /* GPIO22 (15) (16) GPIO23 */ 23,
    -1, /*    3V3 (17) (18) GPIO24 */ 24,
    10, /* GPIO10 (19) (20) GROUND */ -3,
     9, /*  GPIO9 (21) (22) GPIO25 */ 25,
    11, /* GPIO11 (23) (24) GPIO8  */  8,
    -3, /* GROUND (25) (26) GPIO7  */  7,
     0, /*  GPIO0 (27) (28) GPIO1  */  1,
     5, /*  GPIO5 (29) (30) GROUND */ -3,
     6, /*  GPIO6 (31) (32) GPIO12 */ 12,
    13, /* GPIO13 (33) (34) GROUND */ -3,
    19, /* GPIO19 (35) (36) GPIO16 */ 16,
    26, /* GPIO26 (37) (38) GPIO20 */ 20,
    -3, /* GROUND (39) (40) GPIO21 */ 21
};


/* Function prototypes. */
void dispError(char *Msg, char *Name, int errorid);
int ioGetPin(int fd, int line);


/******************************************************************************
* Function: main()
* Purpose: Main function entry point for the GPIO port pin information
*     display using a GPIO character device in the /dev directory.
*     This application uses device lines in an order specific to
*     the Raspberry Pi IO header.
*
* Returns: 0 = OKAY, or ERROR
******************************************************************************/
int main(void)
{
   int charDevfd, errorid, cnt;
   int retval = 0, result = 0;
   char state = '\0';
   char LineName[MAX_LINE_NAME+1];
   char ConsumerName[MAX_CONSUMER+1];
   char BCMNum[4], Dir[4];

   struct gpiochip_info gpioInfoStruct;
   struct gpioline_info signal;

   /* Open the character device that controls access to the header GPIO pins.*/
```

```c
charDevfd = open("/dev/gpiochip0", O_RDONLY);

if (charDevfd != ERROR)
{
/* Clear gpio information structure memory. */
memset(&gpioInfoStruct, 0, sizeof(gpioInfoStruct));

/* Get the GPIO chip information using an input/output
/* control (IOCTL) call. The header file <linux/gpio.h> has the
/* definitions for the  various IOCTL options for GPIO. */
result = ioctl(charDevfd, GPIO_GET_CHIPINFO_IOCTL, &gpioInfoStruct);
if (result != ERROR)
{
   printf("\n\n Device: %s, Label: %s, Num IO: %u",
   gpioInfoStruct.name, gpioInfoStruct.label, gpioInfoStruct.lines);

   /* Display the table header. */
   printf("\n DIR Values: POW(Power), GND(Ground), IN, or OUT.");
  printf("\n V Values: 1 (3.3V), 0 (GND 0V), or X(busy or kernel owned)\n\n");
   printf("._____");
   printf("_____.");
   printf("\n");
   printf("| Consumer  |BCM|  Name   |V|DIR|  Pins");
   printf("  |DIR|V|  Name   |BCM|  Consumer   |");
   printf("\n");
   printf("|_____|___|_____|_|___|");
   printf("_____|___|_|_____|___|_____|");

   /* Display individual GPIO information and current value for each. */
   for(cnt = 0; cnt < NUM_HDR_PINS; cnt++)
   {
       if(iPin[cnt] >= 0)
       {
           /* Save the BCM number in text format. */
           snprintf(BCMNum, 3, "%d", iPin[cnt]);

           /* Get the current pin state. */
           retval = ioGetPin(charDevfd, iPin[cnt]);

           /* If line consumed by another process. */
           if(retval == 16)
               state = 'X';

           /* There was an error accessing the line state. */
```

```
        else if(retval > 1 || retval < 0)
            printf("\nIOCTL Error: %s", strerror(retval));

        /* Line is either 1 = High (3.3V) or 0 = Low (0V) */
        else
            state = (retval == 1) ? '1' : '0';

        memset(&signal, 0, sizeof(signal));
        signal.line_offset = iPin[cnt];

        /* Get the current gpio pin information. */
        result = ioctl(charDevfd, GPIO_GET_LINEINFO_IOCTL, &signal);

        /* Act on results for the current line information. */
        if (result != ERROR)
        {
            /* Display the gpio name. */
            if(signal.name[0] == '\0')
                snprintf(LineName, MAX_LINE_NAME, "GPIO%.2d", iPin[cnt]);
            else
                snprintf(LineName, MAX_LINE_NAME, "%s", signal.name);

            /* Display the gpio owner info. */
            if(signal.consumer[0] != '\0')
                snprintf(ConsumerName, MAX_CONSUMER, "%s", signal.consumer);
            else
                sprintf(ConsumerName, "None");

            /* Display the pin's active flags. */
            if(signal.flags & GPIOLINE_FLAG_IS_OUT) sprintf(Dir, "OUT");
            else sprintf(Dir, "IN");
        }
        else
        {
            /* Display pin default name and error info. */
            if(signal.name[0] == '\0')
                snprintf(LineName, MAX_LINE_NAME, "GPIO%.2d", iPin[cnt]);
                snprintf(ConsumerName, MAX_CONSUMER, "%s", strerror(errno));
        }

        /* Force buffered text to be sent to the terminal. */
        fflush(stdout);
    }
}
// Must be a power or ground pin.
```

```c
else
{
    /* Power-ground pins have no BCM. */
    sprintf(BCMNum, "   ");
    ConsumerName[0] = '\0';

    /* -1 = 3.3V, -2 = 5V, -3 = Ground.   */
    switch(iPin[cnt])
    {
        case -1:
            sprintf(Dir, "POW");
            sprintf(LineName, "3.3V");
            state = ' ';
        break;

        case -2:
            sprintf(Dir, "POW");
            sprintf(LineName, "5V");
            state = ' ';
        break;

        case -3:
            sprintf(Dir, "GND");
            sprintf(LineName, "GND");
            state = ' ';
        break;

    }
}

/* Display Even pin numbers. */
if(cnt % 2) /* Test for even/odd pin numbers. */
{
    printf("(%-2d)|%-3.3s|%c|%-9.9s|%-3s|%-13.13s|",
            cnt+1, Dir, state, LineName, BCMNum, ConsumerName);
}
/* Display Odd numbered pins. */
else
{
    if(cnt == 0) // Pin 1
        printf("\n|%13.13s|%3s|%9.9s|%c|%3.3s|[%2d]",
        ConsumerName, BCMNum, LineName, state, Dir, cnt+1);
    else
        printf("\n|%13.13s|%3s|%9.9s|%c|%3.3s|(%2d)",
```

```c
                            ConsumerName, BCMNum, LineName, state, Dir, cnt+1);
                }
            }

            /* Table end. */
            printf("\n");
            printf("|_____");
            printf("_____|");
            printf("\n\n\n");
        }
        else
        {
            /* Failed to access the GPIO device so print error message. */
            dispError("IOCTL Error for device: ", "/dev/gpiochip0", errno);
            retval = ERROR;
        }

        close(charDevfd);
    }
    else
    {
        /* Failed to open device so print error message. */
        dispError("Error opening device: ", "/dev/gpiochip0", errno);
        retval = ERROR;
    }

    return retval;
}


/*****************************************************************************
* Function: ioGetPin()
* Purpose: Read the value of the specified gpio pin.
*
* Receives: int fd - Open file descriptor to the character device that
*                    controls the port pin.
*           int line - The line number of the gpio pin. On the Raspberry
*                      Pi this is often referred to as the BCM number.
*
* Returns: Pin state 0 or 1, else error code.
*****************************************************************************/
int ioGetPin(int fd, int line)
{
    int retval = 0;
```

```
    struct gpiohandle_request    lineHandle;
    struct gpiohandle_data       lineData;

    /* Clear gpiohandle request structure memory. */
    memset(&lineHandle, 0, sizeof(lineHandle));

    /* Set ioctl request fields. */
    lineHandle.lineoffsets[0] = line;
    lineHandle.lines = 1;
    lineHandle.flags = 0;

    /* Get a handle to the gpio line through the character device if not busy.*/
    retval = ioctl(fd, GPIO_GET_LINEHANDLE_IOCTL, &lineHandle);
    if(retval != ERROR)
    {
        /* Clear gpiohandle data structure memory. */
        memset(&lineData, 0, sizeof(lineData));

        /* Get the current state of the selected line. */
        retval = ioctl(lineHandle.fd, GPIOHANDLE_GET_LINE_VALUES_IOCTL, &lineData);
        if(retval != ERROR)
        {
            /* Save the line value 0(LOW) or 1(High). */
            retval = lineData.values[0];
        }
        else retval = errno;

        close(lineHandle.fd);
    }
    else retval = errno;

    return retval;
}


/*****************************************************************************
* Function: dispError()
* Purpose: Function to display error based on the setting of errno.
*
* Receives:
*        char *Msg1 - Message to display with the error information.
*        char *Name - Name associated with message or NULL.
*        int errorid - The system errno for the fault.
```

```
 *
 * Returns: void
 **************************************************************************/
void dispError(char *Msg, char *Name, int errorid)
{
    printf("\n%s%s, Error number:%d, %s\n", Msg, Name, errorid,
        strerror(errorid));
}
```

The two previous examples were informational, providing insight into using the GPIO character device drivers, and provided a way to view the current status of the GPIO pins on the 40-pin header. Now it's time to explore the character device driver as a means of GPIO control. There are basically four steps that need to be taken in the code to use a character device driver for GPIO set and get operation:

Step 1 - Open the character device driver for access by obtaining a device file descriptor.

Step 2 - Using the device file descriptor obtained in Step 1, make an ioctl() function call to get access to the desired GPIO pins and set the direction as either input or output for each. Making a call to the ioctl() function using the GPIO_GET_LINEHANDLE_IOCTL option will return a file descriptor specific to the GPIO pin specified.

Step 3 - With the previously obtained GPIO pin file descriptor from Step 2, use an ioctl() function call with either the GPIOHANDLE_GET_LINE_VALUES_IOCTL or GPIOHANDLE_SET_LINE_VALUES_IOCTL to read or write the value of the specified GPIO pin. Note that if a pin is configured as an output it can either be written or read while a pin configured as an input can only be read.

Step 4 - Before exiting the application the GPIO pin file descriptors and then the main device file descriptor need to be closed.

See Program Listing 10.3 for an example of using the steps above to take ownership of several GPIO pins. The application will read the state of GPIO2 as an input and then blink GPIO3 and GPIO4 several times. If using external LEDs or the RPI-LED board described in chapter 8, a visual result can be seen. This example provides a way to understand how to use the character device driver to control GPIO pins by reading and writing the pin states.

Notice the line **#define RPi** in the example code. When included in the code, this definition results in the use of the BCM numbers that correspond to the Raspberry Pi. If the define is not used or commented out then this code will work with the Orange Pi Lite single board computer. As stated initially at the beginning of this chapter, character device drivers can be used across many platforms and are not specific only to the Raspberry Pi. Using the Orange Pi Lite GPIO pins is a perfect example of code portability between platforms when using operating system device drivers versus custom code specific to only one platform.

To generate this example follow these steps:

1. At a Terminal Prompt, change into the chapter10 directory: **cd /home/pi/webproj/chapter10**

2. Using either a favorite desktop editor or nano, create a file with the name gpioex.c:

    nano gpioex.c

3. Enter the code from Program Listing 10.3 below.

4. When finished entering Program Listing 10.3, type CTRL + O then ENTER to save then CTRL + X to exit nano.

5. Compile the program by typing the following at the Terminal Prompt:

   gcc gpioex.c -o gpioex

6. Make sure the program is executable: **chmod +x+r gpioex**

7. To run the application from the Terminal Prompt, type: **./gpioex**

Program Listing 10.3: gpioex.c

```c
/*******************************************************************************
* File: gpioex.c
* Description: GPIO Set/Get example program using the GPIO character
* device driver.
* ******************************************************************************/
#include <unistd.h>
#include <dirent.h>
#include <stdio.h>
#include <stdlib.h>
#include <string.h>
#include <fcntl.h>
#include <errno.h>
#include <sys/ioctl.h>
#include <linux/gpio.h>


#define RPi

#define ERROR -1

/* Defines */
#define GPIO_IN       0
#define GPIO_OUT      1
#define ON            1
#define OFF           0
#define MAX_CONSUMER 32

#ifdef RPi  /* Using the Raspberry Pi */
#define BCM_2        2
#define BCM_3        3
#define BCM_4        4

#else /* Using the Orange Pi Lite. */
```

```c
#define BCM_2         12
#define BCM_3         11
#define BCM_4         6


#endif



/* Function prototypes. */
int gpioInitPin(int devfd, int bcm, int inout);
int gpioGetPin(int fd);
int gpioSetPin(int fd, int value);



/****************************************************************************
* Function: main()
* Purpose: Main function entry point for the gpio_example app.
*
* Returns: 0 = OKAY, or ERROR
****************************************************************************/
int main(void)
{
   int retval = 0;
   int Devfd;
   int state = ERROR;

   int fd_GPIO2_Pin3 = ERROR;
   int fd_GPIO3_Pin5 = ERROR;
   int fd_GPIO4_Pin7 = ERROR;

   printf("\n\n*** Running gpio_example application ***\n");

   /* STEP 1: Open the character device driver for access. */
   Devfd = open("/dev/gpiochip0", O_RDONLY);

   if(Devfd != ERROR)
   {
       /* STEP 2: Get access to the desired I/O and set direction. */
       fd_GPIO2_Pin3 = gpioInitPin(Devfd, BCM_2, GPIO_IN);
       fd_GPIO3_Pin5 = gpioInitPin(Devfd, BCM_3, GPIO_OUT);
       fd_GPIO4_Pin7 = gpioInitPin(Devfd, BCM_4, GPIO_OUT);
```

```c
/* STEP 3: Read/Write GPIO by File Descriptor. */

/* Read GPIO 2. */
if(fd_GPIO2_Pin3 != ERROR)
    state = gpioGetPin(fd_GPIO2_Pin3);
if(state != ERROR)
    printf("\nGPIO 2 = %s", state ? "1 (3.3V)" : "0 (0V)");
else
    printf("\nError reading GPIO 2, Pin 3");

printf("\nBlinking GPIO3 and GPIO4 several times.");

 /* Force terminal text to screen now. */
fflush(stdout);

/* Blink GPIO 3 and 4 several times. */
for(int loop = 0; loop < 10; loop++)
{
    gpioSetPin(fd_GPIO3_Pin5, ON);
    gpioSetPin(fd_GPIO4_Pin7, ON);

    /* Wait 1/2 second. */
    usleep(500000);

    gpioSetPin(fd_GPIO3_Pin5, OFF);
    gpioSetPin(fd_GPIO4_Pin7, OFF);
    /* Wait 1/2 second. */
    usleep(500000);
}

/* Leave the pins set to 3.3V to demonstrate the
    default state when the driver is released.  */
gpioSetPin(fd_GPIO3_Pin5, ON);
gpioSetPin(fd_GPIO4_Pin7, ON);

/* STEP 4: Close the character device driver. (cleanup) */
if(fd_GPIO2_Pin3 != ERROR)
    close(fd_GPIO2_Pin3);
if(fd_GPIO3_Pin5 != ERROR)
    close(fd_GPIO3_Pin5);
if(fd_GPIO4_Pin7 != ERROR)
```

```c
        close(fd_GPIO4_Pin7);
        close(Devfd);


    }
    else
    {
        /* Failed to open device so print error message. */
        printf("Error %d opening device: /dev/gpiochip0, %s",
                errno, strerror(errno));

        retval = ERROR;
    }

    printf("\n\nEnd of gpio_example application.\n\n");

    return retval;
}



/*************************************************************************
* Function: gpioInitPin()
* Purpose:  Gain access to the desired gpio pin through the character
*           device driver.
*
* Receives:
*           int devfd - File descriptor of the character device.*
*           int bcm - The BCM number of the gpio pin.
*           int inout - 0 = Input Pin, 1 = Output Pin.
*
* Returns: Pin file descriptor else ERROR
*************************************************************************/
int gpioInitPin(int devfd, int bcm, int inout)
{
    int result = ERROR;
    struct gpiohandle_request lineHandle;

    /* Clear gpiohandle request structure memory. */
    memset(&lineHandle, 0, sizeof(lineHandle));

    /* Set line values for the gpio pin. */
    lineHandle.lineoffsets[0] = bcm;
```

```
    lineHandle.lines = 1;
    lineHandle.default_values[0] = 0;


    /* Set the name of the consumer of the line. */
    strncpy(lineHandle.consumer_label, "gpio_example", MAX_CONSUMER);


    /* Set pin as output. */
    if(inout)
        lineHandle.flags = GPIOHANDLE_REQUEST_OUTPUT;
    else
    lineHandle.flags = GPIOHANDLE_REQUEST_INPUT;


    /* Get gpio pin fd through the line handle. */
    result = ioctl(devfd, GPIO_GET_LINEHANDLE_IOCTL, &lineHandle);


    /* If successful.*/
    if(result != ERROR)
        result = lineHandle.fd; // Save the gpio pin fd.
    else if(errno == 16)    // gpio line is in use already.
    {
        printf("\n gpio pin %d is in use.", bcm);
        fflush(stdout);
    }
    else
    {
        printf("\n Error %d opening gpio %d.", errno, bcm);
        printf("\n\t %s", strerror(errno));
        fflush(stdout);
    }


    return result;
}



/*****************************************************************************
* Function: gpioGetPin()
* Purpose: Function to read IO pin state either 1 (3.3V) or 0 (0V).
*
* Receives:
*          int fd - gpio line handle file descriptor*
```

```
 *
 * Returns: Pin value (0 or 1) else ERROR
 *************************************************************************/
int gpioGetPin(int fd)
{
    int retval = ERROR;
    struct gpiohandle_data lineData;

    if(fd != -1)
    {
        /* Clear gpiohandle data structure memory. */
        memset(&lineData, 0, sizeof(lineData));

        /* Get the current state of the selected line. */
        retval = ioctl(fd, GPIOHANDLE_GET_LINE_VALUES_IOCTL, &lineData);

        if(retval != ERROR)
        {
            /* Save the line value 0(LOW) or 1(High). */
            retval = lineData.values[0];
        }
    }

    return retval;
}


/*************************************************************************
 * Function: gpioSetPin()
 * Purpose: Function to set/clear IO pin value. SET = 3.3V, CLEAR = 0V
 *
 * Receives:
 *           int fd - gpio line handle file descriptor
 *           int value = Clear = 0, Set = 1 (3.3V)
 *
 * Returns: OK or ERROR
 *************************************************************************/
int gpioSetPin(int fd, int value)
{
    int retval = ERROR;
    struct gpiohandle_data lineData;
```

```
if(fd == ERROR)
    return ERROR;

if(value > 1) value = 1;

if(fd != -1)
{
    /* Set the gpio line to either 3.3V or 0V. */
    lineData.values[0] = value;
    retval = ioctl(fd, GPIOHANDLE_SET_LINE_VALUES_IOCTL, &lineData);
}

return retval;
}
```

One trait of the GPIO character device on the Raspberry Pi is that the device driver only holds the state of the GPIO signals when it is open for access. Once the application closes the character device, the GPIO signals return to the default state. This means that if the default states for all GPIO pins are set to off or logic zero, then the GPIO pins will turn off once the device is closed or the application exits. This is not an issue when being used with a local application, but if the desire is to turn on a GPIO pin over a web interface then as soon as the CGI call returns the pin will turn back off. Some GPIO device drivers behave differently depending on the OS and device driver version. For instance, the Orange Pi Lite GPIO driver keeps the last state when the device is closed on application exit.

Since the character device driver on the Raspberry Pi does not hold the GPIO pin state after the application has exited it cannot be used directly for a web-controlled process because a CGI call needs to complete and return as quickly as possible resulting in the GPIO pin returning to the default state. The next chapter will provide a method that can be used to allow the GPIO pins to retain the state set by a CGI call and will be called WebIO.

One additional note about the GPIO pins is that every pin can carry an alternate function. Not every pin has the same alternate functions, but any pin configured for an alternate function cannot be used for standard input/output operations. See the Broadcom datasheets for the various alternate pin functions. When a pin is in use, the ioctl() function will not provide a handle to the resource and will return error 16 "Device or resource busy." Pin info can be obtained but a handle to read or write a pin state is only available when the pin is not in use by another process.

11

WEB IO & IPC

This chapter will explore the use of Interprocess Communications (IPC) to create a new set of applications for controlling gpio pins over a web page using CGI. Two programs will be created that will use IPC to communicate. The first application will run as a service and directly control the gpio pins through a character device driver similar to the example code presented in the previous chapter. This service will always be running unless purposely stopped and will retain the gpio states between CGI calls. The second program named "webio" can be called from either the command line or from a web page through a CGI script to read and write gpio pin values.

The idea is that the service will take ownership of all the gpio pins and then wait for the webio application to use IPC to read or write the gpio values. Once set, a gpio pin will retain the last set value until the service is stopped.

There are several main IPC communication methods that can be used to provide communications between two applications and they are as follows:

- Sockets
- Shared Memory
- Pipes
- Message Queues

File Sharing, Signals, and Semaphores can also be used for limited application synchronization and communications. Many times there is a need to combine multiple methods for cross communication between two or more applications. This need arises quite often when developing applications with a parent process and one or more child processes. The examples used here will be single-threaded for simplicity and will only make use of IPC Sockets.

Sockets used for communications come in two flavors; Unix Domain sockets for IPC and Network sockets. Unix Domain sockets rely on a local file as a socket address whereas Network sockets require an underlying protocol like TCP/IP. Network sockets can communicate between applications on the same or different servers whereas Unix Domain sockets are only used for applications running on the same server or platform. The examples used here will make use of Unix Domain IPC sockets having a local file for the communication mechanism.

Before jumping into the WebIO solution, a more simplified example will be presented showing the IPC basics for using Unix Domain sockets. This first example will provide the source code for both a server and client application. The server application will create a listener that waits for input from a connecting client and will remain running. The client application will open and communicate with the server to exchange some information and then exit. The client can be run over and over again while the server remains open. The methods used for this example will carry forward to the WebIO gpio control solution.

Follow these steps to create the initial IPC server application:

1. At a Terminal Prompt, change into the project directory: **cd /home/pi/webproj**

2. Create a new directory where the Chapter 11 code will be stored:

   mkdir chapter11

3. Change into the chapter11 directory: **cd chapter11**

4. Using either a favorite desktop editor or nano, create a file with the name serverex.c:

   nano serverex.c

5. Enter the code from Program Listing 11.1 below.

6. When finished entering Program Listing 11.1, type CTRL + O then ENTER to save then CTRL + X to exit nano.

7. Compile the program by typing the following at the Terminal Prompt:

   gcc serverex.c -o serverex

8. Make sure to fix any errors or warnings before continuing.

9. Be sure the program is executable by typing: **chmod +x+r serverex**

10. Note that when the serverex application runs it will not return until a CTRL-C is typed at the Terminal Prompt to terminate the server application.

11. To run the application from the Terminal Prompt type: **./serverex**

12. Leave the terminal open with the serverex application running. Open a new Terminal Window to work in before continuing.

13. In the new Terminal Window, change into the chapter11 directory:

    cd /home/pi/webproj/chapter11

14. View the newly created socket file named "ipc_socket" by typing the following at the Terminal Prompt: **ls -als**

Program Listing 11.1: serverex.c

```
/******************************************************************************
 * File: serverex.c
 * Purpose: To provide an example server using IPC. Creates an
 *               ipc_socket file for IPC communications between the two
 *               programs to send and receive simple messages over the
 *               stream socket.
 ******************************************************************************/
#include <stdio.h>
#include <sys/socket.h>
#include <sys/un.h>
#include <sys/types.h>
```

```c
#include <unistd.h>
#include <string.h>
#include <errno.h>
#include <sys/stat.h>

#define OK 0
#define ERROR -1

#define MAX_PATH     256
#define MAX_BUFFER   256
#define SOCKET_PATH "ipc_socket"

/* Function Prototypes. */
int process_cmd(int ipc_stream);

/***************************************************************************
 * Function: main()
 * Purpose: Main entry point for the serverex service.
 * Receives: void
 *
 * returns: OK or ERROR
 ***************************************************************************/
int main(void)
{
   struct sockaddr_un unix_sock_addr;
   socklen_t addr_length;
   int socket_fd, ret = 0;
   int ipc_stream;
   pid_t pid_handler;

   /* Delete exiting socket if exists from previous run. */
   remove(SOCKET_PATH);

   /* Create a socket. */
   socket_fd = socket(AF_UNIX, SOCK_STREAM, 0);
   if(socket_fd < 0)
   {
      printf("\nError! Could not create socket!");
      return ERROR;
   }
```

```c
/* Remove previous symbolic link if exists. */
unlink(SOCKET_PATH);

/* Clear the socket address structure memory. */
memset(&unix_sock_addr, 0, sizeof(struct sockaddr_un));

/* Set up socket address information. */
unix_sock_addr.sun_family = AF_UNIX;
snprintf(unix_sock_addr.sun_path, MAX_PATH, SOCKET_PATH);

/* Bind the socket address to the open socket. */
if(bind(socket_fd, (struct sockaddr*) &unix_sock_addr,
       sizeof(struct sockaddr_un)) != 0)
{
    printf("\nError! Could not bind to the socket.");
    return ERROR;
}

/* Set permissions for accessing the file based IPC Socket. */
chmod(SOCKET_PATH, S_IRWXU | S_IRWXG  | S_IRWXO );

/* Listen to the socket for incoming connections. */
if(listen(socket_fd, 2) != 0)
{
    printf("\nError! Failed to listen on IPC Socket.");
    return ERROR;
}

/* Process incoming connections. */
while(ret != ERROR)
{
    addr_length = sizeof(unix_sock_addr);

    /* Wait for incoming connection. This is a blocking call. */
    if((ipc_stream = accept(socket_fd,
       (struct sockaddr*) & unix_sock_addr, &addr_length)) == -1)
    {
        printf("Error! Accept connection failed with error: %s\n",
            strerror(errno));
        break;
    }
```

```
      /* Handle the incoming gpio command. */
      ret = process_cmd(ipc_stream);

      /* Close the current stream connection. */
      close(ipc_stream);
   }

   /* Close the socket and exit the application. */
   close(socket_fd);
   unlink(SOCKET_PATH);

   return OK;
}



/*****************************************************************************
 * Function: process_cmd()
 * Purpose: To handle a new process to communicate with client.
 * Receives: int ipc_stream - The stream socket file descriptor (fd).
 *
 * returns: OK or ERROR
 *****************************************************************************/
int process_cmd(int ipc_stream)
{
   int ret = 0;
   int numBytes;
   char strBuf[MAX_BUFFER+1];

   /* Read data from the ipc stream connection. */
   numBytes = read(ipc_stream, strBuf, MAX_BUFFER);
   if(numBytes == ERROR || numBytes == 0)
      return ERROR;

   /* Receiving a string so add null termination. */
   strBuf[numBytes] = 0;

   /* Print the string received from the client application. */
   printf("Client sent: %s\n", strBuf);

   /* Create a message to send to the client in return. */
```

```c
    numBytes = snprintf(strBuf, MAX_BUFFER, "Server is alive!");
    write(ipc_stream, strBuf, numBytes);


    /* Close the ipc stream connection. */
    close(ipc_stream);


    return ret;
}
```

With the serverex application still running and the socket file "ipc_socket" created for IPC communications, the clientex application will be created and run by following these steps:

1. In the Terminal Window opened in the previous section, change into the chapter11 directory if not already there:

    cd /home/pi/webproj/chapter11

2. Using either a favorite desktop editor or nano, create a file with the name clientex.c:

    nano clientex.c

3. Enter the code from Program Listing 11.2 below.

4. When finished entering Program Listing 11.2, type CTRL + O then ENTER to save then CTRL + X to exit nano.

5. Compile the program by typing the following at the Terminal Prompt:

    gcc clientex.c -o clientex

6. Make sure to fix any errors or warnings before continuing.

7. Be sure the program is executable by typing: **chmod +x+r clientex**

8. Run the application from the Terminal Prompt: **./clientex**

9. Try running the clientex application several times. Notice that the server continues to run and send a reply message back to the client each time it's run. Both terminals should show the messages sent from the application being run on the other terminal.

10. When finished running the clientex application, go to the terminal running the serverex application and type CTRL-C to terminate the serverex program.

Program Listing 11.2: clientex.c

```c
/******************************************************************************
 * File: clientex.c
 * Purpose: Example IPC client to be used in conjunction with the serverex
 * example app.
 * Note: Requires the serverex application be up and running to get an IPC
 * connection.
 ******************************************************************************/
#include <stdio.h>
#include <stdlib.h>
#include <sys/socket.h>
#include <sys/un.h>
```

```c
#include <unistd.h>
#include <string.h>

#define OK 0
#define ERROR -1

#define MAX_PATH      256
#define MAX_BUFFER    256
#define SOCKET_PATH "ipc_socket"

/***************************************************************************
 * Function: main()
 * Purpose: Main entry point for the clientex example application.
 * Receives: void
 *
 * returns: OK on success else ERROR
 ***************************************************************************/
int main(void)
{
    struct sockaddr_un unix_sock_addr;
    int socket_fd;
    int numBytes;
    char strBuf[MAX_BUFFER+1];
    int retval = OK;

    /* Open a socket for communication with the serverex server. */
    socket_fd = socket(AF_UNIX, SOCK_STREAM, 0);
    if(socket_fd < 0)
    {
        printf("\nError! Failed to open IPC socket!");
        return ERROR;
    }

    /* Clear the socket address structure memory. */
    memset(&unix_sock_addr, 0, sizeof(struct sockaddr_un));

    /* Set up socket address information. */
    unix_sock_addr.sun_family = AF_UNIX;
    snprintf(unix_sock_addr.sun_path, MAX_PATH, SOCKET_PATH);

    /* Connect to the IPC socket. */
    if(connect(socket_fd, (struct sockaddr *) &unix_sock_addr,
        sizeof(struct sockaddr_un)) != 0)
    {
```

```
        printf("Failed to connect to the serverex server.\n");
        printf("Make sure the server is running.\n");
        return ERROR;
    }


    /* Create a message to send to the server. */
    numBytes = snprintf(strBuf, MAX_BUFFER, "Client is alive!");
    write(socket_fd, strBuf, numBytes);

    /* Get reply from the IPC server. */
    numBytes = read(socket_fd, strBuf, MAX_BUFFER);

    /* Receiving a string so add null termination. */
    strBuf[numBytes] = 0;

    /* Print the string received from the server application. */
    printf("Server sent: %s\n", strBuf);

    /* Close the ipc socket. */
    close(socket_fd);

    return retval;
}
```

In the previous example, when the IPC socket is created, it uses a filepath for the address that creates a file for streaming input and output as defined in SOCKET_PATH. This file path will change for the next example. The next two applications that will be created will provide a full standalone solution to controlling gpio pins through a character device driver while maintaining the gpio states between access. The server-side application, called gpioctrol, will eventually be used as a service and can receive client commands from either the webio application or from the final Web Control Panel Solution provided in the next chapter. The webio application can also be used to easily terminate the service at will without having to use system calls. The webio application can be used in scripts to send and receive multiple commands sequentially. The gpioctrl service has two main parts:

- GPIO control interface
- IPC socket server-side communications

The webio application also has two main parts:
- Command line input processing
- IPC socket client-side communications

The gpio control interface takes ownership of all gpio pins except the ones currently in use by other applications. The gpio pins are all set as inputs initially. When a command is sent to set a gpio output to a value, the server will automatically change the gpio pin to an output and set the requested value. To change an output back to an input the **webio dir** command has to be used. If a pin is desired to be used by another application then the **webio rel** command can be used to release the pin. Once released, a **webio dir** or a **webio set** command can be used to regain access to the released pin. To force the gpioctrl service to exit, use the **webio**

rel EXIT command.

If the webio application is run without proper arguments then the following output can be seen on the terminal showing the command syntax:

pi@raspberrypi:~/webproj/temp/webio $ ./webio

Syntax: webio <Option> <Variable 1> <Variable 2>

Options:
> **get <BCM #> (Returns the state of the gpio by BCM number.)**
> **get ALL   (Prints the state of all gpio pins.)**
> **set <BCM #> <value 0|1> (Sets the state of the gpio by BCM number.)**
> **dir <BCM #> <IN | OUT> (Sets the gpio pin direction.)**
> **rel <BCM #> (Release the gpio pin and remove from use.)**
> **rel EXIT   (Cause the server to close.)**

Example: webio set 21 1
> **webio get 21**
> **webio dir 5 IN**
> **webio get 5**
> **webio rel EXIT**

If using the RPI-LED board for easy indication of gpio pin state changes, note that gpio2 and gpio5 are set up to be able to work as inputs and have external pull-up resistors that will read back as a logic "1" when a **webio get** command is sent. All other pins except for gpio0 and gpio1 have LEDs connected that can be used for verifying the gpio output state visually.

The webio client and gpioctrl server (service) share a common header file and a common makefile. These two files will be created first. To create the common header file follow the next steps:

1. In a Terminal Window, change into the chapter11 directory:

   cd /home/pi/webproj/chapter11

2. Using either a favorite desktop editor or nano, create a file with the name ipchdr.h:

   nano ipchdr.h

3. Enter the code from Program Listing 11.3 below.

4. When finished entering Program Listing 11.3, type CTRL + O then ENTER to save then CTRL + X to exit nano.

Program Listing 11.3: ipchdr.h

```
/******************************************************************************
 * File: ipchdr.h
 * Purpose: Header file for both the gpioctrl and webio applications. Contains
 *          common definitions and structures used in both apps.
```

```
 *
 **************************************************************************/

#define MAX_PATH      256
#define MAX_BUFFER    256
#define NUM_HDR_PINS 40
#define NUM_MAX_GPIO 28
#define SOCKET_PATH "/var/www/webapp/webio_socket"

#define OK 0
#define ERROR  -1
#define INV    -2
#define EXIT   -256

/* Command variable values. */
#define IO_IN 0
#define IO_OUT 1
#define IO_EXIT -3
#define IO_ALL -2

/* Command values. */
#define CMD_SET 0
#define CMD_GET 1
#define CMD_DIR 2
#define CMD_REL 3


/* IPC command structure. */
typedef struct gpio_struct
{
   int Command;
   int arg1;
   int arg2;
   int bcm[NUM_MAX_GPIO];
   int value[NUM_MAX_GPIO];
} gpio_struct;

/* gpio control structure */
typedef struct gpio_pin
{
   char direction; /* Either IO_IN, IO_OUT, or -1 if not used. */
   int bcmNum;      /* BCM Number. */
   int gpio_fd;    /* The gpio pin file descriptor. */
} gpio_pin;
```

```
typedef struct gpio_ctrl
{
    int char_dev_fd; /* File descriptor for the character device. */
    gpio_pin gpio_array[NUM_MAX_GPIO]; /* Array of gpio pin info. */
} gpio_ctrl;

/* Array map of pins versus GPIO BCM numbers.
 * These are specific to the Raspberry Pi.
 * Change the gpio values if using an Orange Pi or
 * if a new Raspberry Pi version comes out with
 * different BCM numbers.
 * -1 = 3.3V, -2 = 5V, -3 = Ground.  */
int iPin_bcm[NUM_HDR_PINS] =
{
    -1, /*     3V3  [1] (2)  5V     */ -2,
     2, /* GPIO2   (3) (4)  5V     */ -2,
     3, /* GPIO3   (5) (6)  GROUND */ -3,
     4, /* GPIO4   (7) (8)  GPIO14 */ 14,
    -3, /* GROUND  (9) (10) GPIO15 */ 15,
    17, /* GPIO17 (11) (12) GPIO18 */ 18,
    27, /* GPIO27 (13) (14) GROUND */ -3,
    22, /* GPIO22 (15) (16) GPIO23 */ 23,
    -1, /*     3V3 (17) (18) GPIO24 */ 24,
    10, /* GPIO10 (19) (20) GROUND */ -3,
     9, /* GPIO9  (21) (22) GPIO25 */ 25,
    11, /* GPIO11 (23) (24) GPIO8  */  8,
    -3, /* GROUND (25) (26) GPIO7  */  7,
     0, /* GPIO0  (27) (28) GPIO1  */  1,
     5, /* GPIO5  (29) (30) GROUND */ -3,
     6, /* GPIO6  (31) (32) GPIO12 */ 12,
    13, /* GPIO13 (33) (34) GROUND */ -3,
    19, /* GPIO19 (35) (36) GPIO16 */ 16,
    26, /* GPIO26 (37) (38) GPIO20 */ 20,
    -3, /* GROUND (39) (40) GPIO21 */ 21
};
```

Next, the common makefile will be created by following these steps:

1. In a Terminal Window, change into the chapter11 directory:

   cd /home/pi/webproj/chapter11

2. Using either a favorite desktop editor or nano, create a file with the name makefile:

   nano makefile

3. Enter the code from Program Listing 11.4 below.

4. When finished entering Program Listing 11.4, type CTRL + O then ENTER to save then CTRL + X to exit nano.

Program Listing 11.4: makefile

```
# type 'make <target>' to build the desired project.

all: webio gpioctrl

webio: webio.o
        gcc -lm -o webio webio.o

webio.o: webio.c
        gcc -c webio.c

gpioctrl: gpioctrl.o
        gcc -lm -o gpioctrl gpioctrl.o

gpioctrl.o: gpioctrl.c
        gcc -c gpioctrl.c

# type 'sudo make install' to copy files and change their attributes.

install:
        if test -d /var/www/webapp; then echo -n;  else mkdir /var/www/webapp/; fi
        cp ipc.cgi /usr/lib/cgi-bin
        cp webio /var/www/webapp
        chmod 755 /var/www/webapp/webio
        chmod 755 /usr/lib/cgi-bin/ipc.cgi

# type 'make clean 'to remove objects for a fresh build.

clean:
        rm *.o webio gpioctrl
```

Next, the webio client source code will be created. The makefile was created in a way that will allow both the webio client and the gpioctrl server to be compiled at the same time; however, these steps will compile the client source code first with the server files missing so that any errors in the client can be fixed before moving on to creating the server code. This will help to make things less confusing if there are any typos in the code entered into the nano editor for the client code.

Follow these steps to create the client application code:

1. In a Terminal Window, change into the chapter11 directory:

    cd /home/pi/webproj/chapter11

2. Using either a favorite desktop editor or nano, create a file with the name webio.c:

> **nano webio.c**

3. Enter the code from Program Listing 11.5 below.

4. When finished entering Program Listing 11.5, type CTRL + O then ENTER to save then CTRL + X to exit nano.

5. Next, run the makefile to compile the webio application by typing the following at the Terminal Prompt:

    > **make**

6. Ignore any reference to "No rule to make target gpioctrl.c" since that file has not been created yet. Fix any errors due to typos when entering webio.c using nano before proceeding.

Program Listing 11.5: webio.c

```c
/******************************************************************************
 * File: webio.c
 * Purpose: Used for either command line or web access to gpio port pins through
 * IPC. Requires the gpioctrl server be up and running to get an IPC connection.
 ******************************************************************************/
#include <stdio.h>
#include <stdlib.h>
#include <sys/socket.h>
#include <sys/un.h>
#include <unistd.h>
#include <string.h>
#include "ipchdr.h"

/* Function prototypes. */
void dispSyntax(void);
int isBCMValid(int);
int runCommand(long, long, long);

/******************************************************************************
 * Function: main()
 * Purpose: Main entry point for the webio application.
 * Receives: int argc - Number of command line input strings.
 *           char ** - Command line input strings.
 *
 * returns: gpio state 0|1 or OK on success else ERROR
 ******************************************************************************/
int main(int argc, char *argv[])
{
    long arg1 = 0, arg2 = 0, cmd = 0;
    char *tmp = NULL;
```

```
int retval = OK;

/* If no usr command line input. */
if(argc <= 2)
{
    dispSyntax();
    return ERROR;
}

/* Parse user command line input. */

/* Get BCM number or "ALL" or EXIT option. */
if((strncmp(argv[2], "ALL", 3) == 0) && strlen(argv[2]) == 3)
{
    arg1 = IO_ALL;
}
else if((strncmp(argv[2], "EXIT", 4) == 0) && strlen(argv[2]) == 4)
{
    arg1 = IO_EXIT;
}
else
{
    /* Get the BCM number. */
    arg1 = strtol(argv[2], &tmp, 10);
    if(tmp[0] != '\0')
    {
        printf("\nInvalid BCM number!");
        dispSyntax();
        return ERROR;
    }
    else
    {
        /* Make sure the BCM number matches a
         * valid BCM number from the table. */
        if(!isBCMValid(arg1))
        {
            printf("\nInvalid BCM number!");
            dispSyntax();
            return ERROR;
        }
```

```
        }
    }

    /* Get the second command line argument, if any. */
    if(argc > 3)
    {
        if((strncmp(argv[3], "IN", 2) == 0) && strlen(argv[3]) == 2)
        {
            arg2 = IO_IN;
        }
        else if((strncmp(argv[3], "OUT", 3) == 0) && strlen(argv[3]) == 3)
        {
            arg2 = IO_OUT;
        }
        else
        {
            /* Get the gpio value 0|1 number. */
            arg2 = strtol(argv[3], &tmp, 10);
            if(tmp[0] != '\0' || arg2 > 1 || arg2 < 0)
            {
                printf("\nInvalid option for third parameter!");
                dispSyntax();
                return ERROR;
            }
        }
    }

    /* Parse the requested command type. */
    if((strncmp(argv[1], "get", 3) == 0) && strlen(argv[1]) == 3)
    {
        cmd = CMD_GET;
    }
    else if((strncmp(argv[1], "set", 3) == 0) && strlen(argv[1]) == 3)
    {
        if(argc <= 3)
        {
            printf("\nInvalid gpio output value!");
            dispSyntax();
            return ERROR;
        }
        cmd = CMD_SET;
```

```
    }
    else if((strncmp(argv[1], "dir", 3) == 0) && strlen(argv[1]) == 3)
    {
        if(argc <= 3)
        {
            printf("\nInvalid gpio direction!");
            dispSyntax();
            return ERROR;
        }
        cmd = CMD_DIR;
    }
    else if((strncmp(argv[1], "rel", 3) == 0) && strlen(argv[1]) == 3)
    {
        cmd = CMD_REL;
    }
    else
    {
        printf("\nInvalid input: %s", argv[1]);
        dispSyntax();
        return ERROR;
    }

    /* Create and send an IPC call to execute the command. */
    retval = runCommand(cmd, arg1, arg2);

    return retval;
}



/****************************************************************************
 * Function: dispSyntax()
 * Purpose: To display the command line help options.
 * Receives: N/A
 * Returns void
 * ***************************************************************************/
void dispSyntax(void)
{
    /* Display command line usage. */
    printf("\nSyntax: webio <Option> <Variable 1> <Variable 2>\n");
    printf("\nOptions:");
    printf("\n\tget <BCM #> (Returns the state of the gpio by BCM number.)");
```

```
    printf("\n\tget ALL     (Prints the state of all gpio pins.)");
    printf("\n\tset <BCM #> <value 0|1> ");
    printf("(Sets the state of the gpio by BCM number.)");
    printf("\n\tdir <BCM #> <IN | OUT>  (Sets the gpio pin direction.)");
    printf("\n\trel <BCM #> (Release the gpio pin and remove from use.)");
    printf("\n\trel EXIT    (Cause the server to close.)");
    printf("\n\nExample: webio set 21 1");
    printf("\n             webio get 21");
    printf("\n             webio dir 5 IN");
    printf("\n             webio get 5");
    printf("\n             webio rel EXIT");
    printf("\n");
}




/****************************************************************************
 * Function: isBCMValid()
 * Purpose: To verify the BCM is valid for this target relative to the BCM table.
 * Receives: int bcm_num - The BCM number to check.
 *
 * Returns 1 (true) or 0 (false) if not valid.
 ****************************************************************************/
int isBCMValid(int bcm_num)
{
    int retval = 0;
    int loop;

    /* Loop through the full BCM table looking for the BCM number. */
    /* For some targets the gap between valid BCM numbers can be large. */
    for(loop = 0; loop < NUM_HDR_PINS; loop++)
    {
        if(iPin_bcm[loop] == bcm_num)
        {
            retval = 1;
            break;
        }
    }


    return retval;
}
```

```
/*****************************************************************************
 * Function: runCommand()
 * Purpose: To send an IPC message to the server to run the current
 *          command request.
 * Receives:   long cmd - The command type.
 *             long arg1 - The first argument normally BCM number.
 *             long arg2 - If used will normally be set to ON, OFF, IN, or OUT.
 *
 * Returns: gpio state 0|1 else ERROR
 *****************************************************************************/
int runCommand(long cmd, long arg1, long arg2)
{
    struct sockaddr_un unix_sock_addr;
    int socket_fd, retval = 0, loop, pin;
    char strBuf[MAX_BUFFER+1];
    int numBytes;
    gpio_struct pkt;

    /* Clear the message structure memory. */
    memset(&pkt, 0, sizeof(gpio_struct));

    /* Set up IPC message structure. */
    pkt.Command = (int) cmd;
    pkt.arg1 = (int) arg1;
    pkt.arg2 = (int) arg2;

    /* Open a socket for communication with the gpioctl server. */
    socket_fd = socket(AF_UNIX, SOCK_STREAM, 0);
    if(socket_fd < 0)
    {
        printf("\nError! Failed to open IPC socket!");
        return ERROR;
    }

    /* Clear the socket address structure memory. */
    memset(&unix_sock_addr, 0, sizeof(struct sockaddr_un));

    /* Set up socket address information. */
    unix_sock_addr.sun_family = AF_UNIX;
    snprintf(unix_sock_addr.sun_path, MAX_PATH, SOCKET_PATH);
```

```c
/* Connect to the IPC socket. */
if(connect(socket_fd, (struct sockaddr *) &unix_sock_addr,
    sizeof(struct sockaddr_un)) != 0)
{
    printf("Failed to connect to the gpioctl server.\n");
    printf("Make sure the server is running.\n");
    return ERROR;
}


/* Send command packet to server over IPC connection. */
numBytes = sizeof(gpio_struct);
write(socket_fd, (char *) &pkt, numBytes);


/* Get reply from the IPC server. */
numBytes = read(socket_fd, strBuf, MAX_BUFFER);

/* If command packet size is incorrect. */
if(numBytes != sizeof(gpio_struct))
{
    printf("\nReceived malformed packet from server.");
    retval = ERROR;
}
else
{
    /* Copy the packet into the command structure. */
    memcpy(&pkt, strBuf, sizeof(gpio_struct));

    /* Used for debugging. */
    /*
        printf("\nCommand: %d\n", pkt.Command);
        printf("arg1: %d\n", pkt.arg1);
        printf("arg2: %d\n", pkt.arg2);
    */

    /* Handle response based on command. */
    switch(pkt.Command)
    {
        case CMD_SET:
            if(pkt.arg2 == ERROR)
```

```c
            printf("\nServer Error processing set command.");
        else if(pkt.arg1 == INV)
            printf("\nOperation failed, pin in use by another consumer.");
        else
            printf("\nPin BCM %d value: %d", pkt.arg1, pkt.arg2);
        retval = pkt.arg2;
    break;


    case CMD_GET:
        if(pkt.arg2 == ERROR)
        printf("\nPin not configured! Try configuring with dir command.");
        else if(pkt.arg1 == IO_ALL)
        {
            /* Print list of gpio values. */
            for(loop = 0; loop < NUM_MAX_GPIO; loop++)
            {
                printf("\nP%d:%d", pkt.bcm[loop], pkt.value[loop]);
            }
        }
        else
            printf("\nPin BCM %d value: %d", pkt.arg1, pkt.arg2);
        retval = pkt.arg2;
    break;


    case CMD_DIR:
        if(pkt.arg2 == ERROR)
            printf("\nServer Error processing dir command.");
        else if(pkt.arg1 == INV)
            printf("\nOperation failed, pin in use by another consumer.");
        else
            printf("\ndir bcm %d direction: %s",
                    pkt.arg1, pkt.arg2 ? "IO_OUT":"IO_IN");
        retval = pkt.arg2;
    break;


    case CMD_REL:
        if(pkt.arg2 == ERROR)
            printf("\nServer Error processing release (rel) command.");
        else if(pkt.arg1 == IO_EXIT)
            printf("\nServer termination command sent.");
        else
```

```
            printf("\nrel bcm %d %s.",
                    pkt.arg1, pkt.arg2 ? "Failed" : "successful");
        retval = pkt.arg2;
      break;

      default:
        printf("\nInvalid server response.");
      break;
    }
  }

  printf("\n\n");

  /* Close the ipc socket. */
  close(socket_fd);

  return retval;
}
```

The last file that needs to be created so that the server can be compiled is the gpioctrl.c source code.

To create this file follow the following steps:

1.   In a Terminal Window, change into the chapter11 directory:

   cd /home/pi/webproj/chapter11

2.   Using either a favorite desktop editor or nano, create a file with the name gpioctrl.c:

   nano gpioctrl.c

3.   Enter the code from Program Listing 11.6 below.

4.   When finished entering Program Listing 11.6, type CTRL + O then ENTER to save then CTRL + X to exit nano.

5.   Next, run the makefile to compile the gpioctrl application by typing the following at the Terminal Prompt:

   make

6.   Fix any errors due to typos when entering gpioctrl.c using nano before proceeding.

Program Listing 11.6: gpioctrl.c

```
/*****************************************************************************
 * File: gpioctrl.c
 * Purpose: To take ownership of the gpio pins through a character device driver
 *          and provide a way for a user to change and hold the gpio states.
 *****************************************************************************/
#include <stdio.h>
#include <sys/socket.h>
```

```c
#include <sys/un.h>
#include <sys/types.h>
#include <unistd.h>
#include <string.h>
#include <errno.h>
#include <sys/stat.h>
#include <dirent.h>
#include <stdlib.h>
#include <fcntl.h>
#include <sys/ioctl.h>
#include <signal.h>
#include <linux/gpio.h>
#include <sys/shm.h>
#include "ipchdr.h"


/* Function Prototypes. */
int process_cmd(int ipc_stream, gpio_ctrl *gpiostruct);
int gpioInit(gpio_ctrl *gpiostruct);
int gpioInitPin(gpio_pin *gpiopin, int bcmNum, int dir, int fd);
gpio_pin *gpioGetPinStruct(int bcm, gpio_ctrl *gpiostruct);
int gpioGetPin(int bcm, gpio_ctrl *gpiostruct);
int gpioSetPin(int bcmNum, gpio_ctrl *gpiostruct, int value, int fd);
int gpioSetDir(gpio_ctrl *gpiostruct, int bcmNum, int value);
int gpioRelease(gpio_ctrl *gpiostruct, int bcmNum);

/* For testing only. */
void tmp_prn_gpio_struct(gpio_ctrl *gpiostruct);

/*****************************************************************************
 * Function: main()
 * Purpose: Main entry point for the gpioctrl service.
 * Receives: void
 *
 * returns: OK or ERROR
 ****************************************************************************/
int main(void)
{
    struct sockaddr_un unix_sock_addr;
    socklen_t addr_length;
    int socket_fd, loop, retval = OK;
    int ipc_stream;
    pid_t pid_handler;
    gpio_ctrl gpio_info;
```

```c
gpio_ctrl *gpiostruct = &gpio_info;

printf("\nServer Initializing...");
fflush(stdout);

/* Delete exiting file IO socket, if exists, from previous run. */
remove(SOCKET_PATH);

/* Init the gpio interface. */
if(gpioInit(gpiostruct) != OK)
{
   printf("\nError! Could not initialize the character device.");
   retval = ERROR;
}

if(retval != ERROR)
{
   /* Create a socket. */
   socket_fd = socket(AF_UNIX, SOCK_STREAM, 0);
   if(socket_fd < 0)
   {
      printf("\nError! Could not create socket!");
      retval = ERROR;
   }

   /* Remove previous symbolic link if exists. */
   unlink(SOCKET_PATH);
}

if(retval != ERROR)
{
   /* Clear the socket address structure memory. */
   memset(&unix_sock_addr, 0, sizeof(struct sockaddr_un));

   /* Set up socket address informaiton. */
   unix_sock_addr.sun_family = AF_UNIX;
   snprintf(unix_sock_addr.sun_path, MAX_PATH, SOCKET_PATH);

   /* Bind the socket address to the open socket. */
   if(bind(socket_fd, (struct sockaddr*) &unix_sock_addr,
         sizeof(struct sockaddr_un)) != 0)
   {
      printf("\nError! Could not bind to the socket.");
      retval = ERROR;
```

```c
      }
}

if(retval != ERROR)
{
    /* Set permissions for accessing the file based IPC Socket. */
    chmod(SOCKET_PATH, S_IRWXU | S_IRWXG  | S_IRWXO );

    /* Listen to the socket for incoming connections. */
    if(listen(socket_fd, 4) != 0)
    {
        printf("\nError! Failed to listen on IPC Socket.");
        retval = ERROR;
    }
}

printf("\nInitialization Complete.");
printf("\nWaiting for commands...\n");
flush(stdout);

/* Process incoming connections. */
while(retval != ERROR)
{
    addr_length = sizeof(unix_sock_addr);

    /* Wait for incoming connection. */
    if((ipc_stream = accept(socket_fd,
        (struct sockaddr*) & unix_sock_addr, &addr_length)) == -1)
    {
        printf("Error! Accept connection failed with error: %s\n",
            strerror(errno));
        retval = ERROR;
    }

    /* Handle the incoming gpio command. */
    if(process_cmd(ipc_stream, gpiostruct) == EXIT) break;

    /* Close the ipc_stream to accept the next connection. */
    close(ipc_stream);
}

/*** Clean Up ***/

/* Close the socket and exit the application. */
```

```
      close(socket_fd);
      unlink(SOCKET_PATH);

      /* Free character device driver and all pin fd's. */
      if(gpiostruct->char_dev_fd != ERROR)
      {
         for(loop = 0; loop < NUM_MAX_GPIO; loop++)
         {
            if(gpiostruct->gpio_array[loop].gpio_fd != 0)
               close(gpiostruct->gpio_array[loop].gpio_fd);
         }
         close(gpiostruct->char_dev_fd);
      }

      printf("\nServer exiting...\n");
      fflush(stdout);

      return retval;
}


/****************************************************************************
 * Function: process_cmd()
 * Purpose: To handle a new gpio command send through IPC.
 * Receives: int ipc_stream - The stream socket file descriptor (fd).
 *           gpio_ctrl *gpiostruct - Pointer to the gpio info structure.
 *
 * returns: OK, ERROR, or EXIT if command to quit the app received.
 ****************************************************************************/
int process_cmd(int ipc_stream, gpio_ctrl *gpiostruct)
{
   int ret = 0, loop;
   int numBytes;
   char strBuf[MAX_BUFFER+1];
   gpio_struct pkt;
   gpio_pin *pin;

   /* Read a command packet from the webio client. */
   numBytes = read(ipc_stream, strBuf, MAX_BUFFER);

   /* If command packet size is incorrect. */
   if(numBytes != sizeof(gpio_struct))
   {
      printf("\nReceived malformed packet.");
```

```
      ret = ERROR;
}

/* Copy the packet into the command structure. */
memcpy(&pkt, strBuf, sizeof(gpio_struct));

/* Used for debugging. */
/*
   printf("\nCommand: %d\n", pkt.Command);
   printf("arg1: %d\n", pkt.arg1);
   printf("arg2: %d", pkt.arg2);
   fflush(stdout);
*/

/* Handle the gpio command based on type. */
switch(pkt.Command)
{
   case CMD_SET:
      /* printf("\nCMD_SET\n"); */
      ret = gpioSetPin(pkt.arg1, gpiostruct, pkt.arg2,
         gpiostruct->char_dev_fd);
      if(ret >= 0)
         ret = gpioGetPin(pkt.arg1, gpiostruct);
      pkt.arg2 = ret;  /* Return to client 0|1|INT|ERROR */
   break;

   case CMD_GET:
      /* printf("\nCMD_GET\n"); */
      /* if the get ALL command sent. */
      if(pkt.arg1 == IO_ALL)
      {
         /* Save list of gpio values. */
         for(loop = 0; loop < NUM_MAX_GPIO; loop++)
         {
            pkt.value[loop] =
              gpioGetPin(gpiostruct->gpio_array[loop].bcmNum, gpiostruct);
            pkt.bcm[loop] = gpiostruct->gpio_array[loop].bcmNum;
         }
      }
      else
      {
         /* Get selected gpio value. */
         ret = gpioGetPin(pkt.arg1, gpiostruct);
         pkt.arg2 = ret; /* Return to client 0|1|ERROR */
```

```
            }
        break;

        case CMD_DIR:
            /* printf("\nCMD_DIR\n"); */
            ret = gpioSetDir(gpiostruct, pkt.arg1, pkt.arg2);
            pkt.arg2 = ret;
        break;

        case CMD_REL:
            /* printf("\nCMD_REL\n"); */
            if(pkt.arg1 == IO_EXIT)
                ret = EXIT;
            else
            {
                /* Release gpio pin. */
                ret = gpioRelease(gpiostruct, pkt.arg1);
                pkt.arg2 = ret;
            }
        break;
    }

    /* Send command reply back to the client application. */
    numBytes = sizeof(gpio_struct);
    write(ipc_stream, (char *) &pkt, numBytes);

    /* Close the ipc stream connection. */
    close(ipc_stream);

    return ret;
}


/*****************************************************************************
 * Function: gpioInit()
 * Purpose: To open the character device and initialize the gpio pins.
 * Receives: gpio_ctrl *gpiostruct - Pointer to the gpio info structure.
 *
 * returns: OK or ERROR
 *****************************************************************************/
int gpioInit(gpio_ctrl *gpiostruct)
{
    int loop, offset, bcmNum;
    int ret = 0;
```

```
    /* Open the character device driver for access. */
    gpiostruct->char_dev_fd = open("/dev/gpiochip0", O_RDONLY);

    if(gpiostruct->char_dev_fd != ERROR)
    {
        for(loop = 0, offset = 0; loop < NUM_MAX_GPIO; loop++, offset++)
        {
            /* Get the next BCM number from the BCM array. */
            while( (offset < NUM_HDR_PINS) &&
                        ((bcmNum = iPin_bcm[offset]) < 0) ) offset++;

            /* Make sure the gpio_fd is initially set to 0 so the
             * pin init will not try to close an fd that is not open. */
            gpiostruct->gpio_array[loop].gpio_fd = 0;

            /* Set up all pins as inputs initially. */
            /* Calling a gpio set command will automatically
             * change the gpio to output. */
            gpioInitPin(&gpiostruct->gpio_array[loop], bcmNum, IO_IN,
                    gpiostruct->char_dev_fd);
        }
    }

    return ret;
}


/******************************************************************************
* Function: gpioInitPin()
* Purpose:  Gain access to the desired gpio pin through the character
*           device driver. This function can only be called from the
*           parent and never from a child (listener) process.
*
* Receives:
*           gpio_ctrl *gpiostruct - Pointer to the gpio info structure.
*           int bcmNum - The BCM number for the gpio pin.
*           int dir - Either IO_IN or IO_OUT
*           int fd - Character device driver file descriptor.
*
* Returns: OK, INV or ERROR
******************************************************************************/
int gpioInitPin(gpio_pin *gpiopin, int bcmNum, int dir, int fd)
{
```

```c
int result = OK;
int gpioline = 0;
struct gpiohandle_request lineHandle;

/* If pin fd already open then close it. */
if(gpiopin->gpio_fd != 0)
{
   if(close(gpiopin->gpio_fd) == -1)
       printf("\nFailed to close GPIO handle fd.");
}

/* Save pin info. */
gpiopin->direction = dir; /* IO_IN, IO_OUT, or -1 if not used. */
gpiopin->bcmNum = bcmNum;

/* Clear gpiohandle request structure memory. */
memset(&lineHandle, 0, sizeof(lineHandle));

/* Set line values for the gpio. */
lineHandle.lineoffsets[0] = bcmNum;
lineHandle.lines = 1;
lineHandle.default_values[0] = 0;

if(dir == IO_OUT)
  lineHandle.flags = GPIOHANDLE_REQUEST_OUTPUT;
else
  lineHandle.flags = GPIOHANDLE_REQUEST_INPUT;

/* Set the name of the consumer of the line. */
strncpy(lineHandle.consumer_label, "WEBIO", 32);

/* Get a line handle to the gpio pin. (fd) */
result = ioctl(fd, GPIO_GET_LINEHANDLE_IOCTL, &lineHandle);

/* If successful.*/
if(result != ERROR)
{
    gpiopin->gpio_fd = lineHandle.fd; /* Save the line fd. */
}
else if(errno == 16)  /* gpio line is in use already. */
{
    /* Set pin to "not used". */
    gpiopin->direction = -1;
    gpiopin->gpio_fd = 0;
```

```
            result = INV;
            printf("\n gpio bcm %d is already in use.", bcmNum);
        }
        else
        {
            /* Set pin to "not used". */
            gpiopin->direction = -1;
            gpiopin->gpio_fd = 0;
            result = ERROR;
            printf("\n Error %d opening gpio bcm %d.", errno, bcmNum);
            printf("\n\t %s", strerror(errno));
        }

        fflush(stdout);

        return result;
}


/******************************************************************************
 * Function: gpioGetPin()
 * Purpose: To read the state of an IO pin.
 *
 * Receives:
 *         int bcmNum - The BCM number of the gpio pin.
 *         gpio_ctrl *gpiostruct - Pointer to the gpio info structure.
 *
 * Returns: Pin value (0 or 1) else ERROR
 ******************************************************************************/
int gpioGetPin(int bcmNum, gpio_ctrl *gpiostruct)
{
    int retval = ERROR;
    struct gpiohandle_data lineData;
    gpio_pin *pin;

    /* Get the gpio pin info structure. */
    pin = gpioGetPinStruct(bcmNum, gpiostruct);

    if(pin != NULL)
    {
        /* Clear gpiohandle data structure memory. */
        memset(&lineData, 0, sizeof(lineData));

        /* Get the current state of the selected line. */
```

```
        retval = ioctl(pin->gpio_fd, GPIOHANDLE_GET_LINE_VALUES_IOCTL, &lineData);

        if(retval != ERROR)
        {
            /* Save the line value 0(LOW) or 1(High). */
            retval = lineData.values[0];
        }
    }

    return retval;
}


/**************************************************************************
 * Function: gpioSetPin()
 * Purpose: Function to set/clear IO pin value. SET = 3.3V, CLEAR = 0V
 *
 * Receives:
 *        int bcmNum - The BCM number of the gpio pin.
 *        gpio_ctrl *gpiostruct - Pointer to the gpio info structure.
 *        int value - New pin output value.
 *        int fd - Char device driver file descriptor.
 *
 * Returns: OK (0), INV (-2) if pin set to input else ERROR (-1)
 **************************************************************************/
int gpioSetPin(int bcmNum, gpio_ctrl *gpiostruct, int value, int fd)
{
    int retval = OK;
    struct gpiohandle_data lineData;
    gpio_pin *pin;

    /* Get the gpio pin info structure. */
    pin = gpioGetPinStruct(bcmNum, gpiostruct);

    if(pin != NULL && (value == 0 || value == 1))
    {
        /* If the gpio pin is set to be an input then change to output.*/
        /* If gpio pin is not currently being used then try to open it. */
        if(pin->direction == IO_IN || pin->direction == (char) -1)
        {
            /* Try and configure the gpio pin as an output. */
            retval = gpioInitPin(pin, bcmNum, IO_OUT, fd);
        }
```

```
      if(retval == OK)
      {
          /* Set the gpio line to either 3.3V or 0V. */
          lineData.values[0] = value;
          retval =
              ioctl(pin->gpio_fd, GPIOHANDLE_SET_LINE_VALUES_IOCTL, &lineData);
      }
   }

   return retval;
}



/*******************************************************************************
* Function: gpioSetDir()
* Purpose:  Sets the gpio direction to either IO_IN or IO_OUT.
*
* Receives: gpio_ctrl *gpiostruct - Pointer to the gpio info structure.
*           int bcmNum - The BCM number of the gpio pin.
*           int value - IO_IN or IO_OUT
*
* Returns: INV, IO_IN, IO_OUT, else ERROR
*******************************************************************************/
int gpioSetDir(gpio_ctrl *gpiostruct, int bcmNum, int value)
{
   int retval = value;
   gpio_pin *pin;

   /* Get the gpio pin info structure. */
   pin = gpioGetPinStruct(bcmNum, gpiostruct);

   /* Check if the pin is already set to the desired direction
    * and that the bin is in use. */
   if(pin->direction != value)
   {
      retval = gpioInitPin(pin, bcmNum, value, gpiostruct->char_dev_fd);
      if(retval == OK)
         retval = value;
   }

   return retval;
}
```

```
/*****************************************************************************
* Function: gpioRelease()
* Purpose:   Releases the file descriptor of the selected bcm pin.
*
* Receives: gpio_ctrl *gpiostruct - Pointer to the gpio info structure.
*           int bcmNum - The BCM number of the gpio pin.
*
* Returns: OK or ERROR
******************************************************************************/
int gpioRelease(gpio_ctrl *gpiostruct, int bcmNum)
{
   int retval = OK;
   gpio_pin *pin;

   /* Get the gpio pin info structure. */
   pin = gpioGetPinStruct(bcmNum, gpiostruct);

   /* If pin fd open then close it. */
   if(pin->gpio_fd != 0)
   {
      if(close(pin->gpio_fd) == -1)
      {
         printf("\nFailed to close GPIO handle fd.");
         retval = ERROR;
      }
      else
      {
         pin->direction = -1;
         pin->gpio_fd = 0;
      }
   }


   return retval;
}



/*****************************************************************************
* Function: gpioGetPinStruct()
* Purpose:   Gets a pointer to a gpio pin struct based on the BCM number.
*
* Receives:
*           int bcmNum - The BCM number of the gpio pin.
*           gpio_ctrl *gpiostruct - Pointer to the gpio info structure.
*
```

```
* Returns: gpio_pin structure pointer else NULL if pin is not used.
*************************************************************************/
gpio_pin *gpioGetPinStruct(int bcmNum, gpio_ctrl *gpiostruct)
{
   int loop;
   gpio_pin *pin = NULL;

   /* Search for the bcm number in the gpio info structure. */
   for(loop = 0; loop < NUM_MAX_GPIO; loop++)
   {
      if(gpiostruct->gpio_array[loop].bcmNum == bcmNum)
      {
         pin = &gpiostruct->gpio_array[loop];
         break;
      }
   }

   return pin;
}



/****************************************************************************
* Function: tmp_prn_gpio_struct()
* Purpose:  Used only for testing, this function will print to terminal
*           the current values of the gpio info structure.
*
* Receives: gpio_ctrl *gpiostruct - Pointer to the gpio info structure.
*
* Returns: void
*************************************************************************/
void tmp_prn_gpio_struct(gpio_ctrl *gpiostruct)
{
   int loop;
   for(loop = 0; loop < NUM_MAX_GPIO; loop++)
   {
      printf("\nbcm: %d  dir: %d  fd:  %d",
         gpiostruct->gpio_array[loop].bcmNum,
         gpiostruct->gpio_array[loop].direction,
         gpiostruct->gpio_array[loop].gpio_fd);
   }
}
```

The following exercises will explore a few options for invoking the gpioctrl server for use by either the webio application or the Web Control Panel, which will be covered in the next chapter. These steps will show the following methods of invoking the gpioctrl server:

- Run at the terminal and keep the terminal open but unusable while the server is running.
- Run from a terminal as a background application so the terminal can still be used.
- Run as a service that can either start automatically at boot or start manually when used.

Each of the three options listed above will now be explored:

Part 1 - Running the Server from Its Own Terminal

1. At a Terminal Prompt, change into the chapter11 directory:

   cd /home/pi/webproj/chapter11

2. Run the gpioctrl server by typing the following:

   sudo ./gpioctrl

3. Next, open a new Terminal Window and run the webio client by typing the following:

   ./webio get 2

4. If using the RPI-LED board, the program output should show the input for BCM 2 at a logic 1:

   Pin BCM 2 value: 1

5. Try typing **./webio** without any options to see the command syntax and available commands. Try typing different commands to manipulate the gpio pins. One very useful command is the **./webio get ALL** command that will show all of the gpio pin states.

6. **Note:** The gpiodisp application developed in chapter 10 can be run in a different Terminal Window to view the state of the GPIO pins as the webio **dir** and **rel** commands are used.

7. Before moving on, close the server by typing the following command:

   ./webio rel EXIT

8. The Terminal Window running the gpioctrl server should show that server has exited and the terminal is now available to enter commands.

Part 2 - Running the Server as a Background Task

1. At a Terminal Prompt, change into the chapter11 directory if not already there:

   cd /home/pi/webproj/chapter11

2. Run the gpioctrl server as a background task by typing the following:

   sudo ./gpioctrl &

3. At the same Terminal Prompt, press enter then enter the following command:

   ./webio get ALL

4. Notice that both the server and the client application can be run in the same terminal.

5. Next, exit the server by typing:

   ./webio rel EXIT

6. Notice that the server exited but that the server's output is still shown in the terminal. If this is not desired, start the server using the following command:

   sudo ./gpioctrl > /dev/null 2>&1 &

7. Now all server output is suppressed. The ID of the server should have been displayed on the terminal when the previous command was run. Any applications currently running on the terminal instance can be viewed by typing:

jobs -l

The output should look similar to the following:

[1]+ 2834 Running   sudo ./gpioctrl > /dev/null 2>&1 &

8. Type **./webio rel EXIT** at the prompt then run the **jobs -l** command again to see that the server application has closed and there are no jobs running.

9. Another option for terminating the server running as a background task is to use the kill command:

kill -9 <App ID>

Part 3 - Running the Server as a Service

Running the server in the background is great for implementing both the client and server in the same terminal, but when being used with the Web Control Panel it may be desirable to run the server as a service. To run the server as a service a new file will need to be created and copied to the /lib/systemd/system/ directory. Once the steps are completed to allow the gpioctrl application to be run as a service, it can be set up to run automatically when the system boots or it can be started manually whenever the webio or Web Control Panel applications are used.

Initial Service Setup Steps:

1. At a Terminal Prompt, change into the chapter11 directory if not already there:

cd /home/pi/webproj/chapter11

2. Copy the gpioctrl application built in the sections above to the /etc/systemd/system/ directory:

sudo cp gpioctrl /etc/systemd/system/gpioctrl

3. Set permissions for the application:

sudo chmod +x /etc/systemd/system/gpioctrl

4. Next, create a unit file for a systemd service using the app name.service. Be sure to include the full path to the file location:

sudo nano /lib/systemd/system/gpioctrl.service

5. Enter the text from Listing 11.7 below.

6. When finished entering Listing 11.7, type CTRL + O then ENTER to save then CTRL + X to exit nano.

7. Force the loading of the new service file by typing the following at the Terminal Prompt:

sudo systemctl daemon-reload

8. If desiring to run the service at boot without needing to manually start the service each time it is used, type the following command, otherwise skip this step:

sudo systemctl enable gpioctrl.service

9. If at a later time it is desirable to stop the service from loading at boot then the following command can be used to undo step 8 above:

sudo systemctl disable gpioctrl.service

10. Next, it's time to start the program as a service for the first time:

sudo systemctl start gpioctrl.service

11. The service start can be verified by typing the following:

sudo systemctl status gpioctrl.service

12. Type CTRL-C to exit the service status command.

13. Another method of verifying the service is to simply type a webio command:

    ./webio get ALL

14. To stop the service, two commands can be used:

    sudo systemctl stop gpioctrl.service

    or

    ./webio rel EXIT

Service unit file Listing 11.7: gpioctrl.service

```
[Unit]
      Description=GPIO Control Service for WEBIO

[Service]
      ExecStart=/etc/systemd/system/gpioctrl

[Install]
      WantedBy=multi-user.target
```

Manually Starting the Service after Boot:

Manually starting the gpioctrl server after boot only works if the initial service setup steps were followed. If the initial steps were followed then these next steps will provide a way to manually start the service after a reboot of the system:

1. Type the following at a Terminal Prompt:

    sudo systemctl start gpioctrl.service

2. The service start can be verified by typing the following:

    sudo systemctl status gpioctrl.service

3. Another method of verifying the service is to simply type a webio command:

    ./webio get ALL

4. To stop the service, two commands can be used:

    sudo systemctl stop gpioctrl.service

    or

    ./webio rel EXIT

In the next chapter, the webio interface will be incorporated into the Web Control Panel application; however, a simple CGI example of using the webio interface from the web will be presented here. In the following example script, a simple call to webio will run the following command, **webio get ALL,** from a web browser. This example is simply to demonstrate a basic method of calling into the webio interface through CGI, for reference. Feel free to experiment or use the webio interface with a script of your choosing.

Follow these steps to create the example webio CGI script:

1. In a Terminal Window, change into the chapter11 directory:

   cd /home/pi/webproj/chapter11

2. Using either a favorite desktop editor or nano, create a file with the name ipc.cgi:

   nano ipc.cgi

3. Enter the code from Program Listing 11.8 below.

4. When finished entering Program Listing 11.8, type CTRL + O then ENTER to save then CTRL + X to exit nano.

5. Next, run the makefile to make sure everything was compiled and no changes were made. If the previous steps were followed then nothing should be done for the make:

   make

6. Next, type the following to install webio and ipc.cgi so that a CGI call can be made from a web browser:

   sudo make install

7. Make sure the gpioctrl service is running by typing the following at the Terminal Prompt:

   sudo systemctl start gpioctrl.service

8. Using the IP address of the Raspberry Pi, open a web browser either on the Raspberry Pi or another computer on the local network and type the following into the address bar:

   (IP Address)/cgi-bin/ipc.cgi

The web page output should look similar to the following:

P2:1 P3:1 P4:0 P14:0 P15:0 P17:0 P18:0 P27:0 P22:0 P23:0 P24:0 P10:0 P9:0 P25:0 P11:0 P8:0 P7:0 P0:1 P1:1 P5:1 P6:0 P12:0 P13:0 P19:0 P16:0 P26:0 P20:0 P21:0

Ran ipc.cgi client successfully
IT WORKED!

Program Listing 11.8: ipc.cgi

```perl
#!/usr/bin/perl -w

print "Content-Type: text/html\n\n";
print "<!DOCTYPE html>\n<html>\n<head>\n";
print "<title>webio ipc test</title></head>\n";
print "<body>\n";

my $retval = system("/var/www/webapp/webio", "get", "ALL");
if($retval != 0)
{
```

```
    print "<h1>Error! \'ipc.cgi\' failed.\n";
    print "<br />See Apache error log...</h1>\n";
}
else
{
    print "\n<center><h1>Ran ipc.cgi client successfully</h1>\n";
    print "<h1>IT WORKED!</h1>\n</center>\n";
}

print "</body>\n</html>\n";
```

12

WEB CONTROL PANEL & SECURITY

In this chapter, webio will be added to the CGI backend to read and write the GPIO pins as controlled by the Embedded Web Control Panel. This will be a slight change to the code developed in chapter 9 to replace the Python Scripts with 'C' code that will then access the gpioctrl service created in the last chapter.

Secondly, an example security configuration for the Apache HTTP Server will be provided that can be used to enforce security when accessing the Raspberry Pi over the internet or a local network.

Most of the files and code needed for the Chapter 12 project were created or set up in chapter 9. Only the files that will change for the new modifications will be listed here.

Alternatively, the project source code for all chapters may be downloaded as shown in chapter 3, if not already completed.

Follow these steps to set up the environment for the chapter 12 project code:

1. At a Terminal Prompt, change into the project directory: **cd /home/pi/webproj**

2. Create a new directory where the chapter 12 code will be stored:

   mkdir chapter12

3. Change into the chapter12 directory: **cd chapter12**

4. The Embedded Web Control Panel code created in chapter 9 will serve as the starting place for the chapter 12 modifications. Copy the contents of the chapter9 directory to the newly created chapter12 directory. Type the following at the Terminal Prompt:

   cp ../chapter9/* ./

5. Next, the ipchdr.h file from chapter 11 will be needed. Copy the header file by typing the following at the Terminal Prompt:

   cp ../chapter11/ipchdr.h ./ipchdr.h

6. The two Python files can be deleted from the chapter12 directory, if desired, since they will not be needed for this project:

   rm *.py

7. Clean up the old object files by typing the following at the Terminal Prompt:

   make clean

8. Verify the full list of files now in the chapter12 folder by typing: **ls -als**

9.   The output should look similar to the following:

```
pi@raspberrypi:~/webproj/chapter12 $ ls -akls
total 96
 4 drwxr-xr-x  2 pi pi  4096 Feb 14 10:34 .
 4 drwxr-xr-x 15 pi pi  4096 Feb 14 09:00 ..
12 -rw-r--r--  1 pi pi  8792 Feb 14 09:05 cgidebug.c
 4 -rw-r--r--  1 pi pi   389 Feb 14 09:05 cgidebug.h
16 -rw-r--r--  1 pi pi 13752 Feb 14 09:05 cgimain.c
 4 -rw-r--r--  1 pi pi   496 Feb 14 09:05 cgimain.h
16 -rw-r--r--  1 pi pi 13701 Feb 14 09:05 cgitools.c
 4 -rw-r--r--  1 pi pi  1570 Feb 14 09:05 cgitools.h
 8 -rw-r--r--  1 pi pi  4282 Feb 14 09:05 index.html
 4 -rw-r--r--  1 pi pi  2477 Feb 14 10:30 ipchdr.h
12 -rw-r--r--  1 pi pi 10396 Feb 14 09:05 main.html
 4 -rw-r--r--  1 pi pi   882 Feb 14 10:27 makefile
 4 -rw-r--r--  1 pi pi   547 Feb 14 09:05 webpanel.cgi
pi@raspberrypi:~/webproj/chapter12 $
```

As in chapter 9, the Web Control Panel will make use of two sound files. If chapter 9 was followed then the files **RaspberryPi.wav** and **test.wav** should already exist in the /var/www/html directory. If not then they will need to be added by entering these terminal commands:

1.   Change to the /var/www/html directory:
      cd /var/www/html

2.   If test.wav is not already in the /var/www.html directory then type the following:
      sudo wget https://www.mstmicro.com/projects/test.wav

3.   If the RaspberryPi.wav is not already in the /var/www.html directory then type the following:
      sudo wget https://www.mstmicro.com/projects/RaspberryPi.wav

If not already completed from either chapter 6 or chapter 9, the www-data user must be added to the audio group to be able to play a sound from a web page. If not already completed, follow these steps to update the Raspberry Pi to allow the web user, www-data, to access audio services:

1.   From a Terminal Prompt, add the web user to the audio group:
      sudo usermod -a -G audio www-data

2.   This next step is very important. For the new change to take effect the web server must be restarted:
      sudo service apache2 restart

The next step in updating the Embedded Control Panel Framework is to make the changes necessary to incorporate the webio interface in the CGI backend. Only two files need to be modified to incorporate the changes and they are the **makefile** and the 'C' source file **cgimain.c**.

The changes to cgimain.c are limited and the updated code listing will be provided below. For reference, an overview of the changes to cgimain.c are as follows:

1. Added several header definitions to the top of the file that include:

   #include <sys/socket.h>

   #include <sys/un.h>

   #include <unistd.h>

   #include "ipchdr.h"

2. The SetGPIO() function was rewritten.

3. The DynamicUpdate() function was heavily modified.

4. A new function named runCommand() was added.

5. A function prototype was added near the top of the file as follows:

   int runCommand(gpio_struct *pkt);

Follow these steps to update the cgimain.c source code file:

1. Change into the chapter12 directory:

   cd /home/pi/webproj/chapter12

2. Using either a favorite desktop editor or nano, edit the cgimain.c source code file:

   nano cgimain.c

3. Edit cgimain.c to match the code from Program Listing 12.1 below.

4. When finished entering Program Listing 12.1, type CTRL + O then ENTER to save then CTRL + X to exit nano.

5. Compile the program by typing the following at the Terminal Prompt:

   make

6. Make sure to fix any errors or warnings before continuing.

Program Listing 12.1: cgimain.c

```
/****************************************************************************
* File: cgimain.c
* Purpose: Program to control various Raspberry Pi operations from the web.
*
****************************************************************************/
#include <stdio.h>
#include <string.h>
#include <stdlib.h>
#include <time.h>
#include <sys/socket.h>
#include <sys/un.h>
#include <unistd.h>

#include "cgimain.h"
```

```c
#include "cgitools.h"
#include "cgidebug.h"
#include "ipchdr.h"


/* Global Post data linked list variable. */
CGIPostData CGIData;

/* New function prototype, must be declared here. */
int runCommand(gpio_struct *pkt);



/*****************************************************************************
* Function: main()
* Receives: int argc - Number of command line arguments.
*           char *argv[] - Command line argument strings.
*           char *env[]  - Optionally add for systems that support
*                          environment variables passed to the main function.
*
* Returns 0 = OK or ERROR CODE
*****************************************************************************/
int main(int argc, char *argv[], char *env[])
{
    int retval = 0;
    CGIPostData *CGIDataPtr = &CGIData;

    /* Preinitialize the linked list to prevent unallocation errors. */
    CGIData.ListHead = NULL;
    CGIData.Count = 0;

    /* Start of web page. */
    printf("%s%c%c","Content-Type:text/html;charset=iso-8859-1",10,10);
    printf("<!DOCTYPE html>\n");

    /* Verify the application is called by the CGI script. If the argument
     * text "CGI" is not found then don't run anything. */
    if(argc > 1 && strncmp(argv[1], "CGI", 3) == 0)
    {
        /* Load CGI POST data, if any. */
        ReadCGIPostData(CGIDataPtr);
```

```
        /* If debug operations specified. */
        if(argc >= 3 && strncmp(argv[2], "DEBUG", 5) == 0)
        {
            retval = DebugOperations(argc, argv, env);
        }


        /* Act on control panel POST data, if any. */
        else
        {
            retval = PostDataOperations(argc, argv, env);
        }

    }
    else
    {
        printf("<html>\n<head>\n\n<title>Execution Error</title>\n\n</head>\n\n");
        printf("<body bgcolor=\"#669999\" text=\"#FFFFFF\">\n\n");
        printf("<br/><br/><center>\n<h1>Application Error!</h1>\n</center>\n");
        printf("<br/><br/>\n</body></html>\n");
        retval = 0;
    }

    /* Free CGI POST data allocated memory, if any. */
    DeleteLinkedList(CGIDataPtr);

    return retval;
}



/*****************************************************************************
* Function: PostDataOperations()
* Purpose: Act on POST data form information to perform various control
*          panel operations.
*
* Receives: int argc - Number of script command line arguments.
*           char *argv[] - Command line argument strings.
*           char *env[]  - Environment variables passed to the main function,
*                          only on supported operating systems.
*
* Returns 0 on success
*****************************************************************************/
```

```c
int PostDataOperations(int argc, char *argv[], char *env[])
{
    int retval = 0;
    int val1 = 0;
    char *COMMAND = NULL;
    char *VAR1 = NULL, *VAR2 = NULL, *VAR3 = NULL, *VAR4 = NULL, *VAR5 = NULL;
    char buf[512];

    printf("<html>\n<head>\n\n<title>CGI COMMAND RESULTS</title>\n</head>\n");
    printf("<body bgcolor=\"#559BC7\" text=\"#0E1923\">\n\n");

    /* Get the POST command string. */
    COMMAND = GetKeyValue(&CGIData, "COMMAND", 0);

    /* Act on POST data submission. */
    if(strncmp(COMMAND, "PlaySound", 9) == 0)
    {
        /* POST Data command to play a wav file. */
        /* Get the sound file number from the web form data named 'VAR1'. */
        VAR1 = GetKeyValue(&CGIData, "VAR1", 0);

        /* Get the numeric value for the selected sound file. */
        val1 = atoi(VAR1);

        // Modify the file names below to play different sound files.
        // Put any new sound files in the /var/www/html directory.
        // This will play from either HDMI or through the speaker
        // jack on the board depending on the OS settings. Try listening
        // to both sound channels to be sure it is working. See chapter 9
        // details for more information.

        /* Prepare to play the wav file. */
        sprintf(buf, "aplay /var/www/html/");

        // Play the correct sound file based on the button number.
        switch(val1)
        {
            case 1:
                strncat(buf, "RaspberryPi.wav",  16);
            break;
```

```
        case 2:
          strncat(buf, "RaspberryPi.wav",  16);
        break;

        case 3:
          strncat(buf, "RaspberryPi.wav",  16);
        break;

        case 4:
          strncat(buf, "test.wav",  9);
        break;
    }


    /* Make a system call to play the wav file.        */
    /* Be sure the www-data user is in the audio group  */
    /* and the Apache HTTP Server has been restarted.     */
    /* If command fails see the apache error log.        */
    GenericSystemCall(buf);


}
else if(strncmp(COMMAND, "DriveSpace", 10) == 0)
{
    GenericSystemCall("df");
}
/* Received command to set the output state of a GPIO pin. */
else if(strncmp(COMMAND, "GPIOSet", 7) == 0)
{
    /* Get the BCM GPIO number from the web form. */
    VAR1 = GetKeyValue(&CGIData, "VAR1", 0);
    /* Get the new output state either "0" or "1". */
    VAR2 = GetKeyValue(&CGIData, "VAR2", 0);

    /* Call function to handle the GPIO set command. */
    SetGPIO(VAR1, VAR2);
}
else if(strncmp(COMMAND, "DynamicUpdate", 13) == 0)
{
    DynamicUpdate();
}
```

```
      /* Display CGI command information. */
      printf("\n<br><table border='1' cellspacing='2' cellpadding='15px'>\n");
      printf("\n<tr align='left'>\n<th>\n");
      serverTime();
      printf("\n<h3>CGI COMMAND REPLY:</h3><p>");
      printf("\n  COMMAND: %s<br>", COMMAND);
      printf("\n  VAR1: %s<br>", VAR1);
      printf("\n  VAR2: %s<br>", VAR2);
      printf("\n  VAR3: %s<br>", VAR3);
      printf("\n  VAR4: %s<br>", VAR4);
      printf("\n  VAR5: %s\n</p>", VAR5);
      printf("\n</th>\n</tr>");
      printf("\n</table><br><br>");
      printf("\n</body>\n</html>\n");


   return retval;
}



/******************************************************************************
* Function: DebugOperations()
* Purpose: Call various debug functions relative to the script command line
*          options.
*
* Receives: int argc - Number of script command line arguments.
*           char *argv[] - Command line argument strings.
*         char *env[]  - Environment variables passed to the main function,
*                        only on supported operating systems.
*
* Returns 0 on success
******************************************************************************/
int DebugOperations(int argc, char *argv[], char *env[])
{
   int retval = 0;

   /* Request ENV variables by name. */
   if(argc >= 4 && strncmp(argv[3], "ENV_NAME", 8) == 0)
   {
      retval = CGIDebugByName(argc, argv);
   }
```

```c
    /* If environment variable debug information requested.
     * Request variables by name. */
    else if(argc >= 4 && strncmp(argv[3], "ENV_ALL", 7) == 0)
    {
        retval = CGIDebugAll(argc, argv);
    }

    return retval;
}



/****************************************************************************
* Function: GenericSystemCall()
* Purpose: Executes and displays the results of a Raspberry Pi system call.
*
* Receives: char *sysComand - Command line for system call.
*
* Returns: 0 on success else ERROR.
****************************************************************************/
int GenericSystemCall(char *sysComand)
{
    FILE *fp;
    char buf[1024];
    int strpos;
    int retval = ERROR;

    /* Make a system call based on the sysCommand string. */
    fp = popen(sysComand, "r");

    /* Create a table to hold any command line output. */
    printf("<center><table width='95%' border='1' cellspacing='2' ");
    printf("cellpadding='1'>\n<tr bgcolor=\"#65ABD7\">\n\t<th>\n\t\t<h3>");
    printf("COMMAND OUTPUT - IF ANY</h3>\n\t</th>\n</tr>\n");
    printf("<tr align='left'>\n\t<th>\n");

    if(fp == NULL)
    {
        printf("<br/><h1>ERROR: Could not execute command! bye...</h1>\n");
    }
    else
    {
```

```c
    retval = 0;

    printf("\n\t<div style='color:#00134F;font:14pt,courier, arial;'>\n");
    printf("\t<strong><font face='FreeMono, Lucida Console, Consolas'><p>");
    printf("\n\t ");

    /* Display command output on the web page, if any. */
    while(fgets(buf, sizeof(buf), fp))
    {
        /* For each character in text string. */
        for(strpos = 0; strpos < strlen(buf); strpos++)
        {
            switch(buf[strpos])
            {
                case '\n': printf("\n<br>");
                break;

                case ' ': printf(" ");
                break;

                case '\t': printf("    ");
                break;

                default: putchar(buf[strpos]);
                break;
            }
        }
    }

    printf("\n\t</P>\n\t</font>");
    printf("\n\t</strong>\n\t</div>");
    /* Close the file pointer to the command. */
    pclose(fp);
}

/* Close the table. */
printf("</th>\n\t</tr>\n");
printf("\n</table></center>\n<br><hr>\n\n");
}
```

```c
/*****************************************************************************
* Function: SetGPIO()
* Purpose: Sets the output value of a Raspberry Pi GPIO pin based on BCM value.
*
* Receives: char ioNumStr - Char string holding the GPIO number.
*           char ioStateStr - Char string of either "0" or "1".
*
* Returns: 0 on success else ERROR.
*****************************************************************************/
int SetGPIO(char *ioNumStr, char *ioStateStr)
{
    gpio_struct pkt;
    int bcmNum = atoi(ioNumStr);
    int ioState = atoi(ioStateStr);
    int retval = 0;

    /* Clear the message structure memory. */
    memset(&pkt, 0, sizeof(gpio_struct));

    /* Set up IPC message structure. */
    pkt.Command = CMD_SET;
    pkt.arg1 = bcmNum;
    pkt.arg2 = ioState;

    /* Send IPC command to the gpioctrl server. */
    retval = runCommand(&pkt);

    /* If command successful. */
    if(retval == 0 || retval == 1)
    {
        printf("<p><h3>GPIO (BCM): %d", pkt.arg1);
        printf("<br/>Desired State: %d", pkt.arg2);
        printf("<br/>System call exit code: %d</h3></p>", retval);

        /* This javascript command executed in the hidden_frame will dynamically
         * update the button state and color on the static main_frame. */
        printf("<script>parent.DoBtnUpdate('gpio%d', %d);</script>",
            pkt.arg1, retval);
    }

    return 0;
```

```c
}


/*****************************************************************************
 * Function: DynamicUpdate()
 * Purpose: Gets the following information to update the main_frame web page:
 * 1. Gets the server time and date.
 * 2. Gets the current CPU temperature.
 * 3. Gets the current GPIO pin state for all pins.
 *
 * Returns: 0 on success else ERROR.
 *****************************************************************************/
int DynamicUpdate(void)
{
    const int DATA_SZ = 256;
    const int DATA_TMP = 50;

    gpio_struct pkt;
    double cputemp;
    double gputemp;
    char cmd[DATA_SZ+1];
    char tempStr[DATA_TMP+1];
    int retval = 0, loop;

    time_t timeval;
    struct tm *timeinfo;

    /* First create the commnads to get all gpio states. */
    /* Clear the message structure memory. */
    memset(&pkt, 0, sizeof(gpio_struct));

    /* Set up IPC message structure. */
    pkt.Command = CMD_GET;
    pkt.arg1 = IO_ALL;

      /* Send IPC command to the gpioctrl server. */
      retval = runCommand(&pkt);

      /* Set up results for the Web Control Panel. */
      printf("\n\r <script>");
```

```
   /* Dynamically update the main_frame server time text. */
   if(time(&timeval) != ERROR)
   {
      timeinfo = localtime(&timeval);
      strftime(cmd, DATA_SZ, "Server Time: %h-%-d-%Y %I:%M:%S %p", timeinfo);
      printf("\n\r parent.UpdateTime('%s'); ", cmd);
   }


   /* Dynamically update the main_frame CPU temperature text. */
   cputemp = cpu_temp();


   if(cputemp != -255)
      snprintf(cmd, DATA_SZ, "CPU Temp: %.2f&#176;C", cputemp);
   else
      snprintf(cmd, DATA_SZ, "CPU Temp: Error");


   /* Call JavaScript function to update the CPU temp on the main_frame page.*/
   printf("\n\r parent.UpdateTemp('%s'); ", cmd);


   /* Display the results of the webio get ALL command ran above. */
   if(retval != ERROR && pkt.arg1 == IO_ALL)
   {
       /* Print list of gpio values. */
       for(loop = 0; loop < NUM_MAX_GPIO; loop++)
       {
           /* Only update pins that are user accessible. */
           if(pkt.value[loop] != ERROR && pkt.bcm[loop] != 0 && pkt.bcm[loop]!=1)
           {
               /* Create JavaScript to update the main_frame button objects. */
               printf("\n\r parent.DoBtnUpdate('gpio%d', %d); ",
                               pkt.bcm[loop], pkt.value[loop]);
           }
       }
   }


   printf("\n\r </script>");


   return 0;

}
```

```
/*****************************************************************************
* Function: cpu_temp()
* Purpose: Open the CPU temperature file and read the current CPU temp.
* *
* Returns: CPU Temperature in Deg. C or -250 on error.
*****************************************************************************/
double cpu_temp(void)
{
    const int DATA_SZ = 200;
    char tempStr[DATA_SZ];
    double temperature = -250;
    FILE *fp;

    /* Open the cpu temperature file for reading. */
    fp = fopen("/sys/class/thermal/thermal_zone0/temp","r");

    /* Read temperature data and convert to Deg. C */
    if(fp != NULL)
    {
        memset(tempStr, 0, DATA_SZ);  /* Zero memory buffer. */
        fread(tempStr, DATA_SZ, 1, fp);
        fclose(fp);

        temperature = atoi(tempStr);
        temperature /= 1000;

        if(temperature > 140 || temperature < -60)
          temperature = -250;
    }

  return temperature;
}



/*****************************************************************************
* Function: runCommand()
* Purpose: To send an IPC message to the gpioctrl server to run a gpio
*          command. Requires the gpioctrl server to be running.
* Receives:  gpio_struct *pkt - Pointer to a gpio message structure used to
*                            communicate with the webio interface.
*
```

```c
 * Returns: gpio state 0|1 or else ERROR
 **************************************************************************/
int runCommand(gpio_struct *pkt)
{
    struct sockaddr_un unix_sock_addr;
    int socket_fd, retval = 0;
    char strBuf[MAX_BUFFER+1];
    int numBytes;
    int loop;

    /* Open a socket for communication with the gpioctrl server. */
    socket_fd = socket(AF_UNIX, SOCK_STREAM, 0);
    if(socket_fd < 0)
    {
        printf("\nError! Failed to open IPC socket!");
        return ERROR;
    }

    /* Clear the socket address structure memory. */
    memset(&unix_sock_addr, 0, sizeof(struct sockaddr_un));

    /* Set up socket address information. */
    unix_sock_addr.sun_family = AF_UNIX;
    snprintf(unix_sock_addr.sun_path, MAX_PATH, SOCKET_PATH);

    /* Connect to the IPC socket. */
    if(connect(socket_fd, (struct sockaddr *) &unix_sock_addr,
        sizeof(struct sockaddr_un)) != 0)
    {
        printf("Failed to connect to the gpioctl server.\n");
        printf("Make sure the server is running.\n");
        return ERROR;
    }

    /* Send command packet to server over IPC connection. */
    numBytes = sizeof(gpio_struct);
    write(socket_fd, (char *) pkt, numBytes);


    /* Get reply from the IPC server. */
    numBytes = read(socket_fd, strBuf, MAX_BUFFER);
```

```c
/* If command packet size is incorrect. */
if(numBytes != sizeof(gpio_struct))
{
    printf("\nReceived malformed packet from server.");
    retval = ERROR;
}
else
{
    /* Copy the packet into the command structure. */
    memcpy(pkt, strBuf, sizeof(gpio_struct));

    /* Used for debugging. */
    printf("\nCommand: %d\n", pkt->Command);
    printf("<br>arg1: %d\n", pkt->arg1);
    printf("<br>arg2: %d\n", pkt->arg2);

    /* Check for errors. */
    switch(pkt->Command)
    {
        case CMD_SET:
            if(pkt->arg2 == ERROR)
                printf("\nServer Error processing set command.");
            else if(pkt->arg1 == INV)
                printf("\nOperation failed, pin in use by another consumer.");
            retval = pkt->arg2;
        break;

        case CMD_GET:
            if(pkt->arg2 == ERROR)
                printf("\nError processing the CMD_GET command.");

            retval = pkt->arg2;
        break;

        default:
            printf("\nInvalid server response.");
        break;
    }
}
```

```
    /* Close the ipc socket. */
    close(socket_fd);


    return retval;
}
```

Next, the makefile needs to be updated. Only one line of code will be changed. The following line will be commented out or removed:

cp *.py /var/www/webapp

Follow these steps to update the makefile text:

1. Change into the chapter12 directory:

    cd /home/pi/webproj/chapter12

2. Using either a favorite desktop editor or nano, edit the makefile text:

    nano makefile

3. Edit the makefile to match the text from Program Listing 12.2 below.

4. When finished entering Program Listing 12.2, type CTRL + O then ENTER to save then CTRL + X to exit nano.

5. Now the updated application files are ready to be installed. Type the following at the Terminal Prompt:

    sudo make install

Program Listing 12.2: makefile

```
# type 'make cgimain' to build the project.
cgimain:     cgimain.o cgitools.o cgidebug.o
        gcc -lm -o cgimain cgimain.o cgitools.o cgidebug.o


cgimain.o:   cgimain.c
        gcc -c cgimain.c


cgitools.o:  cgitools.c
        gcc -c cgitools.c


cgidebug.o:  cgidebug.c
        gcc -c cgidebug.c


# type 'sudo make install' to copy files and change their attributes.
install:
        if test -d /var/www/webapp; then echo -n;  else mkdir /var/www/webapp/; fi
        cp cgimain /var/www/webapp
        cp webpanel.cgi /usr/lib/cgi-bin
```

```
#cp *.py /var/www/webapp
chmod 755 /var/www/webapp/cgimain
chmod 755 /usr/lib/cgi-bin/webpanel.cgi
cp *.html /var/www/html
# Allow permissions such that the index.html file can be accessed.
sudo chown -R `whoami` /var/www/html


# type 'make clean 'to remove objects for a fresh build.
clean:
        rm cgitools.o cgimain.o cgidebug.o cgimain
```

There is one additional modification that can be made if so desired. Since the webio interface is much faster than that of the Python GPIO module, the background update rate can be updated to one second or even faster. In the top of the file index.html there is a line of code that sets the background timer update interval. This interval can be changed by changing the line of code from **setInterval(DynamicUpdate, 2000);** to **setInterval(DynamicUpdate, 1000);** for a one-second update rate.

The Web Control Panel can now be accessed by following these steps:

1. If not already running as a service, the gpioctrl server needs to be started. It can be run directly, started in the background, or started as a service. Reference the end of chapter 11 if needed. If it was enabled as a service in the last chapter then it should still be running. Verify that the gpioctrl server is running by typing the following:

   /home/pi/webproj/chapter11/./webio get ALL

2. If the previous command displayed all of the gpio output states then the server is running correctly. If not, the server must first be started.

3. Open a web browser on a device on the local network and type the **<IP Address>** of the Raspberry Pi into the address bar.

4. If the Raspberry Pi is set up in a router DMZ or port forwarding is used for Port 80 then the router's IP address may be entered to access the Embedded Web Control Panel from the Internet.

Adding Security

The control panel web page can be accessed by any computer that has access to the Raspberry Pi over the network or over the internet if the Raspberry Pi is set up in a router DMZ or if Port forwarding is used for Port 80. Port 80 is the normal HTTP access port using the TCP/IP communications protocol, although alternate ports can be used to provide additional security.

If placing the Raspberry Pi in a router DMZ for external internet access, the device is open to attack from external sources or via port scanners. It is best to set up a username and password using the Apache HTTP Server that will prevent anyone from external access unless they know the required credentials.

When using the security options with the Apache HTTP Server, there are two options that can be very useful in this case. The first is to protect all access to the device both locally and over the Internet. This means that whenever the device is accessed using a web browser a username and password will have to be entered, even if on the local network. The second option is to allow open access on the local network while requiring a username and password when accessing the device from the Internet. This is ideal if the local network is trusted so as not to have to enter credentials every time the control panel is accessed. Instructions will be provided here for both options. For reference, the current Raspberry Pi OS uses the following location for the Apache configuration file:

/etc/apache2/apache2.conf

The next steps will need to be followed for either type of security desired. One optional line of text can be added to allow open local access. If this is not desired then that step will be skipped:

1. Before adding the security options, a password file for Apache needs to be created. Type the following command at a Terminal Prompt to make sure the Apache utilities are present on the Raspberry Pi:

    htpasswd

2. If the **htpasswd** command is not found then install the utilities by typing the following at the Terminal Prompt:

    sudo apt-get install apache2-utils

3. Now an admin password will be created by typing the following at a Terminal Prompt:

    sudo htpasswd -c /etc/apache2/.htpasswd admin

    Enter the new desired password when prompted...

4. Next, append the password file with the pi user password by typing the following:

    sudo htpasswd /etc/apache2/.htpasswd pi

    Enter the new desired password when prompted...

5. Before updating the configuration file, make a copy in case it is desirable to change back to the original configuration:

    sudo cp /etc/apache2/apache2.conf /etc/apache2/apache2.conf.bak

6. Next, security will be added to the Apache configuration file by typing the following:

    sudo nano /etc/apache2/apache2.conf

7. Add the following content to the open apache2.conf file. Make sure the entry is after any other entries of the same directory:

    <Directory /var/www/>

    # Authentication

    authtype basic

    Authname "Authorized Personnel Only"

    Authuserfile /etc/apache2/.htpasswd

    require valid-user

    # Controls who can get stuff from this server.

    Order deny,allow

    deny from all

    #allow from 192.168.140

    Satisfy any

    </Directory>

8. Notice that one line is commented out: **#allow from 192.168.140**. When used, this line states that all

users who are on the local network with an address range from 192.168.140.0 to 192.168.140.255 can access the device without needing a username or password. The IP address will need to be changed to match the local network IP address. For instance, if the Raspberry Pi IP address is 192.200.200.5 then the line should be changed to: allow from 192.200.200. If desiring to have open access for local connections, update the IP address to match the local network and uncomment the allow from xxx.xxx.xxx line. Fill in the x's with your local IP address.

9.   When done editing, type CTRL + O then ENTER to save then CTRL + X to exit nano.

10. This next step is very important. The apache2 server must be restarted to use the newly updated security options by typing the following at the Terminal Prompt:

sudo service apache2 restart

Try out access to the Embedded Web Control Panel by opening a web browser and typing the IP address of the Raspberry Pi into the address bar. If the Raspberry Pi is set up in a router DMZ or Port forwarding is used then type in the WAN address of the router into a browser, preferably on a cell phone not connected to the local network, and view the Web Control Panel remotely.

MEET THE AUTHOR

George Babec has been an Electronic Engineer and Software Engineer for over twenty five years. He specializes in the development of data acquisition and control systems hardware, software, and FPGA design. George has extensible experience having developed everything from space-based laser control systems to functional safety devices for theme park rides and factory automation. He has developed control systems for wavelength programmable fiber optic transmitter (XFP) modules as well as media routers for the broadcast industry. George has developed embedded web-based control systems for many real-time applications running on RTOS-based operating systems as well as bare metal interrupt driven programming. His love and excitement for creating something new is only heightened when the opportunity arises to share his passion for design with others.

FROM THE AUTHOR

The desire to learn new things and advance ones knowledge can be very rewarding. As long as there is a desire and willingness to learn then anything is possible. It can be exciting to be able to imagine creating something new and then have the know-how and ability to make it a reality. Even blinking an LED can be thrilling for the first-time programmer of the Raspberry Pi.

There are many ways to control hardware and systems through a web page, many requiring the use of server-side scripts or software using streaming communications along with web applets. The examples provided in this book simply rely on the HTTP protocol, thus they do not require any additional platform support for other technologies.

My desire to write this book started many years ago; however, a common embedded platform to serve as the bases for the examples did not exist until the Raspberry Pi Single Board Computer became popular. My aim was to include as much information about creating web-based embedded control systems as possible in a single book using real-world functional examples that could be useful. I hope that you have enjoyed this technical reference and the technologies provided in the examples.

Authors survive by reviews. If you enjoyed this book then please leave a review. I would much appreciate it!

Feel free to stop by my website and say hi or view my other works.

Visit George Online:

Amazon: Author George L. Babec

Web: http://www.GeorgeBabec.com

Twitter: https://twitter.com/AuthorGBabec

Facebook: https://www.facebook.com/GeorgeLBabec/

PRESENTING A MYSTICAL FANTASY ADVENTURE

An Exciting Historical Fantasy Novel

George L. Babec, an Electronic Engineer and US Army Veteran has launched an exciting new Historical Fantasy Novel. Book details and cover image may be viewed at www.mstmicro.com.

Called "Frog Realm: Artifact of Protection," the novel is inspired by George's love for fantasy adventure and his daughter's love for frogs and animals.

Frog Realm is a mystical and magical experience with strong female characters possessing amazing supernatural abilities. Driven by love and undying devotion a young woman has to find her way and understand her abilities. A lost civilization of ancient days sets the scene.

Deep in the jungle, an ancient power awakens. A young man desiring to prove himself looks to the great one before him.

Conqueror. Father. Deity.

In Necalli's world, life is a struggle of glory and sacrifice, and the youthful successor is ready to give everything he has to save his people. But his father, the venerated Ahau, is at heart a man not a god. And he's been keeping secrets.

Dark, necromantic forces are rising, for the truth has been discovered. Necalli finds himself heir to a shrouded past, while facing a foe he cannot hope to defeat.

Waiting in the dark recesses of time for a foretold promise. A weapon of unthinkable power. A beating heart with a burning fire within, struggling to answer the call. Worlds apart, yet drawn to one another. More than an ally yet less than a worrier.

Together they must find the will to stand and fight or surrender once and for all to the dark ancient artifice desiring to destroy them.

ISBN 978-0-9970222-5-4 (paperback)

ISBN 978-0-9970222-6-1 (e-book)

FROG REALM

ARTIFACT OF PROTECTION

GEORGE L. BABEC

ISBN 978-0-9970222-7-8 (paperback)

ISBN 978-0-9970222-8-5 (ebook)

Printed in Great Britain
by Amazon

79618024R00169